CW00780171

BOYHOODLUM

Also by Anson Cameron

*Nice Shootin' Cowboy*
*Silences Long Gone*
*Tin Toys*
*Confessing the Blues*
*Lies I Told About a Girl*
*Stealing Picasso*
*Pepsi Bears*
*The Last Pulse*

# BOYHOODLUM

Memoirs of a devious childhood

# ANSON CAMERON

**VINTAGE BOOKS**
Australia

*Some pseudonyms have been used in this book and other details altered where necessary to protect the identity and privacy of people mentioned.*

A Vintage book
Published by Random House Australia Pty Ltd
Level 3, 100 Pacific Highway, North Sydney NSW 2060
www.randomhouse.com.au

Penguin
Random House
Australia

First published by Vintage in 2015

Copyright © Anson Cameron 2015

The moral right of the author has been asserted.

All rights reserved. No part of this book may be reproduced or transmitted by any person or entity, including internet search engines or retailers, in any form or by any means, electronic or mechanical, including photocopying (except under the statutory exceptions provisions of the Australian *Copyright Act 1968*), recording, scanning or by any information storage and retrieval system without the prior written permission of Random House Australia.

Random House Books is part of the Penguin Random House group of companies whose addresses can be found at global.penguinrandomhouse.com.

National Library of Australia
Cataloguing-in-Publication entry

Cameron, Anson, 1961– author.
Boyhoodlum/Anson Cameron.

ISBN 978 0 85798 500 2 (paperback)

Cameron, Anson, 1961–
Childhood and youth.
Authors, Australian – Victoria – Biography.

A823.3

Cover design: Design by Committee
Cover photograph: S. Braswell
Typeset in 11/17 pt Palatino by Post Pre-press Group, Brisbane
Printed in Australia by Griffin Press, an accredited ISO AS/NZS 14001:2004 Environmental Management System printer

Random House Australia uses papers that are natural, renewable and recyclable products and made from wood grown in sustainable forests. The logging and manufacturing processes are expected to conform to the environmental regulations of the country of origin.

*To Sarah, Asta and Freya*

# FOREWORD

Memoir is detection, invention, architecture, curatorship and veneration. It is the resurrection and culling of a million lived or imagined moments down to the few you can stomach and sell. In which section does it belong? Fiction? Or the other? The reconstruction of a dead world using the flotsam you find on the beach of your dotage-mind . . . a tusk, a mask and a seed from a fever tree have washed ashore – now recreate Africa.

The vermilion of your favourite pencil, the twisted secrets of a stuffed bear, the moods of a sister, the musk of your waking mother, the topography of your neighbourhood when held aloft in your father's arms, the night sounds of your first house, the high place where a branch joined a trunk, despair's first touch, love . . .

The past is limitlessly malleable. Facts die when tense

1

changes. Memory has lain in a skull-sized crypt, mouldering, curing, mutating. There is no sure tool of archeology to work in such a space with such alchemic stuff. Truths will be different when they come out than when they went in. The lure of humour, the mirrored hall of ego, and the yen for invention, have distorted my boyhood world. If there is a moral responsibility to those who were there that I get this right . . . well, I haven't. So to those people I say sorry. And I say write your own book and see how The Past fucks with you.

I guess I was hoping, during the writing of this boyhood, not to meet myself. To be able to keep that once-upon-a-me at arm's length. Knowing and dreading I was likely to come face-to-face with a solipsistic little prick who used people for play. If I wrote honestly it would be ugly, I was sure of that. So I began to write a lie about a boy I never met. Then I realised, that's just adulthood – that soft calibration of self. And I've been given a chance to tell the truth. To enter the confessional of posterity and sing like a canary.

So, I'm turning myself in. If you meet a little prick here, well, at least you've only had to meet him retrospectively, in the telling. I ask forgiveness from all those who had to meet the flesh-and-blood liar I was as a boy. He was combative, insidious, dishonest, and a vindictive vandal who needed violence visited upon him by someone who knew the line where a kicking turns from altruism to harm.

It will make you smile in wonder at the human gift for redemption that such a despicable boy could turn into such an honest writer and good and gracious man. You might then knit your brow, wonder if the boy was really a good boy, being painted bad by a wicked man for laughs. Don't. That boy, the boy I was, was bad.

But Shepparton was a big enough town that as a kid you could never be known by all its adults. There would always be suckers who didn't suspect I was a manipulative kid whose dreams were realer than their lives. I had blond hair and a smile that was a bigger fraud than organised religion. These gave me an edge.

In my defence – my fate was known from birth. Like a cancer-sufferer, or a Prince, whatever I did in my fledgling years was of little importance – Death or the Kingdom waited regardless. My childhood was always going to end with me being handed a sportscoat and a tie and riding off to a faraway castle for singular young people called Geelong Grammar. And all this – the minor boyhood, the infancy, the neighbours, the schooling, the friends and the town – would be replaced by another boyhood and better schooling and permanent friends and a city. This town and everyone in it, my world, was going to be substituted for a better one when the time came. That was the contract as sold to me in my cot.

So this first chapter of life was mine to do with as I pleased, I figured. I had free rein to treat the town the way other kids treated their ant farms. One day I'd drip honey on it, the next day I'd raise it up and shake it to see its inhabitants run cursing for shelter . . . then, of course, there was fire.

I couldn't lose a friend who wasn't going to be lost anyway when I went away. Like a person of Faith, I was born with a glowing afterlife. But mine would begin at thirteen in the cradle of the plutocracy, where all the habits of living my first baker's dozen years in Shepparton would be slowly unlearnt and my sins forgotten and I would sit at the right hand of some genuine big shots. It made for a pretty free childhood, the knowledge that this life ended at thirteen.

*Anson Cameron*

In the beginning our house in Talinga Crescent was the world entire. Mum prepared meals in the kitchen and wrote letters home on blue airmail envelopes. Dad laughed and gave us horsey rides upstairs to bed and read us stories there. This world slowly expanded with the scream of cicadas and the shouts of football players echoing through the bush across the levee to the Goulburn River where swagmen and blackfellas lived rough on the banks.

Then downtown, to the places a boy was hopelessly drawn to: Halpin's Sports Store and Thompson's Gun Shop, where you would press your nose against the glass to look at the sheath knives and shotguns; and Darveniza's News-agency with the lure of Donald Duck and Phantom comics; or Every's Bookshop which stocked the Secret Seven and penny bungers and sky rockets.

Later, there was Taverna Pizza, exotic and continental, mozzarella and mushrooms, wild new tastes for a mutton and potato town. The Taiwan Cafe, where you could take a billy and have it filled with fried rice. And the cafe in Wyndham Street where we would gather and sip our first cappuccinos and talk to the world's first girls.

Outside The Hurco Cafe, Fido Thompson and his crew smoked and leaned. Flared jeans and long hair and always up for a fight. You didn't look sideways at them as you walked past. The Hurco made the best hamburgers and Blue Heaven milkshakes in the world. Aspiring thugs circled the block endlessly in souped-up Monaros and Chargers and Studebakers, raised high on their wheels, snarling as they passed the cafe.

In summer we went down to the Goulburn River with rafts that took us weeks to scavenge and build and sank immediately and without trace while we watched, sickening ourselves with Marlboros. Then to the Raymond West Pool where we smashed ourselves into the water from frightening heights to impress girls who sat in circles outwardly oblivious but (I still hope to this day) inwardly thrilled. Each year a fruit picker would be pulled duck-egg-blue dead from the brown water and the whisper would go through the crowd, 'A Queenslander. A Queenslander.' As if that word explained how cheap life could be.

We had some poor in town; but they were no-shoes poor, not no-food poor. Back then it was just the Aboriginals and the Greeks and Italians and Turks and us; skips or Anglos or whatever we were. I just thought we were people.

We'd ride our bikes through the bush along the rivers where lone fishermen waited for redfin and couples plied their libidos in old Holdens. Pick our feet up off the pedals and put them on the crossbar away from snakes and dogs. The town was surrounded by orchards and dairy farms and bush and you could ride into them forever.

Older, the world got bigger still – to the north on weekends there was the Murray and water-skiing and fishing and swimming and crayfishing. To the east, a shack in the mountains surrounded by forest and eucalypt air and clear streams. To the south a city with bluestone buildings and skyscrapers and trams and cops wearing white gloves waving endless traffic. But we rarely went there. Many Shepparto-nians had never been. Going to Melbourne meant you had extreme legal or dental problems, or you had an unhealthy desire to see Richmond play football in colour, or to hear *The Mikado* performed with a live orchestra. The few who went to Melbourne often were viewed with suspicion. Aspirational malcontents. There was nothing Shepp didn't have that an honest person could want. And she felt, to us, like the capital of some vast country, a sovereign state, a proud Byzantium. We were an isolated people, and it was easy to feel proud among small neighbours like Mooroopna and Nathalia.

Not everyone knew everyone back then, but everyone at least knew *of* everyone. There was a familial bond that comes with isolation. People didn't move about much and we were all castaway in this hometown together.

But . . . retract from Victoria and its places, into Shep-parton and its people, and further, into the intimacy of our crescent and neighbours, and still further, back into the house, into the conjoined psyche of the family, where only moments ago we met Mum writing letters home to England and Dad giving us horsey rides . . . retract even further . . . before I knew anyone, I was alone in bed, and there was dread.

Dread is my earliest memory. Being the youngest of four, I was made to go to bed early. First. Alone. Upstairs in an old house miles away from my family, who then spent happy evenings clustered around the TV together. Some nights their laughter drifted up the stairs to me. Some nights the sound of my brother Guy breaking a chair over my eldest sister Debbie's head. It was the right thing to do. Everyone who knew that sister wanted to break a chair on her head. But mostly I heard the distant symphony of a loving family, and thus the sound of profound exclusion.

They lay about downstairs guffawing at the idiocies of the hillbilly dolt Pa Kettle, Mum in the big vinyl armchair, knitting jumpers for them, Dad relaxed by beer into lying on the floor alongside his children while they gummed Eskimo Pies with their semi-renovated teeth. They were an antipodean *Ancien Régime*, a debauchery of confectionary and hilarity so acute it invited revolution. And me, I sobbed alone, aloft, a blond dauphin locked in a tower of ghouls. Downstairs was a royal court. Upstairs I lay on the rack. Rattle-Rattle.

Some nights I'd sneak down there and stand pixie-quiet with all my famous smartarsery leeched from me, at the back of the living room, comforted to be . . . well, not in the bosom of my family, but at least in the bleachers. And safe, momentarily, from the ghouls stalking about upstairs. The sounds of family fun would mask my presence for a while. The slurping of hot Milo, riddles and jokes told, compliments and affections passed one to another, wind amusingly broken. But soon enough Dad, without even looking round, would ask,

'What is it this time?' I don't know why he asked. He knew what it was. They all did. The bastards. I'd look down at my bare feet and mumble, 'Rattle-Rattle.'

'Oh, God,' they would say. 'Oh no. Are you kidding? We solved Rattle-Rattle. Rattle-Rattle is debunked, done and dusted. Go to bed, Boyboy.'

But Rattle-Rattle, like all archenemies, had a new life for each volume, a new plan for each episode, fresh dread for each new night. Vampires, werewolves, the Joker, the Vietcong . . . burn them alive and they stalked you next night alive again and giving off a stink of singed hair. So kill off Rattle-Rattle with your assurances it was just the wind. Rattle-Rattle only needs a tiny cluster of cells fertilised by darkness to reform and rise again and stalk the upper floor.

Our house was old and wood framed, and on summer nights as the heat ebbed from it it creaked and cracked as it contracted. I know this now. These many years later I can still hear those sounds, and they make perfect sense; a weary house sighing and relaxing, the sun's warehoused energy leaking back into the night. But as a small boy lying upstairs in bed, each sound was the creak of a loose floorboard as mustachioed men in black fedoras crept toward my room.

Most nights, after lying stone dead breathless in bed for dark eons as these crepuscular creeps crept creakily closer, I would break out and begin to shout, 'Rattle-Rattle. Rattle-Rattle. Rattle-Rattle . . .' I was young with a puny vocabulary and Rattle-Rattle was the only way I could describe the noises. They were without beat or tempo, suggestive of a madman's sporadic gait.

9

No wonder whichever amused family members arrived in my small bedroom to answer my alarm, brushing heart-breaking shards of Violet Crumble from their cardigans, were perplexed at my white-faced terror. A guessing game would begin. 'Was it a willy-wagtail?' Mum would ask. I'd shake my head. 'What about a possum?' Dad would ask. No. 'Cicadas?' What fools they were. Or maybe they were deliberately taunting me with wildly inaccurate guesses. Rattle-Rattle was clearly the sound of a mustachioed man in a big hat creeping up the stairs toward me.

'What colour hat?' Dad would ask, when I got that message across. 'Because blokes in brown hats use a kukri, but blokes in black hats prefer a garrote.'

'Blokes in slouch hats carry a knife and fork,' Guy added. 'And a small bottle of mint sauce. Boys taste best with mint sauce. You didn't smell mint sauce, did you?' Well, no. Not until Guy asked that question. But it was all I smelt after it. The mint patch in our garden became a kind of aromatic *memento mori*, a potpourri of cannibalistic doom.

The guessing game would go on until the family tired of it; there was no pausing the TV, and Pa Kettle, though a lazybones *in excelsis*, could cause about ten different kinds of mayhem during a Rattle-Rattle investigation. They would drift back downstairs calling 'Rattle-Rattle' hilariously, loudly telling each other I was a chicken spooked by a wagtail.

Alone in the dark, given the suggestions they'd made, I was invariably more frightened after my family held a Rattle-Rattle investigation than before. One whole summer I lay awake with my eyes scrunched head-achingly tight waiting for the fatal drip of mint sauce on my forehead. I imagined my skeletal remains lying in my cot surrounded by a puddle of red jelly the way a leg of lamb lay on a plate in the fridge. There'd be a pleasant whiff of mint in the air when Mum found me.

They joked about Rattle-Rattle for years, as if it were a proper topic for reminiscence, me sharing my bedroom with a cannibal in an akubra while they held their hillbilly debauch of Eskimo Pies down below. They told me I was a boy-coward. But I say if you are burdened with an imagination that can transform a stanza of micro-creaks into a fully fleshed, nattily dressed hunchback, then you are a hero to have survived the infinite bestiary of your childhood. Only dimwitted children with slate-grey minds sleep easily. My siblings, when they finally came to bed, after Pa Kettle and Polly Waffles and tickles from Dad, snored like tranquillised rhinos.

Later, with Rattle-Rattle finally dead, sprinklers ticked green time in the garden while I went to sleep. It was a cavernous house, its symphony of faint architectural stresses playing distantly through the night into my dreams. Creeping hoodlums and tiptoeing witches spent themselves in endless, pointless perambulation. But by now the ghouls and I had a détente, we had borders; as long as I stayed in my bed they wouldn't come to me. By dawn they were exhausted, and retreated to rest in their netherworld as the magpies began to carol and the horseclop of the baker delivering warm bread in waxed paper alerted me to hunger and set my stomach rumbling.

Our house was the centre of a crescent, a curved cul de sac, and I'd listen to the horse circumnavigate the cart around us, first clockwise, then counter-clockwise, before I rose and padded down the corridor to my parents' bedroom and climbed into bed between them.

From their window you could see in the distance specks that were men dangling from spider webs on the delicate bones of a half-built telecommunications tower. Mum and Dad would be warmly awake drinking tea, and their night-soured mouths combined with the tannins orangely awash in their teacups gave their breath the muted scent of domestic animals. I would complain. 'Yuck. Tea-breath.' And Dad would catch my head in his hands and breathe at my nose while I squirmed and squealed. My own breath did not smell.

These few minutes were mine. Shortly my brother Guy, seven years older than me, and my two sisters, Debbie five years older, and Vicki three years older, would rise and, by their very existence, dilute my importance. The brother would head downstairs on an early mission to catch, kill or discover something that it had occurred to him during the night was catchable, killable or discoverable. Loud noises and protesting neighbours would soon be heard as a result of this. Perhaps he would set a fence alight or throw some workman's tools down a drain.

The sisters would stump into the parents' bedroom, their faces consistently sullen. I had been enjoying exclusive time with Mum and Dad again. They had heard laughter. Debbie's discontent was regal. She came close to the bed but looked away out the window, maximising the nonchalance she was miming by sighting some enthralling scene on the horizon. Vicki pouted showily, her lips puckering until they quivered and ached. There began a theatre of cheering the girls up.

Five minutes of hugs and tickles and teases and they would be spilling their flaccid dreams in marathon detail. I would go out into the upstairs corridor, swing my leg over the bannister and slide fast backwards downstairs, shooting off the end and rolling heels-over-head across the hall floor. And then to breakfast.

If I was downstairs first I would have the crust, toasted crisp, covered with melted butter and piebald with Vegemite. And the cream, yellowly pyramided in the neck of the bottle of milk. Froot Loops, Frosties, Coco Pops – cover guano with sugar and I'd scarf it down.

Some mornings I would find Dad in the kitchen sitting on his stool at the marble slab running an electric shaver across his face absently, its teeth grinding on his bristles while he read the paper. I would climb up on his knee and we would turn to the comic page where Lil' Abner, outrageously muscled, would crush a robber before trying to evade the congratulatory kisses of a blonde girl with enormous, mesmeric breasts; and Little Sport, a local dumbo, would lose out on a pretty girl; and Ginger Meggs and Dennis the Menace would, coincidentally, end up in the last panel of their different strips across a parent's knees having their bottoms spanked with a spoon or brush and great poufs of dust rising off them like sin. On days when these two were beaten I turned the page quickly so Dad couldn't see how the parents of famous, ne'er-do-wells dealt with them.

I would turn around in Dad's lap and wrap my arms around his massive head and take a few good whiffs of him, because in the morning he combed Yardley English Lavender Brilliantine through his hair. This delicious smell faded through the course of the day, so it was best to smell him early.

* * *

On Friday nights he would come home from drinking with his friends at The Shepparton Club. He'd lie in front of the TV with us and laugh at fatheaded movies. Francis the Talking Mule, Abbott and Costello, Ma and Pa Kettle, these were nothing for a man of Law to laugh at. They were slapsticks and goggle-eyed misadventures designed to break kids free of circumstance and sensibleness. Dad would laugh at our laughter, getting a kick out of our crazy giggles. Nobody had a better dad than that. Red-faced and laughing – poking me in the ribs amping my hilarity off the charts. Nobody. As a family we were gifted at fleeing into hilarity. Dad gave us that licence. Dad gave us that gift.

Dinner has been eaten, the washing-up done, and we are in the living room. As the opening credits to *Rawhide* rise across the black-and-white screen and Guy and Debbie and Vicki settle in for Western adventures, negotiations with my mother are lost. She will not have a six year old witness gunplay. Nor does she admire the low-cut blouses of the floozies who inhabit cowboy Arizona. I trudge from the living room in my orange seersucker shorty pyjamas and chains of self-pity on my way to bed.

But, wait. There is one sanctuary before that upstairs exile. The crack of light under my father's study door. In there, I know, he sits at his desk in a cone of lamplight glum before the Law; applicants and affidavits and appeals and heretofores and extra-judicial proceedings, and plaintiffs and summonses and subpoenas populating the range of open books across his desk.

During World War Two he had gone to Melbourne University. The Law faculty there was a gilded finishing school that readied bright minds for a worthy life where the future was wide and well lit. The Law must have seemed a purposeful, bountiful calling then. One sees that faculty's alumni carrying their chins high. But now, here he sits in midlife, mired in endless human contention. The Law, it turns out, is an infinitely barred cage built to contain the seven deathless beasts of Sin.

I open the door slightly, quietly, and peek in at him before I knock, because this way I get to see his face light with smile when he hears the knock and knows I have come. He is always glad to see me. And I feel important rescuing him from the Law for a brief ride with the Geebung boys. 'Hello, Boyboy. You want me to read a poem?'

'"The Geebung Polo Club".'

'Okay.' I climb into his lap and he pushes back the Law books and reaches for the red clothbound hardback volume of Banjo Paterson's *Collected Poetical Works*. As he opens it the sarcophagal whiff of a venerable obsolete world coils forth. Together we flip past 'The Man from Ironbark', past 'Saltbush Bill J. P.'.

*'It was somewhere up the country in a land of rock and scrub.'*

I listen to the poem and am fascinated again; a moth drawn to light always, by the way those players will sacrifice all for glory. And I'm mortified as the Captain of the Geebungs strikes at goal and misses and tumbles off and dies. Though I knew he would do exactly that, because he always does exactly that.

But the drama inside the poem is nothing to the changes it rings in Dad. And it's these changes I come looking for every night. As he reads his eyes shine with a passionate light and his voice lowers tone, and even so young I recognise that tone is involuntary, it is tracking and elucidating some unbounded adult wonder he is taken by. How does this happen? How can these little rhyming stories bring a man so easily from the greyland of Law to this wide wonderful plain dotted with heroes and gravestones?

And I feel it happening to me too. A shortening of breath in my awe at the evils and braveries and beauties and sad endings. We are travellers together in a hallowed place. And Dad knows I get the wonder and am there with him, and I know he knows I get the wonder, which makes me proud, and there is no better place to be.

As he reads the poems of Paterson and Lawson a holy mood settles over us. 'One more, Dad. Pleeaase,' I whisper. And before you know it he is reading all the favourites covering the laughter and lore of men.

'What about Dan McGrew, Dad? Read Dan McGrew. Last one. Dangerous Dan McGrew.' And Dad takes up that small black volume of poems by Robert Service, and a stranger whose day is done staggers into a Yukon saloon from the great alone and sits at the piano and plays a music that opens up a vast emptiness to the listeners. When the song is finished the stranger tells the bar, '. . . one of you is a hound from Hell . . . and that one is Dan McGrew.' And the lights go out and guns blaze and when they come back on The Lady That's

Known as Lou, Dangerous Dan McGrew's lover, has taken the dead stranger in her arms, and Dad's voice has now thickened, lowered to its profound vocal nadir, a husky quavering whisper, and again this isn't voluntary, there is some wonder awash in this man causing this, and it crosses from him to me and I'm thrilled at the duplicity and complexity of people but even more thrilled by the eventual (so eventual as to be post-mortem) faithfulness of The Lady That's Known as Lou.

'Dad, was The Lady That's Known as Lou the stranger's wife?'

'Almost certainly, Boyboy.'

And by now *Rawhide* is over. I hear the voices of my siblings as they wrestle and race up the stairs for the bathroom, the girls protesting that Guy has shoved them and hauled them back by their hair. Mum finds us in the study and says, 'Oh, come on, you two.' Then to Dad, 'He should be asleep by now.' And the tinkling music of the saloon goes silent and that world falls away. But I know it is there. I know Dad and I can go back.

Later, lying in bed, oblongs of light thrown up on the wall through the grapevine lattice by a downstairs bulb, with the thrill of the reading gone, but the vivid memory of that thrill a thrill itself, I think about the little worlds inside the poems and begin to see the silhouette of the god that stood behind each. A writer made these. A writer got each of these worlds to play just as it did. What other thing could a grown-up person do that was more beautiful than this? Or more important? I had seen the plaintiffs and subpoenas of the Law hunch my Dad into a low morbidity. And I had seen poets draw him up and make him big again and reanimate his smile. The timbre of his voice was proof enough of the magic of stories. I would be a writer.

*   *   *

The first time I remember my imagination taking me beyond the normal behaviour of children was when I assassinated the Cisco Kid. He was a TV vaquero, a Mexican cowboy in skin-tight black suit and wide sombrero all set about with fancy silver stitching. He rode with a delightfully jovial side-kick named Pancho he had clearly stolen from Don Quixote. For a half hour each afternoon, out there among the cactus, he righted wrongs, made fools of robbers, and shot rustlers' hats off from unlikely distances. Sometimes he ran his gloved fingers down the quivering cheek of a homesteader's wife.

One night, while I lay in my bed in a comfortable slumber hugging my companions – Dog Scotty, a stuffed pooch with a fetching tartan saddle, and Raa Raa, the mangy remnants of a cot blanket that I constantly stroked on my upper lip – that immoral vaquero made off with my mother. That thin-hipped greaser. He enticed her from our house with a secret call like that of the brushtail possum. Shkrar . . . krar . . . krar . . . krar . . . She rode on the back of his horse to his hideout, where she lay by his campfire as he stroked her elfin hairdo and the willy-wagtail called into the New Mexico night. She loved him, it was clear.

I woke next morning with my first broken heart. Our world, our happy family, was revealed as a fragile shell, liable to be crushed by the first showboating gunslinger to come along, such was my mother's wanton character. She had ditched me for a pretty boy on a dancing horse. As I dressed, my sorrow turned to anger. I had been a good son. I sliced the beans when she wanted the beans sliced. And Dad had been a good husband. Yet she rode off with the first filigreed vaquero to enter my dreams. Hussy. Deserter.

When I went downstairs to the kitchen she said, 'Morning, Boyboy.' I didn't answer. I objected to her familiarity – carrying on as if nothing had happened. She probably interpreted this as my normal early-morning sullenness. She was in a yellow dress, looking pretty, a sparkle of new love in her eyes.

'What will you have for breakfast? Weet-Bix? Patty on toast?' Patty was paté, but we called it patty because paté sounded stupid. 'What about an egg? Hello . . . Hello . . .' She tickled my earlobe with the redly painted nail of her index finger.

I didn't speak to Mum for a week. Slowly the dream was wearing off. My heartbreak had begun to ease and my hatred of the Kid was waning. I didn't really want to do it. But I had made a pact with myself. A man had his honour. There were lines that, once crossed, could not be recrossed without a debt of blood being paid.

Guy was away at boarding school. His room was a museum of boyish idiocy; of self-tanned snakeskins and fox and rabbit pelts, weapons, whips, war books and cowboy hats. I found his Webley & Scott air rifle in his wardrobe behind an ammunition box filled with what looked like cat skulls. To cock its mighty spring I had to put the end of the barrel on the floor and fold my hands on the butt and place it against my chest and pitch my whole body weight on it, lower and lower, bending the gun beneath me until the spring caught at full stretch. Huffing with exertion I pinched a slug between thumb and forefinger and inserted it into the top of the barrel and slammed the gun closed. It was cocked and loaded and fully as tall as I was. I hefted it and smiled, knowing I held my adversary's life in my hands.

I sat on my yellow vinyl pouf in front of our TV, a wood-bodied behemoth on skinny legs, a twenty-four-inch colourless window into post-war America. I laid Guy's air rifle across my lap and slid my left hand up and down its wood stock nervously, in a noble gunfighter's purgatory, waiting for Cisco to make the first move.

I wouldn't shoot him in the back and I wouldn't shoot him while he was talking to a storekeeper or flipping silver dollars to Mexican waifs. But there would come a moment for gunplay. There always came a moment for gunplay. It was all the West had by way of justice or story endings. Clinical gunplay was the gift Cisco offered that world . . . when he wasn't spiriting mothers away from happy homes.

He appeared disguised as a fancy gambler sitting in a stagecoach, pretending not to be the greatest gunfighter in the West and a scourge to dishonest scum. Pancho sat beside him in a bonnet disguised as an ugly widow. Whenever disguises were required Pancho promptly frocked up as a hag. I found this vexing. He could just as well have donned overalls and been a farmer or got into a silk waistcoat and sold some wonderful new snake oil to suckers.

Anyway, the coach stopped at a stream to water the horses, and the robbers, whooping and yelping like the Indians on this show whooped and yelped, galloped down from a pass and Cisco pulled his gun from the back of his pants. But I pulled mine first. 'Have this, greaser.' I pulled the trigger and the gun flinched and gave a mechanical yap. I think I got him in the breadbasket, and would have been gratified to see him pirouette on his bootheels and gasp, 'Ahhh . . . right in the breadbasket.' But the screen vanished before he could flinch.

The TV imploded. Interestingly, it turns out that a TV implosion is only the first act of a TV explosion. A collapse that ricochets back from itself radially, rejuvenated and nasty. Shit flew everywhere. And I remember thinking, as my reflexes flipped me backward off the pouf, that maybe my marksmanship wasn't so good, maybe I hadn't hit Cisco in the breadbasket, maybe I'd hit the stick of dynamite one of the whooping robbers was brandishing. If I had, and if I had been aiming at that stick of TNT, then my marksmanship was really something. I began to suspect I had, secretly, been aiming at it. In months to come I knew I had.

But now the TV stood gutted on its skinny legs wrapped in the smoke of its own history, all its many stories and programs wreathing about it in a glittery dust. I saw Wilma Flintstone's face in the air, Jeannie reclining with her bare midriff, Rin Tin Tin leaping holographically at a shimmering wolf, Max Smart frowning at me in vague recognition, as if I was a kindred dolt. Glass was all across the floor. Pretty shards of electricity were caroming around the empty innards of the set.

When Mum burst in I was under the dining-room table hiding in a copse of chair legs. I pushed the gun back against the wall with my feet and spread Raa Raa on top of it. I didn't think it was needed now that Cisco and his compatriots and enemies were dead and the whole state of New Mexico lay in ruins. She found me there stunned and wordless and stood me up and looked me up and down for damage and finding none picked me up and hugged me to her. 'What happened, Boyboy?'

'I was watching *The Cis . . . The Flintstones* and the TV blew up.'

'Oh, God. Oh, God. Oh, God.' She was shaking, almost crying, with fear. Over her shoulder I looked at the smoking black husk and mouthed, 'Arrivederci, Cisco.'

She sat me at the kitchen table and made me a cup of Akta-Vite. Then she rang the office. Since Guy had gone away to boarding school, whenever she needed to speak to Dad during working hours it was usually about me.

'Hello, Rhonda. Put me through to Mr Graeme.' Cameron and Cameron was, at this stage, a partnership made up of three male Cameron lawyers. The employees could obviously only call one of them Mr Cameron, and that was naturally enough my dad's dad, old Pa. They called Uncle Bruce 'Mr Bruce', and they called Dad 'Mr Graeme'. But all their wives were called Mrs Cameron, sometimes necessitating a clarification such as 'Mr Graeme's Mrs Cameron is on line one.'

'Mr Graeme's with a client, Mrs Cameron.'

'I don't care if he's with a client, there's been an explosion.'

'Ohh . . . is everybody . . . I'll put you through.'

Dad came straight home, knowing that, even discounting Mum's colourful amplifications, something dangerous had happened to the TV. He unplugged the set and spun it around and looked at it from every side shaking his head with his anger building. Then he loaded it into the ute and said, 'Come on, Boyboy. We're off to see Bloomsy.'

We drove down the street and parked outside Bob Bloom-ington's Electrical Goods. Bloomsy had a comb-over and a leer and a reputation for supplying midday infidelities free with white goods he delivered to white housewives whose husbands were at work and susceptible to white-anting. When we walked in to his store he was telling a couple how a particular tumble dryer leavened and massaged the fibres in cashmere.

'Bloomsy,' Dad called across the shop.

He looked at us testily and waved a hand to say he'd be with us soon, he was about to close a deal. 'Bob,' Dad shouted, 'That twenty-four-inch Hi-Fidelity National Panasonic you sold us just blew up like a landmine. Nearly killed the boy.' He pointed at me and I hung my head like some shell-shocked veteran and leaned on a dishwasher, a consumer maimed and affronted by Japanese junk. Bloomsy winced and couched low under this unexpected and grievous vilifi-cation. He made his apologies to the couple he was currently lying to and hustled over to us.

'What's going on, Graeme? What explosion? The NP's the best set in the whole world.'

'Jesus, Bob. The thing's a bomb. The kid could have been killed.'

We took him outside where the gutted husk of the TV stood in the back of the ute. Bloomsy stared at it in alarm as if it was the vanguard of some vast treachery among elec-trical appliances. 'Bloody hell, Graeme. Bloody hell.' He reached out and touched the TV as a man will touch a fallen comrade. 'That's no good. That's no good at all. Goodness me.'

'No good? I'll say it's no good. You'll kill someone selling this Japanese rubbish, Bloomsy. You'll burn someone's house down.'

'Orr . . . no, Graeme. No risk there, I don't think. It's fire-rated.'

'Happy to hear it. We'll rule out a conflagration. But a piece of shit like this could kill you about five different ways.'

'I don't get it. We've never had any trouble with NP, Graeme. NP's usually right as rain.'

Bloomsy hauled the exploded television inside away from passing eyes. We followed him. I had begun to mutter and shake by now, with shell shock and the desire for a free TV. Bloomsy looked at me, chewing his bottom lip, and he looked at the blackened National and then at me again. Something wasn't right. But because the TV had clearly blown up, and because Dad was a senior partner in the biggest law firm in town, he gave us the latest top-of-the-range thirty-inch Blaupunkt Space-Tone Surround Sound. The best TV in the world and the only one of its type in Shepparton, he said.

I felt proud. I had assassinated the Cisco Kid, would-be lothario who'd stroked my mum's hair by a campfire in a dream. And been rewarded with a new TV. Driving back home with our new Blaupunkt, I recalled the many lumbering gunslingers who had tried to bring Cisco down and I smiled involuntarily and said out loud, 'So he went for his gun, but I drew mine first . . .' Which was a line I liked from a Johnny Cash song.

'What?' Dad asked.

'I didn't . . . What?'

Next day after school I turned on the new TV and the Cisco Kid was alive again. And if I had disliked the Japanese rendering of this Mexican do-gooder, then the German version was larger, sharper, louder and more suavely Latin than ever before. A supra-real presence with teeth white as a cartoon tiger's fangs and far more likely to steal a boy's only mother than the pallid iteration of good Samaritan I had killed. My attempts to defeat him had gifted him an improved aura.

I considered shooting the new Germanically-enhanced Cisco, but reckoned it unlikely I'd get away with gunning down a second TV set, judging by the way Bloomsy had eyeballed me, and was, anyway, pretty sure most things German were booby-trapped for revenge. So the Cisco Kid lived on, and I watched Mum for signs of ongoing infatuation, but her ardour for that cad seemed to have cooled after his first death.

\* \* \*

Cameron and Cameron was a Dickensian office of dark wooden panels and frosted glass and the women who worked in the main office typed at breakneck speed and talked in low voices because clients hovered nervously just over the half-ceiling-height wall in the waiting room. Clients were people who needed the law. Bruised and outraged they sat in the waiting room until being ushered in to see my dad or Uncle Bruce or Pa or Johnno, where their various agonies were dissected and law or justice or, anyway, the closest thing to it they were going to get was delivered.

In the waiting room at Cameron and Cameron fresh widows wept noiselessly alongside fidgeting youths with tattooed knuckles charged with crimes of violence. Hairy-armed dairy farmers in semi-formal dress as incongruous as vaudeville chimps in tuxedos lingered, come to see my father about cutting promiscuous daughters from their wills. Business owners cheated by their partners bristled and paced. Wives frocked smartly, come loaded with grievances against soon-to-be-ex-husbands, sat with their lips pursed. Ex-employees come to unload accusation on and reap compensation from dictatorial bosses silently ticked off these accusations on their fingers learning them by rote.

I came here to see Dad. And not having had much experience of pain, I was fascinated to sit amongst these people with their equanimity disfigured by mean circumstance. I sat quietly and studied them, trying to guess their particular agony and wondering how they had come to this low point.

My investigations into the pain of clients began as the normal boyish wide-eyed staring kind. I would ogle weeping widows with a hypnotic intensity they couldn't ignore and that sometimes sobered them up. It is disquieting to have a flagrantly curious boy in your face when your husband has suddenly fallen off the perch and you are venting emotion. The more evident a widow's grief the more evident my fascination. I leaned at them and boggled. Their twisted mouths and shuddering shoulders were a reaction to death.

If my first explorations into the misery of widows were just by way of goggling showily at them, then, given my quick understanding of serious things that happened to old people, I soon became a counsellor. Rapidly having become a veteran of waiting-room sorrow I began to offer up advice to my father's more chronically heartbroken clientele.

One day after school, while waiting for Dad, I sat next to a dried arrangement of womanhood, leached of colour and whiskered as a hound. She wore a dark woollen suit and sat dabbing tears, giving off mousy squeaks of misery and stifling sobs so they sounded like they might break her bones. I began to watch her. I guess I turned to face her and leaned toward her. I was brazen in my study of pain.

Just as rain falling on earth releases a rich petrichor odour, the tears of a new widow furtively exploring the many crevices of her rumpled cheeks and being wiped on her liver-spotted hands release a reek of history, an arc of life, that make many dead worlds rise up in shimmering vision around her. As this widow cried I saw her as she had been in her girlhood in a corseted dress with gigs and phaetons rushing by, holding the hand of her father who wore a white powdered wig while a town crier shouted 'Hear ye . . . Hear ye . . .' Seeing her swathed in these antique scenes I judged she had had a very long life indeed, and her tears concerning death thus seemed a little indulgent to me.

Anyway, I didn't rate death as much of a problem in those days, not having any experience of it and it seeming a threat as distant and abstract as the Soviet Union. So I didn't believe she was doing the right thing by herself here, in public, in my father's office, with these indecorous mousy squeaks and this dabbing at her eyes. I felt I should straighten her out and give her some perspective, given that there was a man sitting alongside her with a missing leg.

I reached out and took hold of her hand. I was seven. 'From the moment we are born we are sentenced to death,' I told her. It was a thing Dad had told me some nights before while we were doing the washing up, and I was mighty impressed with it.

As a stress-alleviating homily it seemed to work for a few moments too. The old prune went quiet and her eyes became contemplative. I thought she was going to smile. The grave robbers and swindlers and fathers of soon-to-be-disinherited daughters otherwise dotted about the room, and the one-legged litigant alongside her, also appeared to come down out of their own problems and onto the plain of philosophical rumination where I had invited them.

They stopped pacing, the cracking of knuckles and sotto voce plea-bargaining went silent, hopalong stopped caressing his stump, the whole room stilled. And I began to puff my chest at having solved this adult problem of death that lingered in the Cameron and Cameron waiting room. Then the old girl set off hooting like I'd poured something very hot on her and the other clients began to make rough observations about me that, synopsised, pretty much amounted to the fact I was a little prick who needed a foot in the arse.

Another day I sat next to a young woman there who was dressed head to toe in denim, bouncing a baby on her lap while smoking. Both of them were crying, the baby loudly and she noiselessly. 'What's wrong with you?' I asked.

She took the smoke from her mouth. 'What? Who are you?'

'A Cameron. A Cameron-and-Cameron Cameron.'

'Fuck,' she said, and put her squealing baby on her hip and her fag in her mouth and walked out of the office, apparently unwilling to have her legal matters handled by a nosy boy.

Just over a wood and frosted glass partition from the waiting room was a hive of female receptionists, secretaries and clerks, and from it came the sounds of typing and of phones being answered in chirpy voices that fell to grave tones when a crestfallen client was encountered, a manslaughter accused, or an abrupt bankrupt.

The women who worked in here were wary of me. I had a gift for recognising pliable underlings, and at Cameron and Cameron, I had discovered a bottomless pool of servitude. They must have despised me and I'm sure behind my back a semaphore of hatred flashed between them; the shaking of fists, the slitting of throats, the strangling of imaginary pencil necks.

When Dad was working late and the pool of female workers had gone home I tromped around their work stations, sampling the archival smells, the scent of old paper salvaged from the strong room, the legal whiffs of wood and rubber and ink – the law in those days smelt of India ink and old paper. People's lives lay across desk tops in pen and ink documents tied with pink legal ribbon.

I'd wander about adding a few misspelt expletives to any half-typed letter hanging from an Olivetti, opening the drawers, overdubbing nonsense onto the dictaphone tapes a secretary had yet to transcribe: 'Dear Mrs Russell, with relation to the Last Will and Testament of your recently deceased husband Harold, tickle my nuts . . .'

They typed these tapes out at such unthinkable speed they would sometimes weave a 'tickle my nuts' into the dissolution of a local dignitary's estate without noticing it. Which would inevitably lead to a spectacularly hostile widow at the front counter of Cameron and Cameron a day or so after she'd come down from her apex of grief and faced the future and read the aforementioned document.

In the school holidays I visited Dad at Cameron and Cameron to eat lunch with him in his office. We would each eat a meat pie followed by a vanilla slice. He had paintings of stockmen roping cattle on his walls. Which made me think of Clancy and how the guy in that poem somehow fancied Clancy wouldn't suit the office. These outback scenes seemed to me to hint that Dad was a Clancy of the Overflow who had been trapped in an office by expectations and responsibilities – one of which was me. So the paintings of the wide open spaces made me feel guilty, and sad.

The office he was trapped in overlooked a small park in the middle of town where a group of local blackfellas drank beneath a telecommunications tower. One lunchtime we watched as an old white-haired guy, staggering drunk, looked around suspiciously before hiding his bottle behind a rock and entering the public toilet. When he came out he couldn't remember where his precious thing was. While we watched he turned confused circles. He looked behind one bush, and another, then under a bench, scratching his head and swearing.

Until Dad couldn't bear it anymore. He laid down his vanilla slice and opened the window and shouted, 'Billy. It's behind that rock there.' He pointed out the bottle and

Billy swooped. I was wide-eyed at what he'd done. Should a lawyer be propagating public drunkenness? I held my slice and waited. He slid the window closed. 'It's all he's got,' Dad told me.

This bottle hunt happened a few more times while I was having lunch with Dad. Until it got to the stage Billy would hide his bottle and wander off to get something from a shop or to go to the toilet and when he got back he'd go through the motions of doing a mystified three-sixty before looking up at Dad's window and shrugging. Dad would slide the window open and shout down, 'Under the far rock.' 'Behind the bench.' 'The yellow bush. To the left. Further left.'

One day we watched Billy place his bottle in a bin and pull some paper over the top of it before staggering away. When he got back it was gone. He looked up at the window and showed his palms. 'Go on, you tell him,' Dad said. I felt proud to be given the job. I slid the window open and yelled, 'Molo Johnson hooked it. He went into Maude Street.'

'Fuckin Molo. Get fucked, Molo,' Billy shouted up at the building. It made me feel good to help him and I wondered if I wasn't on the wrong path in life. Maybe welfare and charity was my thing.

\* \* \*

Talinga Crescent curled around our house like a moat around a castle. The houses across the road that surrounded ours were smaller, and most were filled with older people. Not people who had lived young through another time and finally found themselves here, in dotage. These people had no past. They were grey animals, born into decrepitude; popped into being as desiccated, humourless, slow-moving, child-hating beasts.

There was Mr Sargood, deaf and roaring loud with his pants hitched high and his Torana ricocheting homeward with neighbourhood shrubs, signage and chattels balancing on its bonnet. And Mrs Quickly next to him, protected by a cloud of camphor and silence and a jungle of agapanthus and canna lilies. Loud radio blatherings sometimes erupted from her bedroom window in the small hours when she was trying to get her new-fangled Panasonic from the choral music station to the station where an old queen pretended to be a hetero-lothario and pitched subtle woo at insomniac widows.

She'd crank the volume button by mistake and then panic and crank the tuner. My summer dreams would be torn open by '*And did those feet in ancient time . . .*' followed by a blurt of static and '. . . so pleased to be keeping company tonight with you sleepless ladies tossing and turning in your beds. Here's something to help you toss. A ballad from the crooner's crooner . . . Mr Crosby. Ooh, Bing. Ooh, Bingedybingbing.' About there, when the closet queen DJ had just shouted Bingedybingbing into the borderland of my dreams, Mrs Quickly would pull the plug. I'd be sitting bolt upright wondering what Bingedybingbing meant and who had shouted it.

There was a vacant block next to Mrs Quickly where we built cubbies, launched rockets and dug for gold. Next to that lived Mr and Mrs Mansell who yearned for the Church of England to rise again and make demands on the towns-folk. She was tall, whitely-coiffed and stiffly regal . . . but she could shout like a town crier who'd swallowed another town crier who'd swallowed a megaphone. From a hundred yards her rantings had such an Old Testament sky-deity timbre that a prickly thrill would course your skin and stand your hair if she caught you unawares – which she deliberately did.

She felt licensed by Christianity to shout at us and correct or admonish us whenever she detected moral error in our play. And she always detected moral error in our play. This gave Talinga Crescent a biblical edginess for us younger citizens. We were light on our toes, ready for voices to come from the sky and put us right on God's opinion and on the riders, codicils, addenda and clauses that accompanied his opinion.

Her pious boomings might break over us at any minute. 'Why play on the road? You have a garden. Go home before you're run down and killed. Thou shalt not trespass.' Her voice would rattle fence palings and dogs would growl low in their throats. She had a white tongue crazed as darkly as a Ming vase. I longed to hit it with a hammer to see if it would shatter.

One day she hollered at me with such force the contraction of her muscles shrank her girth enough for her slip to fall off. I was on my knees in our garden near our low brick fence collecting insects to torture. Enticing a beetle into my new Bug Catcher with a sales pitch partially plagiarised from the Bug Catcher ads on TV and partially made up by me. 'Come on, slater-beetle. Dual top-and-bottom ventilation allows for continually circulating air. Like a palace. So roomy the huntsman mightn't even notice you.'

Then the biblical thunderclap: 'Boy, what are you doing?'

I flinched and snared myself in Dad's roses. 'Nnnn . . . Nnnn . . .'

'You haven't got a ladybird in there, have you?' she brayed. '"He prayeth best, who loveth best all things both great and small."'

Wonderful, I thought. I'm just about to get started burning this collection of Bourbons. (Bugs I caught routinely became members of the usurped and sentenced royal families as seen on TV.) I was going to roast this lot with the white-hot point of light that fell like a miniature star from a magnifying glass on a sunny day. And now this old bag had kicked in with her usual homilies and psalms and associated killjoy crap.

But as she shouted 'both great and small' a silky white undergarment appeared from beneath the hem of her skirt, fluttered down her knotty legs, and pooled at her feet. I goggled high horror. I thought the hag and the Lord had teamed up and were punishing me for my abuse of His small things with a striptease, and that her slip was just the first garment to be loosened by His invisible hand. In a moment she would be standing there naked, undressed by God as a vengeance on me and a lesson to me. I burst into tears and wailed, 'Don't strip. I'll let the beetles go.'

'You cruel boy.' She stepped out of her slip, crossed the road and snatched my Bug Catcher from me and shattered it on our brick fence. My Bourbons, my newly minted Dauphins, the Louis I through XIV, the Maries Antoinette and Stuart as seen on TV, became crickets, beetles and spiders and rained across the horse-manure France of the garden bed and scuttled to freedom.

The Bug Catcher had been my newest favourite thing, a birthday present from Aunty Daphne. But its destruction seemed a let-off when set alongside the threatened striptease.

'Thank you,' I whimpered. 'I'm glad you and Him didn't do it.'

'Do what, you stupid boy.' So loud the roses quivered. 'Who's "Him"?'

'You and God. I don't want to see your bottom.'

Mrs Mansell shivered as if some terrible electricity or idea had got hold of her. She was always so loud and full of advice when we met. But the puff and certainty usually drained out of her by the time we'd swapped a few sentences. Seeing she was now bewildered unto spasms I tried to clear things up for her. 'You don't have to show your vagina to boys so they'll free their beetles.'

She tried to slash me with the jagged neck of my own Bug Catcher. Without the low brick wall between us my throat would have been cut from ear to ear. This woman who annually won prizes for the intricately crocheted doilies she donated to the St Augustine's Church Fete had partially undressed in front of a boy and then attempted murder when her advances were rebuffed.

She skinned both her knees on our brick fence when lunging at me. I was high in our bougainvillea hyperventilating and whispering 'Fuck' repeatedly by the time she waddled straight-legged, with bleeding knees, back across the road and tried to bend to pick up her slip, before giving it up and waddling indoors.

Old people . . . old people were powder kegs, all bound up in hair-trigger sensibilities. They had unknowable proprieties. Who could tell what would set them off? And our crescent was bristling with them. I lived in an asylum roamed by dangerous, liver-spotted pachyderms.

Mr Vagg had been watching from his verandah while this went on. It must have been a mystifying exchange, him only being able to hear Mrs Mansell's side of it – the shouting about God's things, the appearance of the white slip, my tears, the smashing of my toy, and the swipe she took at me. But he spent a lot of time on his front verandah, so he would have seen me lunged at by adults before, and it was kind of him not to come to the conclusion I was a little arsehole, instead of a kid bullied by geriatrics.

Mr and Mrs Vagg lived next to Mr and Mrs Mansell. They were farmers who'd retired into the town and thought neighbours an entertainment and took delight in almost anything we did that wasn't endangering their lives or cats. Mr Vagg was often a fly on the wall when I hit hard times with old people. He saw us Cameron kids as a sort of *cinéma-vérité* and if a rock occasionally came flying out from the action on screen and smashed one of his own windows, then, oh well, our dad was good for the money.

I liked Mr Vagg. He wasn't so tangled in the mysterious decencies other oldies were tangled in. If I had knocked a girl off her bike with a yonnie, there would be Mr Vagg sniggering philosophically over his verandah rail, sipping tea, and eagerly awaiting Act II in which I was hauled inside by an ear leaking excuses. I'd sometimes look over at him imploringly, like he was a chorus in a Greek play and had the wherewithal to sort my problems. 'You'd better go for it, Boyboy,' he'd shout. 'They'll be coming.' He called me 'Boyboy'. I think he liked me. This was a jarringly unusual condition in an adult.

Having seen me with my arm shoved down a roof gutter feeling for blackbird eggs, he took me into his house and showed me his egg collection. It was a worldwide accumulation of wonders set out in trays of cotton wool, divided and labelled with Latin and common names. Australian raven. *Corvus coronoides*. Wedge-tailed eagle. *Aquila audax*. This gave them the legitimate scholastic tang of the museum. Every size and pattern and colour and texture of egg a bird ever laid was surely here. I coveted his egg collection so hard my throat ached and I asked him, 'Can I have these when you're dead?'

He laughed. 'I have two sons.'

'Well . . . are they in Vietnam? Or are they sick?'

'No,' he ruffled my hair to help me through the bad news. 'They're both fighting fit and farming at Congupna.'

* * *

Next to Mr and Mrs Vagg lived a dustman. Old Jeremy Kelly. He didn't have anything to do with dust. 'Dust' was the word Shepparton used for 'rubbish'. He collected the town's rubbish and took it to the tip. He wore sand-coloured bib-and-brace overalls and a cap made of the same cloth. He seemed always sad, but I often confused age with sadness. It was always a surprise to me to hear an old person laugh. And I never got their jokes because I wasn't sure they were jokes, or sure they should be telling jokes, so close to death, oblivion and rot as they were.

Mr Kelly drove a truck shaped like an airplane hangar, its rounded iron roof supposed to seal in the badness he carried around. It didn't. In summer it acted as an oven to stew the foulness therein. The truck was the same tan colour as his overalls and cap. His sheds were the same colour too. His wife was about the colour a wife ought to be, but bigger.

At the back of the truck was a running board on which Mr Kelly and his men stepped to empty the dustbins into its gaping black rear. The truck dripped dark juices that neighbourhood dogs would trot to the road centre for, and would sniff until their eyes rolled back and they became dreamy as mathematicians listening to Beethoven, and they would set to licking the bitumen until their tongues were raw or they were run over. Quite a few dogs lost their canine perspicacity and their lives while tracking the drool of Mr Kelly's truck from pool to pool along the town's roads. His road-daubings were a known hazard to dog owners.

The truck was a Bedford and it gave off stunning smells like a piece of Hell broken off and set adrift from the mothership. When it went past we'd flop to the ground moaning and holding our noses shouting, 'Kelly smelly.' It was often followed home by crows that then sat on the fence posts around his yard.

We were pretty sure the truck was full of the recently murdered, because our friend Langdo had read a book in which a French murderer used ravens to dispose of the bodies of his victims and they'd become so partial to the meat they followed him around cawing for mouldering Parisians. Ravens were French crows, Langdo said. And they gave the game away and the French murderer was scooped up by gendarmes, which were cops.

According to Langdo it wasn't likely to be mouldering Parisians in old Kelly's truck. It was more probably the town's drunks passed out in our parks and murdered and crammed into it before dawn. Mr Kelly was a notorious teeto-taller and it seemed believable he disappeared drunks as a demonstration of alcohol's evil. Langdo's sensible moments gave a frightening veracity to his fantasies.

He had announced Pigsy and I were detectives about two hours before he decided we needed a groundbreaking case to make our reputations and get us recognised alongside the household names like Sherlock Holmes and Hercule Poirot. He had given us walkie-talkies made of wood and we'd crept around the crescent spying on our mums hanging out washing and on the old folk gardening and talking, ducking down when they glanced our way and creeping away behind fences and talking in a code that neither they nor we could understand.

Pigsy and I knew Langdo was right. We needed a big case. We'd detected that our mums hung out washing and we'd deduced it was because it was a sunny day. Other than this our morning as detectives had been pretty meaningless.

'The most important work for a detective is solving murders,' Langdo told us. 'Murders are the top of the tree for detectives.' Being older than us, Langdo was able to walk Pigsy and me into all sorts of traps. He didn't make us detectives to solve crimes of family clothes washing. He'd made us detectives to solve murders, because that's what detectives did. So it was more or less our duty to climb into that infernal truck and search for the bodies of the drunks old Kelly was touring around.

We were sitting rib deep in our compost heap, enjoying the warmth of decomposing lawn clippings, breathing the fungal musk and peering through the wooden lattice at old Kelly's truck parked across the road in his yard.

Great swathes of our days were routinely taken up with arguing over who had to do what. If there was a theft or crime in the offing an argument had to be had over whose turn it was. We'd go and squirm into the compost heap where it was warm. 'I blew up old Rogers' letterbox,' I said, when it had become clear a detective was needed to crawl around in the collected filth of the town looking for bodies.

'So what? He wasn't home,' Pigsy replied. 'I rocked the Gribbles' roof.'

'We all rocked the Gribbles' roof,' I said.

'But I got caught.'

'That was your stupid fault for running on a dry footpath with wet feet and getting followed.'

'I threw that plumber's wrenches down the drain and got belted.'

'He was at your house unblocking a drain. No one else knew he was there. We didn't have a chance. So that doesn't count,' I said. 'Anyway, my dad took us all up the river last week.'

'So what. That doesn't come into it. Your dad takes us everywhere.'

'I'm just saying, if I get in trouble Dad won't take any of us anywhere.'

'That's not fair to bring up.'

'Okay, but neither is your plumber.'

The argument went on for about an hour until I remembered I'd shoplifted two Violet Crumbles a few days before and had made Pigsy beg for one until he said I was his best, best friend and he would do anything for me. This small theft, and gift, tipped the 'missions completed' tally in my favour, and the job of snorkelling for cadavers fell to Pigsy.

He pouted and said he didn't want to be a detective and that a Violet Crumble wasn't worth climbing into the Kelly smelly truck for. But Langdo told him Violet Crumbles had two different values. If you were begging for one as a friend was eating his, then they were treasure. But if you'd already eaten one and were full, and maybe even a bit sick, then they were worthless. Pigsy shouldn't forget that I gave him the Violet Crumble when he was begging for it and so I'd given him treasure. Langdo, being three years older, was a kind of boy-philosopher. He was also part Chinese and could knit his brow and enter a cogitative freeze that approximated deep Oriental ruminations. We thought him wise.

Pigsy could see he was surrounded by justifications and reasons. He stripped to his shorts. We told him we'd make sure the coast was clear and would give him our secret whistle if we spotted danger. We followed him as far as our fence and squatted down there with our wooden walkie-talkies as he ran crouching across the road, holding his wooden walkie-talkie, into the Kellys' yard. I loved to watch Pigsy running in a crouch. It almost always meant he was only minutes away from getting his arse kicked.

The truck hunkered there pinging metallically in the sun, an upwelling of noxious fumes shimmying above it as if it was about to birth an outsized genie. Mr Kelly didn't lock its rear, probably assuming nobody was likely to break in and rifle through tons of detritus. Rubbish wasn't parcelled up in plastic bags then. It mingled and flowed loose and wet and

gooey and rotten and sharp and broken like the whole cast of
Hell in a rugby scrum.

Pigsy, once you convinced him of the virtue of a cause,
was a brave kid. He swung the top half of a door open and
climbed up on the step and then hoisted himself up and
flopped in. Gone. A boy sunk in a black void of rubbish and
bodies and fumes. I was awestruck. It was a courageous thing
to do, and I knew, had I lost the argument and got the job, I
would have found some way out, some excuse. I just flat out
wouldn't have done it. It was also the most disgusting thing
I'd ever seen anyone do. And it made me momentarily sad
that Pigsy was so easily sucked in by us – and that he was so
yellow-dog dirty as to cavort in shit of this sort. The boy was
snorkelling in the world's most disgusting substances with
who knew how many dead drunkards.

Langdo and I looked at each other and back at the truck.
We were dumb with amazement. Amazement might be why,
when Mr Kelly sauntered out of his garden gate and into his
yard in his sand-coloured overalls and his sand-coloured cap,
mooching and pooching his lips suggestive of an agreeable
lunch, we didn't whistle our secret whistle. Langdo whispered, 'Shit. Old Kelly.' I relayed the news into my wooden
walkie-talkie. 'Shit. Old Kelly.' When Old Kelly climbed into
the cab of the truck we also didn't whistle our secret whistle.
'Shit, Old Kelly's in the truck,' Langdo whispered. 'Shit, Old
Kelly's in the truck,' I whispered into the walkie-talkie.

He sat in there a while bobbing about, settling his nuts
in his sand-coloured lap. Then he kicked the thing alive and
accelerated out the gate and Pigsy's head, wet with the juices
and oozings of his murdered comrades, appeared at the back

hatch of the truck with a sad expression as if to protest our lack of secret whistle. I held up my wooden walkie-talkie and looked angry and waggled it to show I'd been trying to get through to him – more or less accusing him of not having his unit turned on.

Forlorn men hung about at the Shepparton tip; veterans of wars and bad marriages and gamblers who, in another age, would have lit out for one gold rush or another. Scrounging there for cast-off pram wheels and planks of wood was akin to gold mining or fishing. It got them out of the house, killed time that needed killing, and there was always the chance of a leviathan or a nugget – a garden bench that only needed all its slats replacing, a briquette bag filled with shards of terracotta. Take these home and lay them out before your woman and see if she has the gall to accuse you of wasting your day and being a no-hoper.

They wandered there, every now and then lifting a hand and pressing a finger to a nostril and snorting a blowfly out the other nostril like a bullet. Lean individuals wearing wide-brimmed hats to keep off the sun that was distilling the rubbish to a noxious wonderment. Kicking at crap, bending to turn some promising item over, calling to one another to come and have a gander at this. And when Mr Kelly's truck hove into view each day and pulled to a halt they gathered around it, feigning nonchalance, their hearts pounding like they were about to break the seal on a pharaoh's tomb.

Mr Kelly was a kind of philanthropist here, at the tip, a Carnegie or a Santa. He sat in the truck, not needing to climb down, and men hurried to undo the swinging doors at its rear end, asking him how he was getting along and how was the missus. Good, he said. And good. Then he revved the engine and started the hydraulic ram and the front of the truck tray raised until the rubbish slid out its rear end making a festering hillock with no part of any murdered individual protruding anywhere from it, but a fully besmirched boy draped face down across its summit as if gripping it and claiming the whole rancid bonanza as his own.

This probably flared a territorial anger in a few of the scroungers. Here was a new player, monopolising Kelly's largesse before they could get a look in. A couple began to call him a little arsehole and to tell him to piss off home before they gave him a kicking, which had no effect at all, him being unconscious.

But the majority of these treasure hunters stepped backwards from the new hillock into the rubbish field, mumbling 'Jesus, Jeremy' and 'What the hell?' Wondering, for the first time, what sort of man their benefactor really was.

When Mr Kelly climbed down to investigate what all the bad language was about, and why the men hadn't fallen on his largesse, he half recognised Pigsy as a neighbourhood lad and half realised he might be all the way dead. He took off his sand-coloured cap and wrung it in his hands and said this was either an act of God or a catastrophe of the boy's own making, but it couldn't be sheeted home to a rubbish man going honestly about his business collecting rubbish.

Some of the scroungers agreed that it couldn't. And some, who had never before called Mr Kelly anything but 'Mr Kelly' now became a pretty unanimous chorus murmuring, 'Jeremy, Jeremy, Jeremy.' Which was an accusation that must have stung.

Mr Kelly shuffled through the cans, bones and rinds to the tip-master's hut to phone the police. The police arrived and called the ambulance and the ambulance woke Pigsy up with oxygen from what they called a 'noxious near-asphyxiation'. Then they gave him a tetanus shot while he squealed nonsense.

But they refused to have so soiled a boy in their ambulance. They said Pigsy would defile an antiseptic environment, possibly permanently. So the police had to take him home. But they weren't going to sit alongside a foul-smelling urchin like this either, so they laid him in the back of their paddy wagon in the manner of a Saturday-night plumber.

When the paddy wagon arrived in Quinlan Parade we were up trees silently watching, half expecting a hearse. But the fool had obviously been arrested rather than killed, which was an anticlimax, but still held some delights for us. A cop supported him as he walked inside giving off the twinned reek of detritus and criminality. Up our trees we itched for information. We began to curse Pigsy for having got a simple detective-based investigation of our own commandeered by the uniformed fuzz. If there were bodies in Kelly's truck, the cops would find them now. Probably they'd get medals and promotions and newspaper photos. This is how sad and pointless it was to hang around with Pigsy. He could ruin almost anything.

The modus operandi of a detective might well look like idiocy to a normal citizen not versed in detective ways. Holmes was a coke-head. Poirot shuffled about in drawing rooms all day stroking duchesses' cleavage for intel. If you didn't know they were groundbreaking sleuths you'd have locked them up. And this is how Pigsy appeared to his parents, Myra and James Pigott, when he told them he'd been doing a grid search of Mr Kelly's rubbish to dredge up executed drunks. An idiot, they said. He's flipped, they assumed. *Executed drunks?* they asked.

Seeing their faces stretched in befuddlement and hearing their voices high in disbelief, it suddenly became apparent to Pigsy that Langdo's theory of Mr Kelly being the leader of a hit squad that preyed on alcos was in error to a degree that made it laughable. He'd been suckered. This is how children learn – not by increment, but in enormous and unsettling waves of revelation.

Pigsy clammed up. He would give his parents no more information as to why he'd climbed into a half-full rubbish truck. The incident seemed like self-harm to all the adults around the crescent. A death wish. After it they suspected Pigsy was a kook and tracked him in their peripheral vision lest he climb into an incinerator or a car boot. I fed Mum and Dad snippets of invented kookiness about him. I found him licking Mr Sargood's chooks. I saw him drink toilet water. He lit his farts and they burnt violet and smelt of gunplay. All of this made my own behaviour look sweet by comparison.

\* \* \*

For the milkman, the baker, a tradesman of any kind, or a gardener, to enter Talinga Crescent was to accept a mission behind enemy lines. My brother and sisters and I knew working men by their overalls, their hair oil, their rough language when our parents weren't around, and their milquetoast deference to our parents when they were around. We didn't rate blue-collar people highly. We were the children of a Lawyer, a professional man, and the repercussions of our bad behaviour were muted by our rank. This meant we were freer to be badder than normal children. Freer to ping yonnies off the poor. It was a freedom we took full advantage of.

Not too far from us lived the children of the Housing Commission, and black kids, shoeless kids, sore-ridden and spotted with ringworm. They enjoyed a different freedom. A freedom from responsibility. They could eat anything or nothing. They could wag school and never be hunted down. They were never going to need writing or maths, so the idea of chivvying them out of the broken homes and billabongs where they were swinging like scrawny Tarzans seemed pointless.

We didn't have that freedom. We were going to need mathematics and writing where we were going. I resented the poor kids for having worthless lives ahead of them and thus not having to go to school or behave right. But I enjoyed our freedom to treat working folk with contempt. We were at liberty to treat blue-collar men like snot. If I shot every window out of an old house (and I did), then a scapegoat had to be rustled up and some sort of confession, no matter how blatantly counterfeit, biffed from him.

I didn't know whether Mr James, who mowed our lawns, was simple or stoic. It is likely, in hindsight, that he simply knew his place. In the fugue and fug given off by his Victa mower, inside his cirrus of blue fumes and its waspish wail, walking back and forth in lines across our lawns, he was struck by fusillades of clods picked from garden beds. Our shorts hung low because our pockets were filled with the white gravel that covered our drive, and he was pinged by white bullets fired from our shanghais.

A shanghai was more or less a boy's handgun. A vicious wire-framed catapult, a handle and two arms, between which were strung rubber bands knotted together into strands and attached to a leather swatch, into which I nestled the smooth white pebbles from our driveway that flew straighter than sharp-edged blue road gravel.

Our asymmetrical war on Mr James reached its furious zenith at the Battle of the Lost Lobe. The sound of the mower, and the fact he needed his job, meant it was as easy to sneak up on him as on a deaf slave. My brother Guy, riled by Mr James' bovine tolerance of pain and insult, snuck through the grevilleas to within a car length of him and drew back his shanghai until the rubber bands thinned like string and his hands quivered with the stored power. When he released, the stone curved past Mr James' head leaving a comet trail. He didn't blink. And we let out a sigh of relief that this giant-killing shot had missed.

Until he turned the mower at the end of his row and started pushing back toward us and we saw part of the man's left earlobe was gone. He always held the mower's throttle between the thumb and forefinger of his right hand to keep the engine running evenly through grass of variable thick-ness. As Guy fired the shot the engine might have given a slight mewl of discontent above its normal run noise as Mr James' hand twitched with pain. But if I did hear that trifling and momentary and involuntary crescendo then that was his only reaction to the shooting off of part of his ear. He apparently didn't feel entitled to protest at such a crime.

None of us felt good about it. We were all disappointed in Mr James. He clearly lacked dignity if we could trounce and wound him without him making a fuss that might jeopardise his dollar-an-hour gardening job. We lost the appetite for the bombardment of Mr James after he failed to lament his ear in any meaningful way. I mean, I don't think any of us wanted to shoot his earlobe off. But what we wanted from Mr James, and what we figured he owed us, was his fury after his earlobe was shot off. We wanted him to rise up in mutiny against his lot in life, against our parents and us and his own ugly subservience. We wanted to see him kicking at our perennials in speechless rage and wanging the grass catcher through a window as smoke blew from his nostrils and explosions went off in his forehead that kinked his veins and stood his hair. We wanted him yelling through that broken window at my startled mother that this wasn't damned Russia and he wasn't a damned serf and she could shove her job and her little bastards up her arse.

But if the guy didn't have enough dignity to react like a bad-tempered cartoon duck when you shot his ear off, then, quite frankly, we didn't want him working for us ... we didn't want anything to do with that type of menial menial at all. He was the type of guy who might let you sell his molars to a dentist for a box of beer.

An hour later, when he came to collect his money from Dad at the back door, I was hiding behind the boiler watching, so I'd know what sort of repercussions to expect. He was handed a five-dollar note by my father. He left his hand outstretched with the note lying in it. Dad looked at his ear and gave a small nod. His first born was Attila the Hun. He took another five dollars from his pocket and laid it on top of the first. 'Thanks, Mr Cameron.' Mr James tucked the notes in the chest pocket of his bib-and-brace overalls and walked away as if the selling of a body part was a normal daily transaction, as if the James family sold parts of themselves to the Camerons on a weekly basis. Which, I suppose, they did.

Watching from behind the boiler I learnt a working man's earlobe was worth five bucks in late-sixties rural Australia. Valuable knowledge for a boy who aimed to vivisect the proletariat.

*    *    *

We had endless cleaners. All of them thieves, until, later, after their dismissal, we found the thing they had stolen under a sofa or in a wardrobe in the spare room. Housemaids came and scrubbed our place and drank tea with Mum and told her to give me a Tic Toc biscuit when I'd jammed my finger in a drawer. Mrs Macarthur lasted longest. She waddled about the house as rapidly and stiffly as one of those Corn Flake horses you pulled from the pack and assembled and hung a weight off the breakfast table to make it giddy up to the edge. She had a pushy, aspirational daughter who ensnared me in a romance that ended with me becoming a pornographer and that girl's name and vulva thoroughly blackened.

Though I was young, only six, I was an experienced lover of full grown women, having kissed many attractive, though bitter-tasting, housewives in magazines. But my first real love affair was with Mrs Macarthur's daughter who, Dad said later, should have been put in the village stocks and pelted with fruit and anvils. The whole affair, though done in a day, had indelible aspects.

Mrs Macarthur came twice a week to clean our house and sometimes brought the heavy-limbed Suelynne, who should have been at school, but who looked so sickly that feigning illness was a cinch and her education sporadic. Suelynne was a year older than me, carelessly freckled, her face parenthesised by the ears of a cape hunting dog and her mind brimming with sufficient opinions for a pack of them. But she was brave enough to put these shortcomings aside and tell me we were in love.

Love was new to me and I was prepared to see where it led. So while her mother vacuumed our living room we slunk away to be in love alone in my father's study. To Suelynne, who lived in a Housing Commission cottage, being in love meant sizing up all my household chattels for a future in which we married, I died, and she inherited. She was quite open about it. 'I'm going to put in a swimming pool. You'll probably be dead. Your mother can live in the shed. I'll have her room. But she can't swim in the pool.'

While I was trying to come to terms with the rotten luck of dying just before we had a pool, and the thought of Mum living in a shed, Suelynne began to fiddle with my father's belongings, eventually picking up a bottle of black India ink that, its label boasted, was indelible.

I told her it was serious adult ink for writing laws and I wasn't allowed to play with it and thought she probably wasn't either, even though, I had to admit, she would one day, upon my death, own it. But my love wouldn't listen. She sat on the floor and grunted and scowled while twisting the lid until it popped open and she dropped the bottle into her cross-legged lap and the contents gushed down between her legs, dyeing her vulva (whether indelibly or not I can't say, as I never saw any part of her again after this day) and leaving a semi-lewd silhouette of her small bottom on my father's study carpet that no amount of her mother's elbow grease or apologies could shift.

Some weeks later, after he'd cooled down, Dad started referring to this silhouette as the Shroud of Suelynne, as if it were a miraculous representation of a crucified messiah instead of a potato-stamp of a naughty girl's buttocks. I began to bring boys to the house to see it. Money changed hands. Mum bought a burnt-orange Afghan rug and laid it on the study floor covering the mark and forbade me to lift it on pain of losing my pocket money. No matter. The Shroud of Suelynne was a good little earner. I smuggled boys into the house and spruiked the wonder of her buttocks like the top-hatted impresario of a canvased freak show, before lifting the rug and revealing all.

The complete devaluation of Suelynne's posterial profile as a curiosity took two weeks. But I made fourteen dollars in that brief season. And, yes, I now feel somewhat ashamed. There was the whiff of the pornographer about me, a boy-Hefner peddling his paramour's parts to perverts. I can only say in my defence that the Shroud of Suelynne wasn't explicit, it was a meagre and confusing cleavage, a mere hint filtered through underwear, which had half my clients stamping their little sandalled feet demanding a refund and calling me a fraud. This got them nowhere. I had a 'No Refund' policy clearly advertised with a sign that read 'ON FERUNDS' stuck with a drawing pin to my father's cork board.

Suelynne was forbidden to visit our house after staining her vulva and our carpet. Of what avail a cleaning lady who scrubs all your dunnies and mops your kitchen floor sparkling clean if her daughter is all the while indelibly staining your carpets with her bottom? No. We might as well have had Mr James scattering triffid seeds behind him as he did the mowing.

There is constant blather re absence making the heart grow fonder, but I can say our love didn't survive more than a day of Suelynne's exile. Perhaps it was the ears of the hunting dog that made her so easy to forsake. Perhaps the blackened vulva, or the fact she had plans to exile my mother to a shed. I don't know. I suppose the spectral silhouette of her young behind still haunts that room in that house and is, perhaps, a mark of wonder to a new family.

I went back to kissing housewives in magazines. It seemed safer. They doted on me, no strings attached. Though, in a perverse reminder of that keen inheritor Suelynne, they always tasted sourly of ink.

Suelynne held no real fascination for me. Romantic love was not a thing I understood or craved then. But within a year my friends and I found, to our surprise, we wanted to see naked women. We knew they existed, theoretically and momentarily. And we knew each woman – Mrs Gunn, Langdo's aunt, Miss Austin from school, Steve Meredith's mother, my Dad's secretary – was only ever a minute away from being a naked woman. Their daily ablutions, or a doctor, or some moment of sinful abandon, must make them naked. But we were not doctors. Nor did we know, despite endless speculations and a sneaking regard for Cinzano (having heard my Uncle Jim say, 'That Cinzano's a real leg opener') the trigger for sinful abandon. Women always remained that minute, and a world, away from nakedness.

The naked woman was a rumour, a sphinx, her pointed breasts and thatched bifurcation a Chinese whisper passed from one boy to the next, causing her to undergo a panicky evolution from mermaid to Valkyrie and back.

One Saturday four of us sat in throbbing sunlight on our biggest shed roof pulling out roofing nails with a claw hammer to lay on Quinlan Parade and explode Mr Kelly's truck tyres to get back at him for trying to kill Pigsy in his rubbish truck. Out of nowhere Pigsy admitted in a low voice, as he if were venturing something risky, that he wanted more than anything else to see Betty Rubble without her little blue dress. Barney Rubble's wife. A wasp-waisted Flintstone character. A barefoot cartoon honey from the Stone Age, whose blue dress, come to think of it, had no visible means of support.

Langdo and Nuts Almond and I didn't laugh at him or call him a sicko. This surprised us. We should have been assassinating him with a hail of abuse. The guy was hot for a pen-and-ink mum. But we couldn't denounce him. Because, we realised, we were similarly afflicted. The idea sounded . . . sexy. But, Jesus, a cartoon housewife with a kid called Bam Bam? I was a lunatic. Suddenly, knowing Betty was naked under that blue dress, I was bewitched. In a low voice I told the boys, 'I'd give my Malvern Star to Barney

Rubble for a glimpse of her perky bazoomas.' And they didn't laugh. They just nodded reverently, weighing up the worth of their own bikes. Apparently we were a sick, sick crew.

What requirement a boy has for a naked woman I couldn't say. Was some seed of need sending a shoot to the surface of our psyche, flaring momentary pangs of a future appetite? I don't know. But we desperately wanted to see them. As mentioned, Pigsy and I often lay with torches in the dark cupboard under our stairs and kissed bra-clad housewives torn from magazines and stuck to the underside of the steps.

And now, with this Betty Rubble revelation renting our Saturday asunder, something had to be done. The four of us pooled our pocket money and came up with three dollars twenty. We sucked in Pigsy to ask Leah Houston to do a striptease for us for three-twenty. Leah was often over at our place. She was the current best friend of my sister Debbie and a venerable and voluptuous thirteen year old . . . tits and a sweet smile. If Pigsy's suggestion met with outrage he'd be slapped and my mum would be told and he'd be sent home in disgrace and on his way my mum would ring his and she'd be waiting with the wooden spoon when he arrived. No downside there for Langdo, Nuts and me.

But Leah's eyes lit up. She discussed the proposition in whispers with Debbie and they nodded and sniggered and the deal was on. She took the money and agreed to strip naked. My stomach began to flip and wonder and fear settled on me. My God. Women. Three bucks twenty.

The four of us boys perched in a tree outside Debbie's room. We heard Shirley Bassey start up in there singing

'Goldfinger'. Good. Good music to striptease by, we nodded at one another. When they pulled the curtain back Leah was wrapped in a sheet. This was apparently promising. 'In a bed sheet,' Langdo said, 'is how one sort of strippers start off.'

She began to writhe beneath it, mugging sexy smiles at us, punctuated with little scowls as she struggled with this button or that catch. She and Debbie kept breaking from the sexy act into fits of giggles, which we found disconcerting, unprofessional. Leah's hand would disappear beneath the bed sheet and reappear out from beneath its folds holding a piece of clothing, which she'd twirl before the window. This was more contortion than strip tease. It started to feel like a con. She produced her bra, unless Debbie had given her a spare one to hide beneath the sheet. Then she produced some knickers, which also might have been a plant, and twirled them on a finger point and slung them at the window. They sounded like a moth hitting a lamp. Then Debbie yelled through the glass that Luscious Leah was now totally naked under the sheet. Nude. Not a stitch on. And, as such, her contract was fulfilled.

They drew the curtain as we shouted robbery. In the window I saw a reflection of a nonplussed gibbon perched in a tree wearing my favourite shirt. I calculated I could have bought twenty Choo-Choo Bars with the striptease money. And, even gypped, felt right to have spent it this way.

Who do you go to when you've paid a neighbourhood girl to strip and the show hasn't been as advertised and you've seen none of the morsels you coveted? You can't complain to Mum. The ombudsman is a distant authority, unconcerned with frauds of teenage tit. So we hauled her bike up a tree with a rope and left it tied up there, twenty metres high. Ride that home, you fraudulent mole.

In my grandparents' house, in Uncle Bruce's old room, there was a poster on the wall of Marilyn Monroe lying in folds of red velvet with her breasts exposed. In the corners of vacant blocks, or down in the bush beyond the levee, we sometimes found an abandoned *MAN* magazine. Pastel women in soft focus with monumental breasts and, occasionally, a dark triangle as mysterious as Bermuda's. If you look at anything long enough there comes a point where you don't see more, you see less.

One summer night when we were sleeping in hammocks in our garden, Pigsy ran up the Mansells' driveway and jumped up at a window and returned saying he'd seen Mrs Mansell in the shower and got a fat because of it. Pigsy was a stupendously barefaced liar. Perhaps, once, a digger sprawled at midnight in the trenches at Lone Pine had found lust blooming in his half sleep for Mrs Mansell. But that psychological phenomenon had not been possible for half a century. So if Pigsy had seen her naked it was a dubious triumph, and I'm pretty sure he'd have turned to stone, rather than got wood.

The winter I was eleven we went to the Gold Coast for a holiday. In an apartment across the street from ours, a young woman walked around naked all day in front of two men. She ironed and laughed and ate nude. The two guys didn't pay her any mind. Seeing this I felt low. I swore I wouldn't grow up to be a debased nihilist like that pair. I flattened my eyeballs against the glass and stayed there a week. And despite that state being beautiful one day and perfect the

57

next, I came home pallid as a troglodyte. None of my friends believed I'd been further north than the local sewage farm.

*   *   *

Across the road from Talinga Crescent was bush that ran all the way to the next town, Mooroopna. It was cut through by the high-banked, muddy Goulburn River. This bush was where the blackfellas had lived. Some were still there, drunk now, frighteningly ungraceful, loud with whitefella swear-words, throwing bottles and abuse like it was their day job. Nothing like the lethal wraiths that had once drifted through the place.

The bush wasn't as wild as when the whites arrived, but it was still a place beyond adults. Kids buried lead they'd stolen from building sites there. Poisonous snakes and covert fornications wound and unwound in the sun. Here-and-there, now-and-then, stolen cars were burnt there and their blackened carcasses became fortresses for our wars. And the scrawny bodies of abandoned dogs appeared, sporting a vestige of cuteness, before rotting away. Swagmen came and went, leaving humpies in which we'd find empty bottles and fatigued photos of nude women. We saw a lot of Italians rutting in the bush by the levee, cries rising from their various grottos like drunks were beating spaniels with wine bottles.

We went to this bush to play. To build secret forts and make war on Nazis and to have rock fights and to take shallow drags on dizzying cigarettes. To walk about nude with our faces painted with mud and grunt in native tongues. To kill whatever we could. It was a monoculture ruled by a tribe of boys. There were no adult laws and no adult eyes and thus we became cowboys and pirates and secret agents and we saved maidens and declared love to them.

If childhood was an endless yearning to find new worlds, worlds removed from the known adult world, an active search for places beyond the control of grown-ups, then this forest was the Jupiter of the kid solar system. But there were many other places and planets. They were everywhere. Vacant blocks and abandoned houses, building sites, treetops and culverts, woodheaps and garden beds and roof valleys and dry channels. Places we could be protagonists. Places we could test the new things we'd learnt. In the private and wild places beyond adults we became condemned men and escapees and wounded soldiers, we were frequently gutshot and limped while friends applied poultices of dirt and stinging nettle.

A bike increased the world tenfold and joined all the wild places together. Throw yourself over the seat and pump your legs twenty times while standing and you were away, at speed, beyond earshot, beyond recall, a period of freedom stretching out in front and trees and fences whizzing past. Mine was a cherry-red Malvern Star and I rode it with the virtuosity of a circus chimp on a galloping pony.

A bike not only joined the wild adult-free swatches of our world, it meant you could escape any crime scene. How could an adult catch a kid on his bike? As long as you resisted the gravitational obedience to 'Come back here' when an outraged adult called, they either had to run after you, and with a twenty-yard start you could never be caught, or they had to chase by car. But the town was full of shortcuts and tracks where cars couldn't go, gaps in fences and footbridges over channels and alleyways and steps and rough ground and the bush. When chased we vamoosed through secret tunnels into the geometric jungle of our neighbourhoods like pygmies through the vines.

Ride up a back alley and stand on your bike's crossbar and you could lean over a fence and steal peaches and catch a glimpse of a svelte mother in a petticoat and be away, pumping the pedals, shirt tucked in and bulging with fruit, wondering at the emerging skerrick of fascination you felt at a bare-legged woman.

* * *

These days I can think of no good reason for joining a club whose only stated purpose is to collect and store urine in bottles. Maybe no such clubs exist anymore. Perhaps they have gone the way of gentlemen's clubs, hunt clubs and Masonic Halls. But if they do exist I wouldn't become a member. I've paid my dues. Urine has no real value. You can corner the market and still not be king. It is not rare, it has no medicinal properties, nor is it an additive, a taste enhancer, a fixative or a cleanser. Apparently you can drink it if you're lost in a desert. But I wasn't lost in a desert.

Many times I'd heard Dad's friend Lucky Simson say about various people, 'I wouldn't piss on him if he was on fire, Lucky.' He called everyone 'Lucky'. And he said this so often I developed a notion his acquaintances routinely burst into flame and required his hydraulic ministrations. The way he told it, there was some line of demarcation visible to adults, and the people you would piss on if they were on fire were on one side of it, and the people you wouldn't piss on if they were on fire were on the other.

But as a boy I didn't know who to piss on if they spontaneously combusted. This worried me. But I wasn't a good-hearted boy, and I think I would have let most people who weren't family burn.

Through long contemplation of my second-grade teacher, Miss Scott, I realised people's salvation depended largely on how they were treating you at the moment of combustion. If she was making me do my seven-times table I wouldn't piss on her if she went up in a ball of blue flame. But if she was reading us a story in which the Three Investigators were deducing their way to victory over greasy horse thieves, then I would have hosed her head to toe in a trice and told her to mop her brow and read on. At such times I was often holding my dick unconsciously through my shorts, just so as to have my equipment ready. I guess Miss Scott will never know what a state of grace she lived in, that my benevolent reservoir was always hovering, at her disposal should a vengeful Lord light her up.

I joined the Wee Club because my eldest sister, Debbie, told me to and said boys were the most important members of wee clubs because boys had dicks and could wee more accurately than girls could, and that made them, she said with Darwinian acuity, 'especially well adapted'.

Weeing in a bottle wasn't a skill I'd given much weight to before Debbie declared it a God-given male dexterity. I hadn't, to that point, been especially enamoured of accuracy and could hardly care if I hit the toilet bowl or not. After she complimented me on my marksmanship, though, I considered myself a sharpshooter to rival the Sundance Kid, who could hurry a rock across a corral with six consecutive bullets. Little did I know signing up to her Wee Club was like signing up to a voyage with Captain Cook – as his ship's goat. I was force-fed fluids until I bloated and bleated with the need to exude and extrude. Debbie, once her stocks of urine began to build, became insatiable.

We had a large garden and down the back behind a hedge was a shed that had become an aviary and then become a shed again after our finches were eaten by a snake. Dad was at work when the snake ate the finches. On hearing our screams and me, at five, yelling, 'A fucking snake,' Mr Quinlan came over with a shovel and put me on his shoulders and told me to quieten down. He lifted a sack and killed the snake, which had gorged itself torpid on our beloved pets. He cut off its head and ran his hand down its length in a choke hold from the tail end to the bloody neck as dead and drenched finches popped out one by one: Goldy, Rankin, Tweets, Small One, Big One, Zebby, Whitey . . . This snake had caught and swallowed twenty finches. We buried them in a mass grave, a tissue box, in the empty block next door, and I threw the snake over Mrs Spivey's fence. When she found it days later I guess she thought it was alive, because she yelled the same thing I had when I found it swallowing finches.

Now, in the time after finches, we put on amateur theatrical productions in the shed, and it became HQ for clubs we formed for the same reason people always form clubs, to deny membership to persons we were down on. We probably started three or four clubs a month that had no purpose other than the pleasure of telling Pigsy he wasn't allowed to join, because he didn't understand the finer duplicities of international espionage, or because he couldn't empathise with Superman's heart-wrenching loss at leaving his parents and planet so young, or he didn't know just how much salt was needed nor what technique required to tan a tiger-snake skin. One club we denied him entry to because he had a foreskin, which, in hindsight, seems very adult of us.

Pigsy lived across a vacant block at the end of our crescent. He was an only child and his mother was lorded over and browbeaten by his tyrannous father. His father didn't work. Nor did he have any friends. He owned flats and rode round on a rusty old girls' bike to inspect them and collect rent and boss his tenants around. Whenever he saw me he'd say, 'Hello, young Cameron. What have they been feeding you on, nuts and bolts?' He drank champagne in his air-conditioned living room watching black-and-white TV alone, and he slept in an air-conditioned bedroom alone.

Pigsy and his mother spent their time in the uncooled kitchen in a sullen conspiracy that never bore fruit. Mr Pigott drove a gargantuan American sedan with canvas covering the seats. Mrs Pigott didn't drive and when she was allowed in the car she sat in the back, while Pigsy sat proudly up front next to his dad. If I went anywhere with them I sat in the back with Mrs Pigott.

Pigsy played the game from both ends. He would damn his father behind his back while he sat with his mother in the kitchen, then join his father's misuse of his mother when they were all three together. Partly he was mimicking his father, and partly he was showing off to me.

Even I, a boy of six, a known sod with no rights, the lowliest of the low, was able to boss Mrs Pigott around if I wanted. Get me a banana Saturn with nutmeg grated on top. I want some ice cream. But I couldn't bring myself to do it. I never felt anything but sorrow for her. My own mother was an unpredictable woman, important enough to have her hair built big in Hilda's Salon; you treated her with the same caution you treated a drunk who'd dug up a grenade. I'd never seen a mother treated that way.

Whenever Mrs Pigott and I were alone together, when Pigsy was in another room at a piano lesson, or outside mowing the lawn, I spoke softly to her and, though it was her habit to wait on people hand and foot, I never let her do anything for me. And, because you couldn't say such things to adults, I spent a lot of time trying, with temple-throbbing concentration, to stare a beam of goodwill at her that would make her feel better and let her know she was all right and I liked her.

The stare was mostly at the back of her head while she was ironing clothes or making pies, and it was supposed to seep into her brain and make it glow with a kind of holy contentment. Sometimes I'd get locked into the stare, my head would quiver and my eyes cross with concentration and I'd see a beam of care reaching out for her, irradiating her with happiness. And sometimes she'd turn around and catch me with this white-lipped trance on my face as I stared at her. At such moments she must have thought me a very strange boy. What did I want from her, ogling her as audaciously as a hypnotist skewers a chook?

Pigsy, having no brothers and sisters, spent a lot of time

at my place using mine. He was in our house most days. At private family times he would lounge silently as a lizard so as not to be noticed. Dad would see him in his sly hibernation and say, 'Peter, we're having dinner. Go home.'

The Wee Club set up its HQ in the garden shed alongside the sandpit. Debbie was the president and Vicki and I were the members. Pigsy was permitted to join when Debbie realised that I, a scrawny boy, wasn't going to be able to brew enough product for a clientele, or a war, or for whatever other reason the wee might be required.

Pigsy was seven, becoming a man, and unsure about bringing out his dick in front of my sisters and filling jars with urine at their command. Being newly proud of my hydraulic dexterity I found his bashfulness perplexing. 'Go on, Pigsy.'

'Why do they have to watch?' He pointed at my sisters.

'Listen, Pigsy,' Debbie told him, 'if you want to be in the club you have to do it with witnesses. We know you, and we don't trust you. You'll probably go home and squeeze yellow crepe paper into water and bring it back and tell us it's wee.' I looked at Pigsy open-mouthed at this rank deception. What a sneaky kid. Later, after the break-up of the club, I found out all the wee Debbie and Vicki supplied was counterfeit, manufactured with yellow crepe paper squeezed in water.

'The wee has to be authentic,' Debbie told him. 'Otherwise it's not a proper wee club. So I have to witness it for authenticity.'

'Witness for . . . But we don't get to watch you. You just bring it out of your house already in a jar.' He pointed at the house and then at a jar.

'Are you a weirdo? Wanting to watch girls do wee?'

'I don't want to watch . . .'

'Good, then wee in this jar and be quiet or you can go home and start your own wee club with just you and your stupid father,' Debbie said. 'I bet his wee is old and foul.'

Pigsy's face went red and he looked down at his feet. It was excruciating to have his father's private bodily functions brought up in public, his father's actual penis brought into the conversation by implication. Debbie was adept at psychological warfare. She held out a Vegemite jar. 'Here.'

Debbie and Vicki served us water, and when we couldn't drink any more of that, they sweetened it with Cottee's 50-50 cordial, which we liked more than water, and, even overhydrated already, could drink freely. We jumped up and down and you could hear liquid sloshing in our bellies. Eventually, we shook our heads at cordial, so Debbie fetched a large bottle of Marchants lemonade, which, the bright-teethed children in party frocks and Brylcreem on the TV ads sang, was 'sparkle . . . arkle . . . arkling' and which I wasn't allowed to drink except one glass on Saturday morning, and which I usually traded to Guy or Debbie for them telling me I was their favourite brother. The catchy TV jingle and the fact we usually weren't allowed to drink the stuff made it irresistible.

Pigsy and I drank Marchants lemonade unto a sparkle . . . arkle . . . arkling belly ache. Not long after we'd skolled that bottle we began to holler for jars. Even with my noted marksmanship a jar was a more suitable receptacle for the panicky overture of this deluge than a bottle. We dropped our shorts and Debbie turned on a garden tap as a subliminal giddy-up.

But I needed no subliminal giddy-up. I frothily filled a Vegemite jar as Pigsy stood alongside me and filled another. We boasted about what was to come. 'I haven't even started.' 'I've got lots more.' 'You maybe should time me with a stop-watch, this could be a record.' 'Bring me a bucket.' 'Bring me a bushfire.' The deflation of our distended bladders was so palpable we laughed out loud as we pissed.

Vicki decanted the contents of the Vegemite jars into a Vickers Gin bottle using Mum's kitchen funnel, while we filled peanut butter jars. By the time these were full she had our Vegemite jars empty and ready to go again. She was a clumsy girl and throughout the life of the Wee Club her hands and frock were sodden with spillage and she gave off a stale fug that made me blink sharply.

Debbie, being president of Wee Club, wasn't hands on with the product itself. She stood back out of the spray with pride lighting her face and her hands cupped beneath her chin like a Krupp or a Ford whose many years of blue-sky thinking, meticulous design and precise engineering were finally paying off in the form of groundbreaking, next-generation merchandise. She had cornered the market on piss. She was its supreme mogul and monopolist and must have gone to bed at night comforted knowing that no girl for towns around had a vault of urine to compare with hers.

Force-feeding Pigsy and me juices, cordials, pop drinks and flavoured milks in this way, it was only a little over a month before we had more than a hundred and fifty Vickers Gin bottles filled and capped and shelved and ageing sweetly in our shed. My sisters brought their wee from the house and placed it on the lower shelves away from ours. They seemed to lack faith in its vintage. I understood this. Ours was made with lemonade and laughter, shot gold and steaming into Vegemite jars on clear blue summer days. Theirs was smuggled shamefully from indoors beneath their cardigans. It was over-yellow and cool to the touch. Girl wee. Destined for the bottom shelves, never uncorked for its bouquet, nor held to the sun for its lustre.

In our HQ my sisters walked along the shelves of urine admiring the way the sun caught and flashed on the limitlessly faceted glass of the Vickers bottles and flared a variety of yellows and golds that would have beggared Aladdin's few baubles. Debbie would sometimes take a bottle off a shelf and unscrew the top and sniff it showily and pucker her lips in enquiry before announcing, 'Boyboy . . . first piss of the morning . . . pot roast the night before.'

She had the swagger of a connoisseur. I was amazed at how fast she had learnt the game. She'd uncap another bottle. 'Pigsy . . . after beetroot for lunch.'

Pigsy and I also took pride in the groaning shelves weighted with our water. But it came at a cost. She worked us hard, with barely a day's rest. We took Vegemite jars to bed with us. We were run covertly round the clock like a couple of hillbilly stills, and our moonshine was warehoused for we knew not what. Some future in which piss might be myrrh? Some bright day on which the Prime Minister would announce the end of the pound and the introduction of the pint-of-piss as our new currency and thereby make us Midas?

After a month Pigsy and I couldn't see the point. My stomach was sore and I figured my bladder was now large as a li-lo. I felt wounded, gutshot. I checked myself in the mirror and was appalled to see I was developing a pot belly in miniature replica of some of the town's infamous barflies.

The Wee Club ran out of steam, as it were, after about a month and a half, when all the shelves were stocked and we gazed on it with waning pride as we began to realise our hoarded piss, though pretty as jewels, was valueless. We couldn't show it off or boast of it, we had to keep it a secret. So there wasn't even any real value in it as transgression. And wee is readily available if one requires it. There seems no need to store vast quantities against a rainy day or a nuclear winter.

One morning out by the sheds as Pigsy fired his sudsy night-time micturition into a jar he said, 'This is stupid.' My doubts crystallised around his words and I realised it was. I could be inside eating toast and here I was screwing the lid on a jar of warm wee for Vicki to decant. Stupid. Debbie was stupid. She was mad with the lust for our golden water. But you crossed Debbie at your peril. When she said 'piss' we either produced a golden parabola a rat could run up, or an intricate vengeance awaited. Everyone was scared of Debbie.

They became a brooding danger out there in the shed, those hundred or so maturing varietals. By the middle of that second month visualising catastrophe became routine for me.

My Uncle Jim was a home brewer whose beer often exploded in his laundry, staining Aunty Norma's petticoats and sending him to the doghouse. What if our wee exploded? My early-morning brews were as frothy as the pilsner that regularly wrecked his laundry and domesticity. What if it was as chemically unstable?

At night as I lay in bed the bottles began to explode in my imagination. The first few were muted, like depth charges. Just enough noise to invite investigation, but not to cause alarm. Mum wandered down behind the hedge to the sheds in one of her thin flowery dresses to see what the ruckus was. As she swung the shed door wide, these vintages with military gravitas, the super-frothies orange with Coke acids, the viciously viscous varietals coiling sinister with dairy oils, these would be touched off by the rasping of the rusty hinges.

She would be buffeted by shockwaves and gradually tanned orange by a hundred vintages washing over her in staccato waves. Her proud beehive swept into a sodden point behind her like a comet tail.

This night-time anxiety had a sinister veracity while I lay in bed. In the daytime it faded. Wee could not detonate and dye Mum orange. I was sure of that. In daylight that fear was replaced by realer Armageddons ripe with shame and sorrow.

By daytime my worries were clearer and nearer. Even at six I realised if our vault of piss was discovered by Mum or Dad they would be touched by a cold shock that wouldn't turn into anger but would instead play out in a long and silent despair. The thought of this had me throwing sly glances at them over meals to see if they knew that something wasn't quite right with us, that we were macabre kids who treasured urine. I began to be oppressed by the possibility they might catch on, and to feel sad that they would ever have to know.

I imagined Mum and Dad after the story broke, revelations strange enough to make the *Shepparton News*: 'URINE

FOUND IN LAWYER'S SHED'. I imagined them having to face their friends, whose kids didn't establish repositories of urine, but won scholarships and sang in choirs. Their friends wouldn't speak of their own children's achievements anymore, after the headlines. To bring up their darlings' triumphs would be to usher forth a corresponding silence from our mum and dad that spoke of our bizarre proclivities and their shame.

I knew that the world punished parents for the crimes of their children. And that what we were up to was a major and creepy piece of work that would ruin my parents socially and economically. Who seeks legal counsel from a man with a shed full of piss? How can a man debate with dignity in a court of law while shrouded in the ineradicable uric odour of his offspring and assailed by the tittering of school excursions?

We were their shame. But we were their children too. They wouldn't abandon us. We would move, as a family, to live in a humpy made of flattened kerosene tins down by the river. I would beg for food from town boys who were once my friends and who rode out on their bikes to taunt us on weekends. With my gift for faking pain I would be an effective beggar and would share my bounty of half donuts and cold chops with my family.

*   *   *

Then, one Sunday, a straitlaced old lady called Marny came doddering down to the back of the garden calling our names in an aged and broken voice that sounded like the end of all things. This woman was a churchgoer, harbouring the unfeasible values those people are regularly infested with. 'Hello? Debbie? Anson? Vicki? Hellooo . . .?'

I knew the sight of our warehoused wee would upset her dangerously, and hoped, briefly, the shock of it might kill her. We could bury her flaccid corpse in the sandpit and deny she ever visited us. Her disappearance would be a great mystery we would work on side by side with detectives in fedoras for years to come.

'Hello? Debbie? Vicki? Hellooo . . .' Marny was our Dad's mother. She grew up a Furphy in a town where that name rang with the grandeur of famous water carts and classic novels. As a girl she and her siblings rode in a buggy behind a horse while the rest of Shepparton walked. I had seen her in browned-off photographs looking young, but hoarding a prehistory of her vast age in her sharp features, and not a car or a clean-shaven man yet in the world. The Furphys still owned a foundry and ironworks in town and Marny had been, and was still, the daughter of a local dynasty.

She married Frank Cameron, a boy from Orbost, who returned from the First War and finished his law degree in Melbourne before coming to Shepparton to do his articles. He joined the law firm of a man named Sutherland and outlived him, and the firm went on to become Cameron and Cameron when his sons joined. He smoked three packs of Viscount a day with trembling hands, clacking his false teeth on them happily as an infant.

Either age or Passchendaele, or both, had made Frank, who we called 'Pa', a quiet man by the time I met him. He never talked of that war to me, but as an addicted and adept eaves-dropper I overheard him tell another man at a party that he once walked up a hill in France without stepping on anything but dead Frenchmen the whole way. In bed at night I tried to see that hill and the Frenchmen. It seemed a very grand thing to have done. I saw him striding out for the summit, sad but determined, keeping his chin high so he didn't have to discomfit the dead by making eye contact with them in their embarrassing and unusual circumstance. Standing on faces and in crotches as he went. This was not the sort of stuff women or shirkers had to do. It was the dread price of heroism. And I knew full well I would have to walk up a hill paved with men, probably Frenchmen, myself one day.

Marny, though she didn't boast about it over games of bridge with Lady Fairley, was my grandmother. Her hands were covered with liver spots and her face was painted white and in her calf-length frocks a massive bosom lurked like an unholy anachronism. She had seen sufficient generations come and go not to be excited or duped by mine. And had reached that pious longevity where people either see no need for subtlety and diplomacy or the facility for both just withers like one's ability to make love or run a marathon. She didn't like me and it wasn't uncommon for her, on first seeing me, to reel back and say in the most outraged way, 'Whatever do you look like?'

It became a catchcry around our house. If I had a cool new shirt or shorts or bathers or slightly edgy sneakers, to bring me down my sisters would ask incredulously, 'Whatever do you look like?'

Being a religious woman, the only joy Marny ever got from me was when she recognised in my conduct a bright and undeniable refutation of evolution. Look at this newest, youngest member of the family trying to glimpse his own buttocks. Mankind is surely heading helter-skelter back in among the apes, rather than away from them. I think she and her minister flashed polaroids of me to each other on Sunday and laughed at Darwin.

The passion had leached from our Wee Club by now. Debbie, Vicki, Pigsy and I were all there in the dark shed trying half-heartedly to gloat over our monopoly. Debbie was plinking her fingernails on the bottles making pretty tunes. 'No one else has got a shed full of wee like us.' 'No. No one.' 'Everyone would be jealous if they knew.' 'Yeah, wouldn't they.' 'Hoffy hasn't got any.' 'No way.' 'No one has. "Cause no one else thought of it.' 'Yeah. We thought of it.'

Debbie was still addicted to the power of her presidency. And though it was clear the club was faltering in intent, she was still making plans for future expansion. 'We should use flagons. Flagons can hold gallons.'

'Debbie? Vicki . . .?' The desiccated voice of doddering doom. The catch on the shed door began to rattle as Marny tried to get in. 'I know you're in there. Whatever are you doing?'

Debbie was wearing an embroidered felt bolero waistcoat made for her by Marny. She took it off and whispered to me, 'Strip off your clothes and put this on. You're going to be a decoy.'

'A what? I don't want to . . .'

'It's like being a hero. A greater-love-hath–no-man type of hero. You know . . . Lest We Forget. It's honourable.' Seeing my reluctance she turned to look at Pigsy. 'Hmmm . . . maybe I'll get Pigsy to do it. He could probably do it better. It being so honourable.'

'No. He couldn't be a decoy. Only I could. I'll do it.'

Debbie whipped my shorts down and in the half dark I stripped naked and put on her blue felt waistcoat. All the while the door was rattling. A voice from a thousand years ago. 'Let me in. Whatever are you up to? Let me in. I've come to visit. Vicki? I can hear you.'

Debbie whispered, 'Just say "Hello, Marny' and walk straight past her as if you're fully dressed and everything is normal. She thinks you're mental, anyway. She'll chase you back to the house.'

'Mum will be angry.'

'No way. Tell Mum your clothes got wet and I lent you my waistcoat so you wouldn't be cold.'

This made sense to me. Not only was I not affronted by my own nudity, I had heard other people call me cute while I was naked and was eager to exploit this admiration whenever I could.

Debbie opened the door just wide enough for me to slip out. When Marny saw me she put a hand to her mouth and one to her ribs to brace herself against the abrupt descent our once-respected family was taking with me as its newest and most disgusting member. 'Whatever are you up to now?'

The president of our little club had given me instructions to walk straight past this old dame and on into the house, my near nudity inevitably luring her along lecturing and hectoring in my wake. But, seeing the horror on Marny's face, I began to awaken to the power of my performance. The role of decoy was a heroic one that surely needed to be played a little more fully than Debbie had imagined. As I got to Marny I put my left hand into my left armpit and began to flap it as if it was a broken wing; a mother duck, you see, being a decoy, luring the fox from her ducklings. I began to dance around the old woman flapping my broken wing, as her disgust alchemised into horror and fear. 'Hello, I'm Porky Pig's cousin Walter,' I announced.

In hindsight, it was an oblique reference. It is unlikely this old woman watched daytime cartoons or had any idea who Porky Pig was, or that he and his confreres got about in blue felt waistcoats and nothing else. 'Oh . . .' she said. And repeated herself twice as I flapped my broken wing and, playing two roles simultaneously, said, 'Quackquack-quack . . . yibbedahyibbedah . . . that's all, folks.'

Debbie, seeing me veer off script, came out of the shed at a hustle. She needn't have. I had the situation under control. With my unbroken wing I waved her back.

'He's disgusting, Marny. He did wee on his own clothes on purpose and then said he was going to wee on us all if I didn't give him the waistcoat you made for me. Yuck, Marny.' To my amazement she began to cry at the tragedy of her concocted circumstance; a foul lunatic brother set loose amid her innocent girlhood. Vicki emerged from the shed also crying and began pointing at me. I stopped flapping my broken wing.

I was not trained for the role of decoy. And was, at this moment, clueless as to my next move. It seemed, with Debbie saying all this crazy stuff, and hooting like a heartbroken owl, and Vicki copying her and validating her misery and her wild claims, that the part might end up with me in deep shit. I didn't like being accused of stealing the waistcoat Debbie had just tricked me into wearing, nor could I bear the slander that I had deliberately urinated on myself. I was opening my mouth to protest when there was a loud noise close by and stars began to flare and swoop. Someone had hit me hard on the head with something bigger than most things you would consider hitting a boy with.

To this day I don't know if it was Debbie who thumped me, or Marny. I can make a case for either, and it is likely whoever did it only just pipped the other at the post. They were both fond of hitting me. And though they never actually high-fived after landing a good one, I had, from the vantage of the floor, seen their gaze lock in congratulation, had seen Marny license Debbie for future violence via a tiny nod.

I lay sightless and near naked on the nail-bed of our buffalo grass and heard Marny say, 'Quickly, now. Step on him while I pull the waistcoat off. Hurry, before he comes to. How disgusting. Ohh . . .' The waistcoat was hauled off me with no respect for my broken wing and I was thrashed with it a few times, its gilt embroidery scourging me like lead pieces in a cat-o-nine-tails will scourge a pirate. I heard Marny consoling Debbie and Vicki, both crying in loud counterfeit misery, as they hurried back to the house to rail at Mum about the new shame I had nearly brought on the family until they saved the day by beating the shit out of me.

I went to the shed and began to dress. In the half dark, surrounded by the galaxy of our winking wee, Pigsy was silent, solemn, not knowing what to make of how this had played out. He was unsure if I had saved the day, or was a ham actor who had almost led the Wee Club to ruin. As I was tucking my shirt into my shorts he told me, 'Porky Pig doesn't have a cousin Walter. But he does have a brother in

Pennsylvania called Peter . . . if you're ever being a decoy again . . . in only a blue waistcoat . . .'

'Get rooted, Pigsy.'

I crouched beneath the kitchen window, eavesdropping to see if it was safe to go in. Marny was railing and reminiscing, trying to get Mum to see the seriousness of the situation. 'Well, whatever will become of him I just don't know, Linda. He's a fool. And I know you run a good house, but he behaves like he's been brought up by dingoes or Englesens.' The Englesens were a shoeless family that lived in the Commission and sometimes came to our house to beg groceries from us. Mum had recently given them an unopened tub of creamed honey, so I had sworn to get even with them, and had to bite my lip when Marny compared me to them.

The incident came to nothing with Mum. My stepping out naked in the guise of a cartoon pig and talking nonsense was no big deal to her. I think, in the way of mothers, she even saw a spark of creativity, some artistic future, in such harebrained propensities.

Later that day when I complained to Debbie about the lies she'd told and the thrashing I'd been given she said, 'Hey, you were the dimwit who started quacking and quoting pigs. Just say "hello" and walk inside, I told you. Do you even know what a decoy is?'

'Yes.'

'Well, is Porky Pig a decoy or a major star?'

'I wasn't Porky. I was his cousin Walter.'

'You are so dickless.'

Years later I speculated that, given Buenos Aires is five hours ahead of Melbourne, then, every day, as Adolf

Eichmann was at his lunch, regaling his compadres with tales of a concocted boyhood in Zurich, Deborah was dropping her children at school, swapping tales with other mothers at the school gate, and occasionally vacuuming her living room to disguise her true nature.

When anyone mentions Eichmann, or other famous Nazis who camouflaged themselves in the great cities of South America, I think of Debbie and say to myself, 'Ho, ho . . . none of us know the blood-and-urine-steeped yesterdays of our neighbours. None of us are alive to the monster shuffling in sync with the more blameless elements of the supermarket queue.'

The thrashing of Porky Pig's cousin Walter brought the Wee Club to civil war. Pigsy and I came to believe a tyrant had used us as mindless bladders. But we were too scared of that tyrant to take any action against her. As was routine when vengeance was necessary, I started a fight with Vicki so as to have an enemy I could rise heroically against and vanquish.

Vicki was a sweet girl without the dark energy to maintain unpleasantness. In the face of the worst insults, blows, thefts and injustices I could heap on her, she would go silent and brood for perhaps two hours before her stock of bile was depleted and she came out of her cocoon with new ideas and pretty thoughts unfurling like a butterfly's wings. So when the Wee Club went into its vicious decline she was bound to take the rap.

On Monday she brought two friends, Fiona Greeves and Melissa Gribble, to our house after school to talk of love. All three dropped their bikes on our lawn and went inside the house and up the stairs to the girls' room. I snuck into the room with them, staying quiet so as not to attract their attention. They were girls, older girls, and they were contemptuous of me, and their contempt was more powerful than anybody else's because they were vaguely, girlishly, spookily . . . cool.

I sat with my back to the door and ran a Matchbox Thunderbird up and down my thigh, pretending not to listen as they began to talk of the interminable conjoining and division of grade five students; the who liked who and who was going with who and who had dropped who and who was thinking of dropping who. It was an endlessly echoing and amplifying record-keeping and speculation, this newly found topic of love. They talked about it with the passion and certitude of proselytes. 'If Wendy drops Barry it'll break his heart.' 'Break his heart.' 'He'll be soooo heartbroken.' I was fascinated by the breaking of hearts. I had only just learnt of this fatal epidemic. It seemed like a new and subtle form of gunplay to me.

I stopped driving the Thunderbird along my scrawny thigh. I couldn't help myself. I blew my cover. 'Will Barry die?' I asked. 'How does she break it? Is there blood?'

'Don't you have windows to lick, or something?' Melissa Gribble asked.

'I hear the Flintstones calling,' Fiona Greeves said, putting a hand to her ear. 'Ooh, I think Betty Rubble might be doing a striptease.' This was tempting, but I was almost certain Betty Rubble wasn't that sort of woman.

'Be quiet or get out,' Vicki warned.

They went back to love. 'Sharon likes Tim.' 'Yeah. I don't know why.' 'Yuck. She's too good for him.' 'Way too good for him.'

Deciding who was too good for who was one of the most important undertakings of the love conversations. Sometimes they would argue over whether someone was too good for someone else or not. But mostly they knew and agreed. They had some ineffable way of measuring goodness I could only wonder at. And someone who was going with someone else was almost always too good for him or vice versa. No couple ever turned out to be perfectly suited to each other once my sisters and their friends got to measuring goodness.

'But . . . how do you know Sharon is too good for Tim?' I asked. I genuinely wanted to know. They rolled their eyes and shook their heads. How could a grade two kid be expected to get any of this? You might as well recite psalms to a slug as explain love to me.

Fiona Greeves hung her bottom lip out and slit her eyes at me as if I was dangerously stupid. 'What is he even doing in here, Vicki?'

'I'm allowed,' I said. It was a declaration I made frequently. An early summation of the universal rights of man. The universal rights of me. But it wasn't effective. 'We're talking about stuff you don't understand,' Vicki said. 'Get out.'

'I'm allowed.' They grabbed me and threw me out of the room. The door cracked open and my Thunderbird went flying down the stairs, then the door slammed closed. Vicki turned on her portable record player and began playing 'Nowhere Man' by the Beatles in case I was at the door eavesdropping. I listened the song through, but she put it on again.

Pigsy came over and found me angrily gorging Tic Toc biscuits in the kitchen. 'I'm going to get Vicki,' I told him. 'I'm going to get her bitch friends too.'

'How?' he asked.

'The wee.'

He looked solemn and thoughtful. This was a big step. After a few moments he asked me, 'What did they do?'

'I spied on them and heard them. They're going to pour it on our bikes.'

'My bike? What have I done?'

'Pudding bowl haircut.'

He put a hand to his head. 'Bitches.'

We went to the shed and took bottles off the shelves and laid them gently as grenades in Dad's wheelbarrow, perhaps thirty in all, wheeling them across the lawn to the girls' bikes. We unscrewed a cap each and chugged the piss up and down the framework of the bikes, along the handlebars and soaked the seats. One bottle was more than enough to douse each bike, but we were rich in piss so we opened more and poured until the machines lay in a frothy puddle and a fog of foul odour. Neighbourhood dogs began to gather, standing at a distance with their noses twitching and their heads aslant in wonder. Some walked in circles, wanting to leave, but fascinated. Ours was the most emphatic marking of territory they had ever smelt.

And once we started we couldn't stop. Cry havoc and let slip the pints of piss. The size of our stockpile of armaments was for us, as it has been for the Americans, a reason to declare war on everyone. How else were we going to get rid of the stuff? It seemed, by its very potential to bring a tyrant down, to make tyrants of everyone. It was its own justification. Piss was a silver bullet and we were surrounded by vampires.

I crept into the Hoffmans' backyard where Hoffy's footy sat under the verandah in a cane chair like an egg in a nest. I poured a bottle over the footy slowly, giving it time to sponge up the piss, making it sodden, dark and rainy-day heavy to handle. An hour later when I saw Hoffy come home I went to the fence to listen. It was training night. I was behind the fence when he came outside to get his footy. 'Hey?' I heard him bounce it soddenly on the concrete path. Then he must have smelt it. 'Hey? What? Urgh. Urgh. Man!' He dropped the ball and began shouting, 'Mum . . . Mum . . . Ohpa's gotta go. The senile old bastard. Mum. My Sherrin.'

We'd started with the girls' bikes. We next went to Hoffy's football. But then we found ourselves with another ninety bottles, and as war was declared and battle come down, we began a scorched-earth, or doused-everything, policy. Mrs Mansell's doormat, then every doormat in the neighbourhood including, strangely, our own; Mrs Quickly's labrador; Mr Sargood's Torana; the business shirts that hung on the Riordans' washing line; Mr Kelly's golf bag; Dad's Victa mower; Mrs Pogue's mail; Mrs Hoffman's tomatoes; Nanna Langdon's verandah setting; Peter Langdon's motorbike . . .

We became meticulous. We dribbled it up the arms of chairs and down the handles of golf clubs, we coated dogs' beds as if eradicating fleas, Peter Langdon's Suzuki was painted top to bottom, carburettor and throttle, piston and pillion, Nana Langdon's sun bonnet was more meticulously immersed in piss than Achilles in the Styx. It had no heel. We lay hidden in her begonias thrashing and chortling when we saw her wearing it next day in a cloud of coiling air.

During this fluid fusillade we were astounded to discover girl wee had no odour. What type of stainless robots were my sisters? We sniffed deeply, but their piss was heartbreakingly inoffensive, worthless as a weapon of chemical warfare, and we poured it down the gully trap while shaking our heads at this final proof of the irrelevance of girls.

Hours later, when our stockpile of piss was finally exhausted, there hung over Talinga Crescent a toilet block miasma, the smell of a dark ward, the smell of old men en masse, the smell of a black soil swamp. It remained and sharpened until rain came the following week. Adults speculated on what variety of phenomenon the neighbourhood was experiencing: the sewage system had ruptured and was venting ruined air; a plague of possums had descended; someone had covered their garden beds with chook shit; a dog lay dead and green in a corner of someone's garden; Stuart's Meatworks was excreting illegal nocturnal pollutants; Mr Sargood had passed on and was getting ripe. Dad went to knock on his door to check on him. 'Hello, Graeme, would you like some eggs?' he shouted.

'You smell anything, Angus?' Dad shouted.

'Urine,' he shouted. 'But I always smell urine.'

For a while I did charitable work with Mum. Raising four kids ought to have been a full and rewarding enough life for any woman. Mothering was known to be a sacred mission that fit a woman's psychological appetites so snugly she was either left wholly contented or she was some sort of revolutionary freak who wanted to destroy democracy and God. They seldom asked for more from life than a kitchen full of kids and any one of them who did was thought greedy and self-absorbed. Suspicion greeted the few female malcontents who wanted a job, or to open a business, or who aspired to anything other than the constant applying of Band-Aids to scraped knees.

What type of bra-burner needed to be on the town council or a golf-club committee or to open up a frock salon or see live opera in Melbourne? What was wrong with a day spent in the house and garden with a walk to the butcher and green-grocer, a round of gossip here, and then the school pick-up and a round of gossip there, followed by the loving construction of a casserole? Women didn't know how good they had it.

A man, hearing a woman had just opened a hair salon or bought her own car would open the side of his mouth and say, 'Bad case of the "I wants".' And the men listening to this would nod stoically as if hearing another country had fallen to communism. During the sixties and seventies women were infected with a sweeping plague of the 'I wants', an epidemic that confused and saddened the men who sat at bars documenting its advance.

My Mum was English. She had grown up during the Second World War amid the drone of the Luftwaffe and the wail of air-raid sirens and the red fog of brick dust and fear and the neighbours' DNA. After the war she worked for Sir Norman Hartnell at his mirror-lined art moderne salon in London. Sir Norman was an icon of new couture and dress-maker to the stars. He had the Royal Warrant as dressmaker to the royal ladies and they would pop in whenever they needed a new frock – the Queen Mother, the Queen and, most princessly beautiful, Princess Margaret Rose.

Mum was Princess Margaret's body double. That is, they were the same size and shape and Mum was measured for and fitted with the Princess' new dresses and when they were finished and Princess Margaret came in to inspect them Mum would model them for her, walking up and down and twirling and glancing coquettishly over her shoulder as if at a nude matinee idol as the Princess was wont to do. While

Mum acted out being a Princess in the dresses, the real Princess Margaret lounged on a rose-tapestry divan sucking languidly on a Rothmans.

If the Princess liked the dress she would say, 'Yes. Norman, yes.' Or sometimes, 'Gorgeous. Linda, I hope I look half as good as you in the thing.' Mum would go red and wriggle out of the dress then, and standing in her petticoat and heels help the Princess wriggle into it and zip her up.

These dresses then appeared on the front pages of newspapers stumbling from nightclubs, perhaps with a Count's hand on their derrière escorting the Princess from the casino at Monte Carlo in the small hours, and were, presumably, unhitched and unlaced by her infamously inappropriate beaux at one debauch or another that threatened to bring the royal family's reign to an inglorious end. So my mum had the vicarious thrill of watching some of the great scandals of the day play out in dresses she'd been wearing the day before.

My dad, a Shepparton boy, was over in the UK on holiday with friends. England was a rite of passage every ex-private school boy from Australia had to take. It was the only other country in the world. It was our own glorious history represented in architecture, plaques, music and high-stepping Queen's Guards. And all of this was, happily for an Aussie, populated by a runtish, ignorant and insular people that an antipodean, with his perfect teeth and straight back and travel plans, couldn't help but feel superior to. You were at once humbled by history and superior to the present. It was a good time to be an Australian in England.

Mum was sharing a flat with two other girls when a mob of young Aussie blokes called around to visit and there ensued a locking of the gazes, hers and his, that unravelled life plans and leached alternative paths of all colour and bound them in a shared fate. He was an extraterritorial lawyer/sportsman with a pointed moustache. She was the double for the world's most beautiful and dissolute Princess.

They were married on 26 April 1953 in Findon, the village in Worthing where her parents lived. At their wedding reception on the Sussex Downs, when the reverend proposed a toast to Anzac Day the revellers hushed, not in veneration, but in confusion. What, after all, was an Anzac? And how did it deserve a day?

Soon after, the couple embarked on the *Strathaird* from nearby Tilbury for Australia and docked at Station Pier in Melbourne on 18 July 1953. My mother remembers being overwhelmed by Camerons and Furphys. She and Dad spent their first night at the Windsor. No food after five o'clock in Melbourne, but my grandfather rustled up some macaroni cheese from the kitchen.

Then a three-hour drive up a broken road through a landscape that couldn't be understood. To Shepparton, which was about as distant from the milieu of Norman Hartwell's haute couture as a stone orbiting the Pluto that was Melbourne is from the sun that was London. And Shepparton had an equivalent culture to that stone if you'd come from London.

You can hear the sounds of home from a long way away for a long time after leaving if you go to a foreign enough place. And London continued to morph into the swingingest city on the planet. Its prettiest birds began to sing an American slang after a long winter of war and penury. The place began to rebuild using foreign money and freedoms and a backbeat the Beatles stole from black America and used to make a sweet blameless love all up and down Carnaby Street where the young wore ribbons in their hair. A lot to be said for not dying in a war.

News of this breathtaking new London being born must have left Mum with a kind of spiritual tinnitus in the cultural silence of Shepparton. Even the great joy of tying little Anson's shoelaces couldn't deafen her to the opening chords of 'Please, Please Me' or blind her to the twin-set suits of Mary Quant, to Sidney Poitier's smile as he melted school-girls in *To Sir with Love*, or Emma Peel in her leather catsuit emancipating all women by kicking hoodlums over settees.

My brother and sisters and I were a counter-fascination that might have got Mum through breakfast without dreaming of life in that cool Brit city of beehives and minis that she had forsaken, but not much deeper into the day than that. Shepparton was an odyssey from home and a long way from anywhere that mattered a whit.

She first showed her discontent at having every day of her life eaten whole by insatiable and alien piccaninnies in a one-bowser town by signing up to deliver Meals on Wheels. It was a trivial rebellion against housewifely constraints, and cunningly disguised as charity. My father couldn't, in good conscience, whisper, 'Linda's got the "I wants",' to his friends about her delivering sustenance to senior citizens. But he wrinkled his brow and rubbed his face, recognising it as a breakout of some sort.

So, after Mum picked me up from kindergarten, we'd drive over to the red-brick hospital in the neighbouring town of Mooroopna, biggest building in my world and rumoured to be full of the diseased sucking their final breaths and whispering prayers. We'd go round the back to the kitchen to pick up the meals. In this vast industrial space of linoleum and stainless steel and rising steam and robotic stirrings and blue flames and people shouting, the air was heavy with the braided olfactory incarnations of fifty different simultaneous attempts at passable meals.

A selection of these attempted meals was placed hot in metal containers in the back of our station wagon and Mum and I would drive back to Shepparton and begin to go among the hungry old with their wrinkly heads leaned back and their little beaks clapping open and closed as they chirped for food.

Old people were disgusting when I was a boy. They've become much more palatable since. But back then, oh . . . The thick fug of faeces garnished with mothballs in which they were domiciled has diluted and their homes are perfumed these days by candles scented with begonia and jasmine; surgeons have tautened their epidermises making them less like eased bladders, less visually horrific; their conversation isn't so portentous and indecipherable now; the darkness of their homes has become less the wanton dinginess of the bomb shelter, illuminated now by a bluish enfilade of cheap LEDs. It is as if a primitive and foul race has been discovered and civilised – Tierra del Fuegans captured and bathed and clothed and taught grammar; a whole country saved, brought back from a dark ethos.

But the old were a frightening species when I was young. Rather go among the Zulu painted for battle, or the Germans on holiday. If you think I exaggerate when I write of the base lunatic squalor of the aged, then I can only say you never encountered a 1960s octogenarian gurning toothlessly at you and asking what you wanted to be when you grew up.

A boy's nose is a delicate, untested instrument. An olfactory lamb. A fart that might flare a rosy grin of reminiscence on a man's face will cause a boy to reel and gag and blink in a rush of disorderly thought, and in that queasy moment his known world might be undone. Truths might be made plastic and warped permanently by this intestinal hallucinogen escaped into bright air.

By the time your hair has greyed and your children have abandoned you and you are living in the darkening, shrinking circumstance of your evening, your nose, through the million scented explorations and indignities that have been visited upon it, will have become inured to the fog of mould spore, the faecal miasma and the myriad other grey smells of crocheting and the crypt that accompany the bent and infirm. But mine was a Romanesque virgin. So large on a small boy that people sometimes laughed at it outright. Thus the homes of the old were like a physical assault to me.

My mother was a beautiful woman. And it puffed a boy's chest to have a beautiful mum; so lithe among the bevy of maternal dirigibles who came to pick their kids up from school. She had high cheekbones and mod-cut hair and pretty eyes like the women who looked out of magazines while caressing fridges and boxes of self-raising flour.

Mostly I enjoyed her beauty for its effect on men. And the most unguarded of these, the most simple-minded and vulnerable, were the pensioners to whom we delivered Meals on Wheels. Seeing my mother at the door with a steaming casserole, First War veterans would focus out of their glassy-eyed haze into pointed, libidinous reminiscence. Would suddenly hear the bugle of sexuality again and their nostrils would flare, they became confused and aghast, having thought those appetites had decamped and those urges were irretrievably lost. Old blokes, seeing Mum, mumbled nonsense and stammered and ushered us inside their squalid homes.

There were often a great many large flies in the homes of the old, their fly-wires having fallen rattling from the window frames into the weeds in their yards. Mum had become, by necessity, professorial re Australian entomology within a year of stepping off the boat. If a certain variety of large iridescent green fly was blundering sleepily through the rooms like a gorged vulture, she would grab my arm and pull me behind her into the backwater of her skirts and tell me, 'Wait in the car, Boyboy.' But I would sneak around her and rush forward. Those green flies usually meant death. A venerable husk of womanhood sitting in an armchair reproachfully awaiting the steaming casserole that might have saved her, but which would now go to Mr Smith at number twenty-four. Sometimes, I fancied, these cadavers tapped their feet to reprove us. 'Okay, Boyboy, out to the car. Now.' But I had seen enough, I had seen death in all its inglorious untellability and would tell it at kindergarten next day to a fear-hushed circle of tots in whom I planted recurrent nightmares like rows of lettuce.

Usually, the free-mealers weren't dead when we arrived. And when Mum went into the kitchen to put the meal onto a plate, or do the washing up, in the dim sitting room we males would enter a conspiracy. 'Your Mum's a good sort, isn't she,' the old guy would say. 'A real good sort.'

'Yes,' I'd agree. 'She uses hair spray.'

'Does she? My God. Does she? Good boy. Good boy.' He might clap me on the knee as if I'd done something wonderful. Or nod at me and give me a two-fingered V for Victory sign like Churchill. It was gratifying, being praised for having a beautiful mother. It was as if I'd done something no other boy in town could.

I sensed there was something a little off about it, though. Something a touch dirty. I didn't really know what we were talking about, or why we were so agog at her tight skirt or thin ankles. But I detected some dark cathedral of unspoken, unspeakable veneration or yearning in these men's whispered platitudes. I felt, at times, I should carry the meals inside by myself, making her wait outside.

He leant toward me in his deep chair and whispered tuberculently, 'What a . . . what a set of pins, eh?'

'Yes. What?'

'Legs.'

'Orr . . . yes. She has nice legs.'

'Horhor, as hot as a stove,' he wheezed.

Afterwards, outside in our Holden station wagon I broke confidence with the old bastard. 'Mum, that old bloke was talking about your legs.'

'Was he, Boyboy? That's okay. He doesn't see many people now. He forgets what they look like.'

'He says you're a good sort.'

'That's friendly of him.'

'But . . . but it's like . . . a copliment.'

She laughed. 'It's a compliment, but it's not a really big compliment.'

'He says it like it is. "Whoo, your mum's a good sort,"' I mimed his husky lust.

Her face came down out of laughter when I copycatted the old man's tone. 'All right. Mrs Fitzpatrick is next. She has the apricot chicken, I think. Did you draw her a picture? Remember she wanted a picture of our house?'

'"Horhor, as hot as a stove . . ."' I wheezed.

'Stop that.'

\* \* \*

On my first day at North Shepparton Primary School Mum led me into the classroom and introduced me to Miss Stoddard, who took my hand and showed me to a desk and told me I was to share it with another student. Mum then bent down and gave me a hug and told me she'd see me after school. As she walked blithely out the door I realised my childhood had ended. Our partnership was broken in that moment. I had been sold and was now the chattel of an institution.

I felt the air go cold around me, watching her walk away. Until this moment I had had no presentiment that life had an ending – and yet here it was. Our world, the perfect work-aday symbiosis of Mum and me, was over. And our love apparently hadn't even been symbiotic. I'd needed her, but she hadn't needed me. She went out the door without looking back. I tried to imagine tears running down her face, but giggles and glee flashed from her imaginary mouth and my first five years felt like fraud. I should have known. She had form. She'd sold three children before me into the clutches of scholarly servitude – unto this very grimy school.

This crushing revelation of my abandonment may have coloured my view on the new companions. Or perhaps they were just ugly. I looked around at my fellow students and saw girls with runny noses, boys with grey shirts tucked hard into shorts that belonged to much bigger boys. Boys with crew cuts, and others maniacally hirsute. Some kids were smugly pink, having been brutally washed for their educational debut. Others, shoeless and in buttonless shirts, smelt sour and stray. Some few were ironed and portly, and some were all dotted about with scabs and freckles, underfed, silent and bruised. A few black kids showed flit-eyed suspicion of this room decorated with letters and numbers cut from shiny coloured paper, with the seated rows of boys and girls unnaturally silent, stilled by fear.

So. This cast of horrid types with their noses running and their hair growing, these variously unsatisfactory specimens who didn't seem to have any inkling I was the centre of the world, these were to be my schoolmates. Mum and Dad had told me I would make new friends at school. Just another of the lies with which they had lured me to the place. Who could make friends with such macabre children as these? There looked to be about five different species of unsatisfactory infant seated in this room.

As I stared at them I knew school was not for me. And I began to imagine what Mum was up to without me. To see how she struggled at her various tasks alone. Maybe it was golf day. A morning on the broad fairways reciting facts and figures I'd memorised from the *Pears' Cyclopedia* to Mum's perpetually astounded friends was far preferable to this Gomorrah.

I went to Miss Stoddard and told her I was leaving school. It was golf day and Mum needed me to caddy and I didn't like these children she had gathered together. Australia was fifty-three times as big as Nepal and I was sure Mrs Simson and Mrs Newton didn't know this yet. I was off to golf to tell them. It was the kind of surprising fact that would have them lowing like cattle. Miss Stoddard took my hand and led me back to my desk and told me to sit down. I was hers until, sometime deep into the afternoon, someone would ring the final bell, and then I could go home. As she was explaining this a girl sitting at a desk behind me with a haircut like the Jack of Spades and long socks as white as snow who had been giving off occasional whimpers and sobs wet herself. Or rather, wet herself and the girl sitting alongside her. As the urine splashed down, dousing and yellowing her socks and puddling on the linoleum and running along the seat and soaking her deskmate's dress, that deskmate scrambled to her feet and began to cry. The Jack of Spades girl began to bawl as well. Her socks, weighted with piss, fell to her ankles.

Half the class began to cry at the there-but-for-the-grace-of-God-go-I horror of the event and at the sudden humiliation of the girl. The other half burst into laughter. Miss Stoddard led the urine-soaked twosome caterwauling from the room. A dark-skinned boy bolted out the door while she was gone and was brought back by his mother, using his ear as a handle, an hour later. So, it was to be this sort of place. An arena in which profound foibles were paraded as slapstick. A cage where the frailties of my fellows might be put on display and fed peanuts. A place where we could scoff at each other's infirmities and cry havoc and let slip the hilarious mayhem that preyed on pants-pissers. So. A morning of golf with Mum and her amigos suddenly seemed tame. Let those old biddies cram the *Pears' Cyclopaedia* into their buggies and look up their own fascinating facts. I smiled and settled into my desk for further exciting developments. At morning playtime we broke from our lesson, and milk monitors, large boys from senior years, delivered a crate of small bottles of milk and we were given one each. We peeled the red and silver foil tops from our bottles and drank. This milk was warmer and tasted more milky than the milk at home, hinting of a corrupt, cheesy future. I skolled mine to show everyone how fast I could drink milk and spent the rest of playtime eyeing off the milk of more abstemious individuals who sipped and smacked their lips and lorded it over those rash few who had drunk theirs hoggishly. The girls in my class proved to be especially able to ration and enjoy their milk and glowed with an annoying smugness to us guzzlers. They held their bottles up alongside one another to measure who had most left. Every day for my seven years at North Shepparton Primary I hogged down my milk and promptly set about coveting the milk of those who hadn't.

One day, a few years later, the dairy delivered the school seven hundred little bottles of milk gone rancid in such a bacterially covert way that none of us could taste its wrongness. We drank as usual, the greedy coveting the milk of the sippers, the show-offs skolling their own milk and the milk of the unwary, then smacking their lips and aahing theatrically.

Within a half hour the student body became queasy. The colour drained from its many small heads and it laid its palms gently on its seven-hundred fragile stomachs. I feel sick. I feel sick too. I feel really sick. I really feel sicker.

You will have seen that film in which a ping-pong ball is thrown into a room carpeted with mousetraps all set and loaded with two ping-pong balls each. The first trap hit fires off two balls that hit two traps firing four balls etc. The air is suddenly ablaze with flying balls and the white storm of multiplying consequence is over very quickly.

Meredith Hanley was the first metaphorical ball that landed in the queasy campus of North Shepp Primary. She vomited while being comforted by two slightly less ill friends. But not so less ill that they didn't both reflexively vomit in response. Within a minute fusillades of milky spew were raking the campus, dousing would-be medics and drenching educators. Infectious geysers of albino bile sought out the innocent and smartly dressed. Never one to waste a crisis, I chucked up on Terry Holmes because he owned a book called *Stig of the Dump* which I thought might be better owned by me. Terry, being a shy boy and not wanting to disturb anyone, vomited into his own lap.

The desks had flip-up lids, under which was a compartment to store our books and pencils. Two ceramic inkwells sat in holes at the far corners of the desktop. We were too young to be permitted to use ink, so we filled the inkwells with dead or maimed flies and treasurable nose pickings. The classroom smelt of sour children and was full of flies and boy would bet boy as to who could kill the most during the course of an afternoon.

The silent and efficient method was to let one land on your face and then slap it gently, trapping it, so you could roll it down your cheek until it was smeared and maimed, whereupon you'd pop the twitching prize into the inkwell, leaving a few legs tangled in the peach fuzz on your jaw. At day's end the contestants would upend their inkwells and count the flies. Amorphously astounding nose pickings would also tumble forth, but these, while admirable, weren't scored.

Bomber Johnson from the Housing Commission soon became the acknowledged champion of the fly cull. Flies newly born in cowsheds and offal bins in other latitudes picked up Bomber's scent as a guiding star and, bypassing galaxies of cowpats and several town rubbish tips without looking sideways, they made their quavering pilgrimage to him. We knew he was a bit whiffy, but one day he casually revealed his house was unplumbed, and that no one in his family had ever had a bar . . . bar . . . bath or shar . . . shar . . . shower so far as he knew.

We took this badly. It was the sort of advantage about which a fair-minded boy would have told his opponent before entering into a fly-culling contest. It was virtually an admission of professionalism in an age of amateurs. Not quite above board. But we didn't know this until late in the game, and Bomber had many days of glory before we realised he was a bacteriological Siren calling winged Argonauts along a violin-note flight path to certain doom.

\*   \*   \*

Miss Stoddard sat me next to Kelvin Woodhouse. She might as well have sat Charles Darwin next to a whelk. I was curious and I was bristling with quasi-scientific tools of investigation. It was an unhappy day for Kelvin, and if he vectored into criminality and unsociability in later life, became what the news reports call 'a loner', then I accept my portion of the blame. Because he was a sensitive kid and his sensitivity was a Lalique vase to a vandal.

Miss Stoddard was an elfin young woman who sat out front of the class in a short skirt, up which I tried to see, reading to us about John and Betty. Two bigger dicks than John and Betty you've never met. I quickly became disgusted at their goodness and pliability as they frolicked, actually frolicked, with their happy, yappy dog Spot. Illustrations showed Spot never had four legs on the ground at once, which bespoke a limitless capacity to be gay and amusing. John, or Betty, or both, also owned a witlessly personable cat named Fluffy.

I once asked Miss Stoddard what would happen to Fluffy if I fired her from a cannon at a tin shed and she made me stand outside for an hour beating the wadded felt blackboard duster with a ruler and thereby raising a cloud of coloured chalk dust. I beat that duster frequently after that, and always went home hued the colour of that day's lesson. If, for instance, Miss Stoddard drew a red hippo eating yellow grass on the blackboard alongside a song about hippos, I would ask if it was a picture of Deidre Lowe. Deidre Lowe would hunch and snuffle miserably to be compared to a crimson hippo and I would, at lesson's end, be punished by having to erase the blackboard and then take the duster outside and clean it by beating it with a ruler, thereby raising an orange fog made of red hippo and yellow grass. As my skin became wet I would march back and forth through the orange fog and it would settle brightly on me and I would cycle home the colour of an Oompa Loompa.

If Miss Stoddard thought I found this embarrassing, she was wrong. I enjoyed leaving school as gaudily coloured as an *Oz* extra. The eyes of one particular old couple leaning on their wire fence in Cotrell Street would widen as I rode past on my way home. Her eyesight was going and he would narrate my passing for her. 'Look, Doris. It's the coloured boy. Orange today. Orange as orange can be.' I imagined they thought me a sprite leapt from the flagon of sweet sherry that was always plugged into the horse-manured garden bed between them. Most old people were drunk in those days. 'Why is a boy riding around orange?' he'd ask her.

One day Miss Stoddard was teaching us a song from *The Sound of Music*. She had drawn an alpine scene on the blackboard, luring us to sing of a lonely goatherd. But I had substituted 'old turd' for 'goatherd' and sang too loudly, 'High on a hill was a lonely old turd, Oh diddlee oh diddlee oh oh oh . . .' You know how it goes.

My punishment was to erase those mountains and then go outside and clean the duster. Once outside I beat the duster and writhed in the fog made of that obliterated mountain-scape upon which the von Trapps' lonely goatherd had fed his mangy flock.

As I rode home I saw the old couple standing holding onto their fence watching their swatch of streetscape. I pedalled along on the footpath, right up close to them to hear what they said. 'Well . . . jingoes, Doris . . . He's green today. Green as clover.'

'Who? The boy?'

'Yes. The coloured boy.'

'Sing out to him and ask him why he's green.'

'Why are you green?' the old duffer shouted at me.

'Because "goatherd" rhymes with "old turd",' I shouted back. I think that cleared it up for them.

\* \* \*

John and Betty had picnics and held hands. Were they lovers or siblings? I couldn't tell. They seemed to fill both roles at various times. Why read to us of such suspect types? John skipped rope like a girl, and handed the rope over to Betty without a fight when she wanted a turn. John, John, John . . . John made me gag with abhorrence. John sported the invulnerable happiness of a labrador or a sitcom housemaid. What chance did John have of fooling anyone into painting a fence for him? John and Betty were supposed to awaken an appetite for reading in us. They awakened an appetite for throwing John and Betty down a well in me.

Mid-morning, and John and Betty were frolicking as best they could given the stilted, haphazardly emphasised reading of Miss Stoddard. (She would, for instance, read a sentence like, 'John could jump ever so high.' Putting the emphasis on 'John' or 'jump' or 'so' – the only words where it made no sense at all.) I took Kelvin's shiny new red-lead pencil out of the trough where it lay on his side of our desk and bit it clean in half. Kelvin made a noise like a sensitive boy who has had his new pencil bitten in half by a less sensitive boy, and Miss Stoddard stopped reading right when John was admonishing

Spot for barking at a squirrel and invited Kelvin to come out front of the class and explain to us what he was making silly noises about. Kelvin hung his head and sat in his seat. The front of the classroom was bathed in a scarifying limelight that made him wince and squirm. 'Come out here at once, Kelvin.' He drooged draggingly out to where she sat and she spun him around to face us. 'Now, tell the class why you've put an end to story reading with your silly noises.'

'I . . . but . . . Miss Stoddard?'

'Yes, Kelvin.'

'Can I tell on a boy who did something?'

'Yes, Kelvin.'

'Anson bited my red lead in two bits.'

The class laughed wildly at this crazy idea. Though I was a known vandal it was a dentally implausible feat. A boy is not a beaver. Miss Stoddard wandered back and looked down at Kelvin's pencil trough. I had replaced his mauled red lead with my own, which was perfectly unmarked.

'Kelvin.'

'Yes, Miss Stoddard.'

'Go to Mr Schatz's office and tell him you are a liar. Mr Schatz despises liars.'

I stood up. 'It's all right, Miss Stoddard. I don't care about that lie.'

'Don't you? Why not?'

'Kelvin's been telling whoppers all morning.' The class laughed so loud Mr Smith, a grade six teacher, came from next door to make sure Miss Stoddard wasn't injured. And here was my first inkling that I might be an insurrectionist par excellence and a smart-arse of note. The thrill of the class' laughter was like nothing I'd known. My ego took its first intra-aural hit of notoriety and was hooked and I never again strayed too far for too long from the centre of attention. The laughter of schoolmates was an anaesthetic pay-off that denied the pain of the canings and detentions and other punishments it instigated.

Kelvin was allowed to go back to his seat. I was made to stand in the corner facing the wall for my silly joke. But my ego had become another nerve and I could feel the eyes of the class upon my back like early morning sun while lying on a favourite riverbank.

Kelvin was moved. Thus began a rotation of students sitting alongside me that continued right through primary school. Most kids could only last a few days of my incessant persecution. The toughest could last a week or so. I wanted to keep my hands off them and their possessions. But always, in the end, my inability to restrain myself, my overwhelming need to tease and stir, to see what would happen if I took this possession, asked this question, or poked that bit of flesh, led to tears, a fight, or some kid hiding out in the library and refusing to come back to class. Then they would be relocated.

After a few weeks of Betty and John I started to develop a yearning to stand up while Miss Stoddard was reading and say, 'Fuck John.' I had a great faith in swearing then. I saw it as the language of elevated urgency. Adults used it when cars burst into flames or fine porcelain smashed. It was a kind of Latin to speak to the God of emergency.

The word 'fuck' was the greatest act of insurrection I knew, and it seemed right for John, and my yearning grew stronger by the day. I convinced myself it was for the greater good. That by my brave renunciation of John the Banal my classmates would be freed from the pale spell of goodness he had cast over them. I thought through the repercussions time and again, and it seemed to me after a brief outrage people would come around, would blink and shake their heads suddenly aware of the dangerously happy trance in which John had held them captive. Then, having debunked this effete svengali who was taking them on inglorious picnics with his sister/girlfriend, I would be feted.

Nearing the end of first term, having played the triumphant scenes that flowed from my proclamation over and over in my head, having imagined Miss Stoddard gaping in new hostility at the John and Betty primary reader and dashing it to the floor and agreeing with me. 'Quite right, Anson. Fuck John. And fuck Betty too.' And stamping her foot on that book and grinding its pages beneath her heel before whipping a copy of *Huck Finn* from behind her back and announcing, 'Now . . . now we really read.' Having conjured this happy coup so many times, I was ready.

I stood up from my desk while Miss Stoddard read of the dull duo heading out on another maudlin jaunt and I said what I had to say about John.

The outcome wasn't the one I'd fantasised. Teacher and students were stunned silent by me bringing the playground commonplace 'fuck' into the classroom and lobbing it at an adult. A boy alongside me mimed 'fuck' slowly, reviewing the horror of what I'd said. Miss Stoddard laid the John and Betty primary reader on the floor beside herself quietly and came to me and took me with gentle portent by the elbow and led me out of the room. Looking over my shoulder as

I left I saw fear on the faces of my classmates, which sent a flow of heroism through me and straightened my spine.

Remembering this I feel a happy affinity with my young self. For even today I can barely sit through a movie, certainly not an opera, and only napkin-twistingly through a speech, without feeling a deep urge to stand and say the same of the leading man, soprano or blowhard.

To Mr Schatz's office, then. It was our first meeting, and with the sumptuous malevolence only a truly fat man can display, he puckered his lips out and elegantly indicated where I should stand and mimed how I should hold my hand. He unrolled a leather strap as large as a cobra and whipped me across the left hand with it as loudly as a cad is slapped in a pantomime. I walked back to class shaking, breathing a ragged overture to tears, and holding my hand before me as if begging change.

This hand was thereby transformed into a wonder for a day and I became briefly famous. During lunchtime boys from the upper grades crossed illegally from their zones into our infant area to ogle the welt across my palm and say they'd seen worse. But it was clear from their eyes that I had wrestled a croc and lived.

\* \* \*

Buttoned up in grey shorts and shirt and grey school jumper, with socks pulled high and secured by garters, the bike ride from Talinga Crescent to North Shepparton Primary School took about fifteen minutes if you were really going for it. If you went along The Boulevard you rode the gauntlet of fast trucks and their monstrous after-suck, and drunks shouted up at you from the riverside bush. You passed Stuarts meatworks where the pigs that had squealed across the neighbourhood during the night were being portioned into various smallgoods. Then the plasterworks where ghost-white men in dustman caps smoked and leant and called filth at you as you pedalled past.

A few years before, one of these rough spectres caught Guy by the handlebars as he rode along the footpath and bull-dogged him to a standstill, and asked loudly, for his spectral co-workers to hear, 'What's the difference between an orange and a soldier's cock?' 'I . . . I don't know,' Guy said. 'Suck 'em and find out,' he laughed. We rode on the other side of the road after that. The question had become a niggling concern to us in the years since. Why a soldier? Why an orange?

After a kid got maimed by a cement truck on The Boule-vard we were forbidden to ride that way anymore. So we rode along Quinlan Parade, up Knight Street into Erskine Street and into Dans Street, where two warmongering mongrels lingered drooling at the visions of us that played in their heads. One was a heeler cross and the other a lurcher of the sort used to pull down roos.

If I was riding with Debbie and Vicki and Pigsy all talk would cease as we got close to where the dogs lived. We were hoping to sneak past in silence while they slept. But they were devoted to ambush and most mornings would burst from a gate or through a hedge and launch themselves at us, a tirade of threat and fang. You needed to have picked up speed before they hit so you could take your feet off the pedals to kick and wage a mobile war while moving away. The girls lifted their feet onto their handlebars so as not to be bitten, and wobbled and screamed, drifting down the road to neutral territory. I lashed out with my foot and sometimes, on rare perfect mornings, I lifted a dog beneath the chin with the point of my shoe and jacked it yelping onto its back in my wake and I'd boast about that all day. But more often I was bitten, or fell off my bike and had to climb a fence or tree until they lost interest or were called home by a rough voice whose owner lay on a couch inside.

When Guy came home on holiday from boarding school I complained to him about these dogs. Next morning he rode with the girls and Pigsy and me and when the first dog emerged Guy's face lit up. He didn't kick at it or stop to fight it. He urged it on, hissing and meowing and reaching down offering his hand as it leapt at him, shouting, 'Sool onto 'im, ya bastard. Reeoow . . . Sool, sool onto it.'

I regretted telling him about the dogs, then. With his love of danger and mayhem, his regard for the interplay of fang and bullwhip, he was pouring petrol on my fire, goading grudge-bearing predators to frenzied acts of vengeance. He was fifteen and could fight off large dogs. The rest of us were likely to be badly mauled. But that didn't concern Guy. He joked about what chickens we were and said he thought the dogs that bedevilled us would be big dogs not lapdogs with stumpy legs and teeth like a canary. He chided us all the way to school, where he looked grandly across the playground and told us the only lesson this shithole taught him was how to fight.

That night he told me he had reasoned with the pooches and they had reached a détente and I needn't worry about canine hostilities anymore. 'Did you shoot the dogs?' I asked hopefully. 'You don't rate me as a diplomat, do you?' he asked. Which was answering a question with a question and the sort of trick I saw interrogated villains on *Homicide* do all the time. 'Bayonet them through the gut?' I was quite taken with war comics, in which snarling Japanese were bayoneted amidships on every page. 'Détente,' he said. 'It's French for sorting shit out.'

The next day, when Pigsy and the girls and I rode to school the first dog was missing altogether. No sign of the blue-furred brute. This was a good start. I figured it had probably found détente alongside a couple of bricks in a sack in the river. A few houses on and there was the lurcher sitting behind his chain-link fence with his head low, all his property rights null and void and his sinews stilled and his fangs secreted away behind a pout.

You've seen those black-and-white shots of conquered Parisians looking sullenly at stormtroopers as they frogmarch along the Champs Elysées. That's how this lurcher looked at us riding past; hate radiated from his pupils through the fence, but that optic insinuation was the extent of his hostility. He who had once gamboled alongside children airing fang and rhapsodising threat was conquered and forlorn. He remembered the good days, and maybe they would come again, a liberation whereby he could reignite his passion for mauling small humans. But for now Nazis like Guy marched the street and he was a surrendered and broken dog.

It was a short-term solution. There were always new angry dogs in Shepparton, owned and primed by angry people who couldn't make ends meet and whose lives were hard. And dogs were encouraged to bite children then. As a

trespasser and thief I was constantly mottled with Mercurochrome and tattooed with tetanus shots.

* * *

It was in this same stretch of Dans Street that I found Ricky
Pavlidis beating up two black kids a few years later. They
weren't indigenous kids. They were racial rarities who
had appeared from Africa or Papua New Guinea or somewhere. No one else looked like them around here. A small
curly-haired alien walking his tiny curly-haired sister home
hand-in-hand from school.

They'd been caught and backed up against a roller door by
Ricky, a boy my own age who spat deftly and had a few hard
mates and a few fistic victories to his name and was capable
of wisecracks, all of which made him about mid-tier tough
at North Shepp. He had the little boy by the shirt and was in
his face shouting at him when I came riding round the corner.
Seeing the action I slewed sideways with a gravel spray,
dropping my bike and stepping off in my signature cowboy
dismount. 'What have the little pricks done?' I asked. Ricky
smiled – he was a generous boy, happy to share his prey.

'Arseholes,' he explained.

Their fear was accentuated by their eyes blaring doubly
white in such black faces. Tiny kids crying soundlessly and
about as far from home as you could be. The boy was trying
to hide his sister behind himself.

'Which one you going to smack up first?' I asked Ricky.

He shook the boy by a fistful of shirtfront. 'This one. Then
the little black mole.'

'What'd they do?' I asked.

'Hangin' round, staring and shit. They're going to get it now.'

'Yeah, well, if they did it they got to get it.'

'Yeah, I might even kill one. For a lesson. Haven't decided which one yet.' The small boy pressed into Ricky's fist, offering himself.

'Know who I like beating up best?' I asked.

'Fuzzy-wuzzies. Or poofs. Poofs are great to belt up.'

'Dickheads.'

'Yeah, dickheads,' Ricky agreed. He shook the boy and shouted 'dickheads' into his face.

'Dickheads who belt up little kids,' I said.

'Dickheads who . . .' Ricky turned to look at me and I grabbed him by his collarbones and slammed him against the roller door alongside the black kids and punched him in the stomach.

'You think you're so fuckin' tough, eh? Pickin' on little kids, eh? You ever touch these kids again and I'll go through you like a dose of fuckin' salts. You get me?'

'Hey . . . Urggh . . . I was only . . .'

'You fuckin' get me?' I shouted, pushing him into the roller door and it giving off a warlike rattle that incited me to slap his face. He cowered against the door holding his face with one hand and his stomach with the other. 'Fuck off,' I shouted, hauling him toward his bike. 'And don't come near these kids again. Dickhead.'

The kids were standing there blinking, adrift in the drama, not quite knowing what had happened, not quite believing the day had flipped in their favour, that they were free, they had a champion. We watched Ricky ride away. 'You kids'll be okay now. He won't come near you again. You okay?'

He nodded and she nodded after him. 'I like you kids. But don't tell anyone about this. Okay?' The boy nodded, starting his sister nodding again. Their eyes were wider now than they had been when Ricky was assaulting them, suggesting kindness might have been a greater wonder in their world than assault.

I felt good about saving those kids for a long while. The way I'd led Ricky on, then suddenly reversed the direction of the scene and unleashed justice and goodness. It was like something I'd read in a book. It didn't become a habit, though. It didn't set me on a course or anything.

\* \* \*

The school day began at ten-to-nine when the assembly bell rang. Kids would run from all points of the playground and line up in their classes, from preps to grade six. A grade six boy would pull the Australian flag up the flagpole while the school band stood out front of us and played. Two military drummers would alternately flail and caress drums hung athwart their scrawny chests and a bugler would fart dejected half-notes while a few kids tooted recorders and a reluctant cymbalist winced and staggered backward with every clash of his cymbals.

This, amazingly, assembled into a lurching 'God Save the Queen', to which we sang along in deliberately spastic soprano. None of us knew what 'Send her victorious,' meant. It was only years later I realised we were singing a propagandist jig that invited Her Majesty's troops to go forth and invade, slaughter and subjugate various pre-industrial hunter-gatherer societies around the globe in order to make said woman smile, happy and glorious, at her morning tea.

We argued about what 'Long to reign over us' meant. I asked Debbie, who replied, 'You are so dumb it's unbelievable.' I knew, then, she had been singing it for five years with no idea what it meant either.

Dogs of every size and temper were drawn to the school to beg for or steal our lunches, and they roamed the grounds, singly and in packs. They were daintily fed crusts by girls and happily pelted with whole sandwiches by boys. You'd as soon leave your lunchbox unprotected on a seat as a wildebeest would abandon its calf on the high veldt among spotted hyena. One large black libidinous freak named Devil would clutch small children in his front legs and balancing on his hindquarters dance an ungainly, thrusting pas de deux while his human partner either joined in, singing and swinging along, or hollered for release as other kids gathered and laughed thrusting their hips at air and lolling their tongues in mimicry of this sexual predator.

Now and then a kid would be bitten protecting a ham sandwich or cupcake and subsequently splashed with Mercurochrome and given a tetanus shot. Then the dog catcher would arrive with a noose and a net. Followed by a posse of kids barracking in whispers he'd usually bag an entirely innocent pooch and extort twenty bucks from its owner to give it back.

At least once a week a funeral cortege would drive along Balaclava Road, past the school on its way out to the cemetery.

A slate-grey hearse, a Buick, with flowers blooming inside and speakers on its roof giving off sombre European death-music, was followed by thirty or forty cars all at walking pace with their occupants sombre as the music and staring straight ahead, ignoring the young, who were ranged along the school fence, hanging over toward the road ogling this macabre parade and wondering aloud who was dead. 'Who's carked it?' 'Who's the dead one?' 'I heard it was a fella from Congupna who fell off a horse after it stepped on a snake and stampeded.' 'No. It's a old woman they fished out of the lake after burglars threw her in.' None of the horizontal inhabitants of the slate-grey hearse ever died of natural causes.

Once I realised that the lead role in every solemn motorcade was as anonymous to the North Shepp students as Superman was to the citizens of Metropolis, I began to cast the role myself. 'That's your mother in there. Your mother was killed at work today,' I told Terry Langley while we were watching a funeral cortege pass one lunchtime. 'No it's not.' 'Yes it is.' He ran to the bike shed and got on his bike and caught up to the hearse and rode along beside it peering in through the windows, until it stopped, stopping all the mourners in their turn, and a window wound down. The driver of the hearse and Terry swapped a few words and Terry came riding back to school. 'I told you it wasn't my mum.'

'Well, who is it?'

'Don't you read the newspaper? It's the Queen of fucking England.'

'It's not the Queen. The bloke was just saying that. They don't bury the Queen here.'

'Well, it's not my mum.'

'Well, it's not the Queen.'

'Well, it's not just between my mum and the Queen. It can be a . . . a . . . just a dead woman.'

'The bloke's a liar. A dreadful fibber. Have you been home to check?'

Barry Marshall was a boy a few years older than me who had taken a set against me and vowed to get me. Some kid was always going to 'get' some other kid at North Shepp. On a Thursday Barry deliberately crashed his bike into mine, sending me tumbling through a bush into the school incinerator. So on Friday I leaned over to Natalie Oxley, who was balancing on the bottom fence railing watching a passing funeral, and said, 'I'll tell you a secret about this funeral if you promise not to tell anyone else.'

'Oh, I promise. I double promise.'

'Double promise? I don't know.'

'I triple promise.'

'That's Barry Marshall's dad in the dead wagon. He was poisoned this morning.'

'Oh,' she put her hands to her mouth. 'That's terrible.' Natalie broke the terrible news to anyone who would triple promise not to tell anyone else. They all triple promised. And the people they told also triple promised not to tell anyone else. So, soon everyone knew . . . which was good, because they'd triple promised not to tell anyone else, and now they couldn't.

Kids started to commiserate with Barry Marshall about his dad being dead. The first couple of times he called them dickheads and denied his dad was even sick. Poisoned, they told him, happened fast. And they patted him on the shoulder and laid hands on his arms and made other gestures of sympathy they'd seen on TV. They knew it was true because it had been told to them as a secret they triple promised to keep.

Barry's denials of his father's death became less and less emphatic as the commiserations mounted. Some had seen his old man's funeral go past and could furnish details. Witnesses had spotted his relatives in various jalopies in the cortege.

'Does your Uncle Reg drive a blue ute?'

'Yep.'

'That was him, then. He was there.'

'With your grandma in the passenger seat.'

'And your mum went wild hanging out a car window screaming she wanted to drink poison too, she wanted to be taken up. Called heavenward like . . . what's your dad's name?'

'Peter.'

'Yeah, called heavenward like Peter.'

In his first class after lunch, with the teacher writing on the blackboard and her back to the students, a girl leaned across from her desk to Barry's and slipped him a heart she had cut from paper and coloured pink. It was folded down the centre and when Barry opened it he saw a picture of a scrawny bloke whizzing upward through clouds with his ears pinned back as if shot out of a cannon. The words 'Peter . . . Taken Up' were written beneath. This was final proof of his father's death for Barry. And he went for home on the wings of tragedy, ricocheting off this and that in tragedy's miasma.

When he burst into his house and found his mother sitting on the sofa, made breathless by the *Bellbird* rerun she was watching and the Escort Special Filter she was sucking, rather than recognise all was well with the world, Barry called her a bitch with a heart of shit. She chased him around until her anger subsided enough for the pull of *Bellbird* to outweigh it, whereupon she sat and re-entered that pastoral drama and lit up again, shouting threats during the ad breaks. When his father got home he was alive sufficient to wallop Barry on twin counts of wagging school and swearing at his mother.

No one could trace the labyrinth of gossip that killed Barry's father back to its headwaters . . . at first. Too many triple promises had been broken in its distribution for kids to own up to having helped. To the teachers it seemed a school-yard hysteria of the kind that was routine around Easter and Christmas when bunny and Santa sightings caused tides of students to wash this way and that across the playground toward the reported location of the close encounter with either mythical benefactor.

To the pupils of North Shepparton Primary it had been a whole lot of fun. Barry denying. Barry doubting. Barry believing. Barry absconding. Barry bawling through the streets. Barry's mum having a heart of shit. Barry being beaten. How could we repeat this fine adventure?

It became a commonplace at North Shepp, after I killed Barry's father, to give an identity to the deceased. As the slate-grey hearse passed the school with its retinue of wet-eyed relatives trailing, kids would turn to other kids and say, 'That's your mum in there. She got a disease.'

'It is not. It's your dad. He slipped on a turd and fell into a sewer and drowned.' Hundreds of kids would be telling each other some loved one had snuffed it in some exotic way.

But it didn't work anymore. No one believed. Since Barry's embarrassing gullibility we'd become a cynical audience. We knew funerals were for strangers. Only old people who lived three streets away were driven in first gear along Balaclava Road in the slate-grey Buick.

Eventually a portly old teacher by the name of Salter, in his suit and wide tie, smoking his Stuyvesant and patrolling the playground for litterbugs, bullies, fights and intruders, overheard this misuse of the dead. He stood there aghast awhile, sucking deep, eavesdropping as the slate-grey Buick crept by. 'That's your brother Ken in there. He was rolled over by a steamroller.' Hahaha. 'No it's not. It's my Aunty Bette. She died of being a bitch.' Hahaha. 'It's Kevin McConkey's mum with a sex disease.' Hahaha.

They held an investigation and somehow the whole phenomenon of a funeral as a revenge and an entertainment was sheeted home to me. Sitting in the waiting room outside the Headmaster's office I could hear Mr Schatz struggle to outline the gravity of the problem to my parents. 'No, no, no . . . Not normal boyish mischiefs at all, Mr Cameron.' A frightening, distant behemoth, his voice a run of fat tuba notes. 'No. In my thirty years in the department I've never encountered a similar . . . joy of delinquency. He seems driven, riotous, unable to help himself.' There was a long silence. 'I have wondered . . . since this last episode, this sad use of the deceased . . . if he's . . . if he's subject to some . . . Have you ever had him looked at by a . . . behaviourist?'

'A what?' My mother's alarmed voice.

'A psychiatrist.' More silence. I imagined them shaking their heads guiltily. No. They had never had me looked at by a psychiatrist. They had neglected me. They had let this 'joy of delinquency' grow in me like a tumour, when they could so easily have intervened. They were off playing golf, going out to dinner, laughing with friends while this malignant thing assailed me.

I immediately recognised this as a season of forgiveness. With my parents made temporarily penitent by the news I might have some dreadful mental disease they had neither diagnosed nor acted on, and mortified that they'd punished me for mischiefs beyond my control, now was the time to come clean on a couple of outstanding crimes.

I sat on the back seat of our HD Holden station wagon as we drove home. My parents sat in the front, heavily silent. 'Mr Kelly might be coming round to see you this afternoon.' Dad's eyes flashed at me in the rear view. Mum smiled sympathetically over the back of the seat at me, her ill son. 'A mirror I was holding accidentally flashed sun in his eyes and he crashed his truck into his fence.' She reached over and took hold of my knee and squeezed it and said, 'Silly old goat shouldn't be driving.'

'What were you doing with a mirror?' Dad asked. She looked at him darkly, aghast at his heartlessness.

'And . . . we . . .'

'Who's we?' he asked.

'Langdo and Pigsy and me. We picked all Mrs Hoffman's tomatoes to help her because she's old and can't bend down.'

'Did she ask you to pick them?'

'It was initiative.'

'Initiative. Not theft.'

'Graeme.' She silenced him.

119

'Then, we thought, well, she would probably want money more than tomatoes, so we sold them to Mrs Selvey.'

'But Mrs Hoffman didn't get the money,' Dad said softly.

'No, because Langdo and Pigsy and me were thirsty from picking the tomatoes and we thought if we bought lemonade and lollies that would freshen us up to do some jobs for Mrs Hoffman instead of giving her the money, which she probably didn't want as much as some jobs done anyway.'

'But you didn't do the jobs.'

'Well, we were going to. But when Mrs Hoffman found out about the tomatoes she shouted at Mrs Selvey she was an actress Mary after the act.'

'Accessory after the fact.'

'Yes. And then Mrs Selvey called her a rotten old bag and threw the tomatoes over the fence at her. So, Mrs Hoffman got them back anyway. And Langdo said no way known do we have to do jobs for that old bag now because she's got her tomatoes back, even if they were, well, he said "rooted". But some weren't.'

'Did Mrs Selvey get her money back?'

'Remember the lemonade?'

'And Mrs Hoffman's tomatoes are "rooted"?'

'She could make sauce with them. Or chutney.'

'Chutney. And old Mrs Selvey and old Mrs Hoffman are fighting?'

'Well . . . yes. Some of the tomatoes hit Mrs Hoffman when Mrs Selvey threw them back. Then they yelled at each other until Mrs Selvey got dizzy and had to go and lie down.'

'Some tomatoes hit Mrs Hoffman? Did you help Mrs Selvey throw them back over the fence?'

'Well . . . Mrs Selvey is about three hundred and she needs help to do stuff now. That idiot son of hers Peter should help her more.' Dad scowled at this. I was quoting him.

'You pelted Mrs Hoffman with her own stolen tomatoes . . .' He was getting hotter.

But to Mum this episode was further evidence of my illness, and deeper cause for pity. 'Graeme!' she looked across at Dad in the most meaningful way. If he was going to persecute a sick child then he wasn't the man she knew and loved.

'I think they're both coming around to see you. About the mix up,' I mumbled.

'Why not? One has been robbed and assaulted and the other defrauded and defamed. Why wouldn't widows seek legal advice about that?'

'Graeme!' Mum massaged my knee and smiled sadly at me. The world was an unspeakably cruel place if the escapades of feuding hags could be blamed on a mentally ill child. I moved away along the bench seat. None of her wan ministerings could ease the trauma of being me.

*   *   *

Mr Schatz, that hateful zeppelin caroming around his school in slo-mo and a waistcoat, was right. The moment I overheard him question my sanity I recognised in his words a new scam to be worked on the adult world. My eyes widened at the beauty of the dodge. I can hornswoggle the town with this sick-in-the-head shtick for a year at least. Man, I'll limp, gurgle and drool like a boy brought up by dysfunctional wolves. The town will cry for me and set up charities for me while I struggle along under the hump of my feigned illness.

But Schatzy knew better than me. I didn't have it under control. Mine wasn't a normal reaction to serious allegations of mental abnormality. The reaction itself suggests he was right. It wasn't a con. My boyhood was defined by lurid and fantastical delusions that enticed me beyond boyish hijinks into criminality, politics and totalitarianism. I had an imagination that constantly overwhelmed reality. I couldn't believe in my fellow townsfolk as important or real. I couldn't get beyond a deep suspicion that life, the world, the town, the red-faced authoritarians who bent low to offer me advice, the pear-shaped ladies who gave me apricot slice and encouragement, they were all players in a farce. It was all a one-leg-in-the-air pantomime and none of it mattered. Life was plainly a joke the exact size and duration of life, and once the laughter stopped, well, that was death. Death was the end of the joke. Early, I realised everyone else thought this world and life was a serious place. But they were nuts.

\* \* \*

Mr Sargood was as deaf as a post. A big old man in a sweat-stained fedora and a white shirt yellowing at the armpits with its sleeves rolled and his pants hitched to his tits and held aloft by braces. He would get into his Torana in the morning and put it in reverse and rev it like goading a Rottweiler, unable to hear its screaming engine. Dad would mutter, 'I'm telling you, if he slips the clutch he'll go straight through our house. Come out of the street, kids.'

He lived alone, all his family and friends and indeed everyone he ever knew or loved was dead of old age centuries ago. A last citizen of Ancient Rome or Dickens' London, doomed to live on after all his world had perished beneath the sod. A man to wonder at and weave stories around and drape in dark juvenile rumours. He had made a pact with the devil. He had hidden beneath the bodies of dead women when Nazis were scouring his village to finish off survivors; the barking of their Mausers as they butchered the women had made him deaf. He had been the first white man in the Shepparton district and had fathered an entire half-white tribe that was genetically susceptible to exotic influenzas and died out in some dago epidemic started by Italians through their crazy use of garlic. The dying sighs of his caramel-coloured tribe had turned his ears to stone and made them useless evermore. He was all these things, this lonely old man.

But he was disarmingly friendly for a neighbourhood spook. This friendliness continually doused and confounded our red fictions. When you met him he smiled and boomed hello as if to the man in the moon. He'd never learnt to lip-read, so he took your side of the conversation on faith with a grin and a set of nods and shouted at you about the beautiful day or the crisp morning and offered you free eggs from his chooks. And he knew you were agreeing with him about the morning's crispness and the day's beauty, and yes, you would come around and get the eggs tomorrow morning – though you never did. That's the way conversations went with Mr Sargood. He shouted stuff at you and then nodded and smiled, because in his silent happy world there long ago ceased to be disagreements. But I wasn't going to let an old man get away with that.

Having a deaf neighbour was as cool as owning a monkey or a corpse. It was a thing boys wanted to see, and gave me the ability to bestow favours, to take my friends on a tour of the halt and the handicapped. Using Mr Sargood, I made myself a curator of human curiosities. I became a P. T. Barnum to rival Daryl Scott, a boy in the Commission who owned a carpet snake with two heads. Kids would point me out, 'He has a deaf neighbour. Some old giant who couldn't hear a cannon if you fired it in his kitchen.'

Langdo and Pigsy and I had worked out early that conversations with a deaf adult allowed you a creative freedom and an outrageous opportunity for transgression that normal conversations did not. And it turned out I was better at this than either of them. I could ad lib humour and insult into a dialogue with this smiling deaf man that would make my friends flinch and have them choking back eruptions of mirth.

I loved to show off my conversational dexterity, and would cross the road to speak with Mr Sargood if I had friends in tow. And, deafness being an invisible disability, my friends would be spellbound with my brutal use of this towering, seemingly flawless, adult.

'Hello, young Cameron. Are you going all right?' he would shout, smiling and nodding.

I'd smile back at him as if my heart was a second sun built to manufacture bright days for geriatrics. And I'd shout, 'Well, yes, Mr Sargood. Going all right apart from silly old fuckers who smell like shit keep asking me dumb questions. You haven't seen any of them around, have you?'

'Would you lads like some fresh eggs? My pullets are laying,' he'd boom.

'Why, oh why, would we accept eggs from a dreadful fatty who smells like a retriever?' Not everyone can shout such a thing while smiling as if platitudes are blooming on his tongue. I could.

'All right, then,' he'd shout, smiling as if the deal were done. 'I'll leave a bag with two dozen on the back porch.'

'You'll be wearing the bastards if you do,' I blazed my teeth at him and waved.

School friends and semi-friends and, eventually, kids who didn't know me at all would come round to the crescent to see this David and Goliath show first hand. Sometimes I had a posse of a half-dozen admirers as I insulted the old fellow.

At first, as the shouted conversation began, boys who were new to this theatre would go stiff with fear and begin to cast about for hedges, low fences and other escape routes. No one could speak to an adult this way. They looked at me like I was the type of screw-loose fool to call down a shitstorm from on high. Watching their disbelief, their beamed astonishment, their fear, a wave of physical pleasure passed from my stomach to my scrotum as if I'd jumped off a cliff.

I was protective of Mr Sargood, as one might be of a rare beetle. I didn't want to share, and when other kids muscled in on the act I quickly cut them out. Mr Sargood and I were shouting at each other one day. I hadn't got too abusive yet, was just limbering up, booming meteorological facts, about to surprise my cohort of newcomers by asking him if his nuts had been blown off in the First World War, when Lawrence

Abdul, an unwashed kid from the Commission who'd come to the crescent to witness the phenomenon of the deaf man, stepped up to Mr Sargood as if he was mentally shrivelled to idiocy and shouted up into his face, 'You stupid old cunt.' It sounded dirty and mean – really wrong. And he'd said it with anger in his face, beaming disgust at the old man. Mr Sargood smiled unsurely at him.

I grabbed Lawrence by the arm and spun him toward me. 'Hey. You don't yell stuff. He can read some people's lips. He can read "cunt". Anybody can read "cunt".'

'Then he must be one. Because he didn't say he wasn't.'

'Fuck off. Get out of the crescent now or I'll get Guy.'

Boys my age longed to see Guy from a distance, but no one wanted to meet him face-to-face; the mythical absentee big brother, gun owner and explosives expert who had left a dozen boys to drown in the floods. Lawrence wandered away slowly while Mr Sargood looked doubtfully after him.

I should have stopped then. Having been shown by Lawrence Abdul what I was, I should have just stopped, and let my sad use of that old man become a secret shrinking shame. But the lure of the footlights is strong. The stage and the adoration of a group of callous boys called. Just one more performance and I would put the act away forever.

It was Saturday and thunderstorms were skirting the town, lightning strobing a bruised sky. Stephen Newman had come to my place to play. Newmo was the first kid I ever talked about books with. We swapped our favourites. *The Boy's Own Annual*, the Three Investigators, the Secret Seven – he seemed the only other kid in town who had discovered these worlds. It was like we were mediums, people with a rare and special gift for communicating with the unliving in all their limitless fictional glory.

Pigsy was over, as usual. The three of us climbed the lilly pilly and picked a bucket full of berries and were taking turns to stomp them barefoot to make wine. The juice was purple and the berries felt like panicking tadpoles between our toes.

Across the road Mr Sargood came out of his house and into his front garden, staring at the sky, at the lightning. 'Go on,' Pigsy said. 'Show Newmo.'

I jumped over our low brick fence and crossed the road and swaggered halfway up Mr Sargood's drive with my feet stained purple and my hands in my pockets. The other boys trailed a few paces behind, Newmo edgy in the presence of this fabled freak with the thousand rumours coiling about him making every awfulness likely.

'Be a big rain before long, young Cameron.' Mr Sargood shouted.

'Build an ark, you old goat,' I shouted back. 'You and a few wrinkly old grannies can float away in a love boat.'

'Ha ha . . . your feet are purple.'

'Which would make your arse purple if I kicked it forty times.'

Behind me Newmo was big eyed at this exchange, on his toes, ready to go. Kids didn't speak to men like this without a blitzkrieg of adult vengeance. Pigsy was grinning happy fear like a boy on a Tarzan swing. Behind them, standing in our yard beneath the lilly pilly with his hands on his hips, was my dad. The four-ball competition had been called off because of the lightning, so Dad had come home from golf early and, hearing shouting, had wandered around to the side of the house and found me misusing Mr Sargood.

I turned and saw him there, wearing the sporty mustard coloured slacks and paisley knit of a man dressed for victory. He and his partner, Lucky Simson, were both fine golfers and had won the four-ball championship that year. But the look on his face was at odds with his sartorial gaiety. A sort of blank enmity I had never seen before. He'd become a stranger. I've done this to Dad, I realised. I've done this.

'Come here right now.' His words were slow and his voice strained. 'Newmo, Pigsy . . . get out of here.'

The thick ear only hurt for what it told me about Dad's anger and my behaviour. He rarely resorted to corporal punishment. I had done something that had made him, for a few moments, someone else, someone worse, one of those angry, humourless fathers, ground down by life, one of those fathers from the Commission. I had turned him into one of those mythically low men. And I knew I had turned him into that by suddenly revealing myself as a far lesser boy than he had thought me. It seemed to me I had broken his heart.

As I lay in bed, early, banished, with remorse thrust upon me, but no less real for that, I wondered if Mr Sargood knew of my cynical use of him. Was he really so lost in his deafness? Maybe the way I treated him was how the world treated people with a weakness. Maybe he'd come to accept abuse as his due years ago. Was he always deaf? Had he come to expect no better, from strangers, neighbours, kids? Was he the butt of everyone's jokes from such an early age he had come to find cruelty banal . . . except at night, in his bed, just

128

a hundred yards from me now, where he wept loudly and wide-eyed at his ceiling.

For some time that night I tried to hate old Mr Sargood in order to make my use of him acceptable. To get that vision of him crying in his bed out of my mind. But when I thought about him honestly I had to admit I liked him. I was invisible to many adults – but never to him. And he seemed to like me, always told jokes he thought we could both laugh at, though only he ever did. Maybe he was a friend . . . of mine.

Yet I'd made him a famous sideshow that attracted boys from right across town. Lying in bed that night as the wagtails nickered and the sprinklers ticked their watery second hand around themselves, I realised I was the type of person who would cause pain to a friend if the pay-off was right.

Okay, I said to myself, I will be very careful not to sell my friends anymore. Nothing will make me corrupt the sacred bonds of friendship from now on. I will maintain a code, like a knight does. I will become honourable. No price is high enough to sell a friend. Certainly not laughter. I crossed my fingers, I crossed my legs and my toes and made a pact with future friends. I tried to believe all of this, that night, with my ear hot and swollen. But even so young I knew what bounty the world offered traitors, and that I would be bought again.

*　*　*

For my misuse of Mr Sargood Dad forced upon me a number of self-improving activities. I was found a job as a chemist boy. Mr Beneforte, the pharmacist, stood at a raised counter at the back of his shop wearing a white coat grinding powders and stirring slurries to make potions and elixirs that fended off death, or fear of it, in the townsfolk.

A new mother might come in pushing a pram, hiding a prescription in her palm. 'Ahh . . .' Beneforte would shout from his vantage, 'Morning, Mrs Johnson. Don't tell me why you're here. I can see by the way you're hobbling the euca-lypt salve didn't do the trick. Piles are a bugger to get on top of . . . ha ha. A pain in the bum, we might say. Ha ha.' Beau-tiful young Mrs Johnson would hunch and wince to have the travails of her anus broadcast and make damping motions with her hands before abandoning the babe and ducking red faced behind the shampoo spinner. 'Come out, Mrs Johnson. Show me your script. What liniment has Doctor Ferguson prescribed for your ravaged sphincter now?'

Shepparton's ailments were barked by old Beneforte as if he were paid by Big Pharmacy to create panic and suspicion. You had no choice. You had to go and see him for medicines. There were no medical secrets in our valley with Beneforte on his soapbox working his mortar and pestle and screeching of our boils and bodily malfunctions. No lurking fevers or hidden epidemics could creep up and scald our district. They would be caught at inception and their presence broadcast as Beneforte brandished the pestle above his head. 'Hello, young Cameron. How's that tinea? Confined to your feet yet? Or still heading north?'

I delivered drugs on my bike in the dark after school to the homes of people wracked by coughs and beset by fevers. Others were in urgent need of rubbery prophylactics. Those pounded by coughs or standing slick with sweat in their pyjamas would thank me in fervent mumbles for the medicines I brought. The men waiting on frangers would snatch them from my hand and tell me, 'Took your time,' and slam the door in my face and I'd jump on the bike and pedal away before the howls could begin. Being a chemist boy I gained free jelly beans, frequent illnesses and dark dreams of priapic men.

I was also made to enrol in a judo academy and tasked with hefting fat boys gently onto spongy mats. Bidden to stand on one leg, hands cocked like cobras, while white youths gave off anecdotes of Eastern spiritualism in which scrawny old Japanese beat the shit out of foul-minded armies. The parameters of judo were overly civilised and I was constantly cautioned for punching my opponents in combat.

Tennis was essential to a rounded education. So they bought me whites and on Saturday mornings when summer was warping our world with heat I became a D-grade player for St Augustine's alongside other clumsy kids who whaled away at thin air while lobs soared over us into the backcourt and our fathers guffawed at new idiocy.

And I was forced to join the Shepparton Chess Club. I liked chess and was a major force at it – in the chess-phobic Cameron household. I'd nag a sibling or a parent to play with me, and eventually they'd sigh and say, okay, one quick game. Whoever it was then let me win pronto so they could get back to whatever they were doing before I began hassling them to play chess. Being unbeatable at home led me to think of myself as a Spassky in utero. A grandmaster in the offing. And I still think I might have developed well, had I not run into the Chinese boy and, worse, the autistic boy so early in my dash to the top.

At the Shepparton Library on Thursday evenings effete men in cardigans and snide smiles were waging mute battles. Sitting opposite each other at small tables, one would run a forefinger across the bridge of his nose before moving a rook and lolling back in his chair like a Bond villain who'd just snapped out an evil masterstroke, caressing his own forearms in lieu of an albino cat. Chess was an egalitarian and empowering passion. Ice makers and cannery workers and Hungarians and clerks and, preposterously enough, women, were freed this one night a week to become Napoleon.

Benjamin Sheridan, a friend of our family, played here. Benjamin was an obese egotist and laughing stock in his late twenties, temping as a bus driver until the confusion about him not being a QC or an MD or the CEO of a major company was cleared up by his mum writing letters to people begging them to give him a go. He sat way back from the chess table to accommodate his obesity and smug postures.

One night, in his caftan-and-sandals stage, Benjamin leant back in his chair and put an ankle on a knee inadvertently exposing himself to his opponent, a boy who froze and was timed out. Whereupon Benjamin set about boasting of his easy victory and speculating that seeing his opening moves the boy probably realised he was totally outmatched and a goner, though he might have had the good grace to surrender by upending his king rather than freezing like a rabbit in the headlights of Benjamin's excellence.

His next opponent that night was a dairy farmer who, when Benjamin leant back and his left ankle went to his right knee, took an elastic band from his pocket and made a sling-shot between thumb and forefinger and fired the black queen up the gaping caftan where, wearing her pointy crown, she head-butted one of Benjamin's testicles, causing him to collapse onto the carpet tiles and moan, 'Holyfugginchrist,' which was decoded as both a swearword and a blasphemy and cost him two dollars into the swear jar. A new code of dress was drawn up for the Chess Club that prohibited caftans and made underwear obligatory.

Benjamin's opening gambits were strong and as his position on the board became more promising he wore the showy aura of invincibility I recognised from cartoon villains – coyotes and cats and such. His pomp was so blatantly jerrybuilt and transient, and his comeuppance so obviously nigh, that I sat and waited in delicious expectation

When his opponent announced 'Checkmate', which every opponent who hadn't been defeated by the Medusa gaze of his tossil always did, Benjamin collapsed backward twenty years into childhood and pouted and grumbled and whispered, 'Oh, jingoes. Oh . . . crap. Crap, crap, crapola.' For which quadruple expletive he would be tapped on the shoulder by the club president and told, 'Language, Benjamin . . . chess, not football.' And made to pay a tithe into the swear jar. It was a lesson, watching men swell with hubris as their black knights slayed white bishops, only to be grumpily jamming coins through the slot in the lid of a swear jar ten minutes later.

Into this field of serially-usurped Napoleons steps young Anson. Never beaten. In my first few bouts, against other newcomers, I muddled through to victory, sweaty-browed and chewing my lips. Next they put me up against what was then known as a 'Chinaman'. His name was Bernard. Name a Chinese boy anything you want, if he's yours. But I didn't think Bernard much of a name for one.

Chinese boys, it turned out, were being selectively bred for chess. China placed great importance on chess, in those days, and any boy child not a Candidate Master by the age of seven was euthanised and his parents told to try again. In this way they had changed the nature of the Chinese psychology until it was able to rampage heroically inside the sixty-four-square battleground just as successfully as we Aussies had changed the colour of the budgerigar blue to delight the aesthetic of the suburban retiree. Playing chess against a Chinaman, I discovered, was like sword fighting a Three-Musketeer. The whole assault was bewilderingly rapid and I could take no lesson or sense from it.

I played Bernard seven or eight times. Which didn't take long. His chubby little hand kept snaking out for my pieces so frequently, so rapidly, in the end I didn't know if he was taking them fairly or just snatching them at random on spec that he would have them shortly anyway. After only minutes he would quietly and solemnly say, 'Checkmate.' Then, a few seconds later he'd break into a grin and, much louder and several octaves higher, say 'I do it', with genuine surprise and delight. Always in the brief span between him saying 'Check-mate' and 'I do it', I hoped he wouldn't say 'I do it'. But he always did.

When I went home and told Dad I'd been whipped by a Chinaman called Bernard he fell about laughing. Next Thursday he came along to watch me get beaten. There was something hilarious to him about me being beaten by a Chinese boy. As we walked home, between bouts of laughter he chided me. 'You'll get him next week, Boyboy. That last game you got two of his prawns.'

'They're pawns.'

'A Chinaman,' he laughed. 'Bernard the Chinaman.'

Chess-wise, things couldn't get any worse than being beaten by a Chinaman. Until they did. Until Randall. Randall was a very different kid. He could neither talk to you nor look at you and pulled nervously at his fingers, ears and buttons and made strange noises while saliva ran freely from his lips. He probably went on to design rockets or carve out a bio-dynamic nirvana from deep scrub and grow perfect peaches. But I was scared he might do something really strange, possibly violent or disgusting, at any moment.

We knew nothing of autism. Kids in that place at that time who were mentally or behaviourally unusual were known as 'retarded' or 'retards' by those of us with no medical knowledge and not much compassion and no reason not to dump everyone who was different into the one collective category. This shy, internally focused boy came across as a lunatic to me. Potentially violent, liable to vomit or strip . . . hell, I didn't know. The president of the club sat me opposite Randall and set the game clock ticking. And inside this architecture of tics and tocs a world was created in which Randall became omniscient, omnipotent, a perfect predator . . . God.

Dad was sitting in an armchair with *The Herald* up in front of his face when I got home. From this papery cul-de-sac he asked, 'How'd you go, Boyboy?'

'Mmm . . . not too good.'

'Who did you play?'

'The retard.'

He lowered the paper and looked at me. 'A retarded boy beat you?'

'The retarded boy is . . . He's . . . You couldn't beat the retarded boy, Dad. Nobody in this whole family could beat the retarded boy. Not even the Chinaman can beat the retarded boy.'

Dad wasn't going to miss me being clobbered by a retarded boy. He came along the following Thursday night to watch. And if you think he enjoyed watching the Chinaman beating me, he was in seventh heaven now I was being thrashed by a boy who could neither talk nor unwrap a biscuit. He couldn't hide his hilarity at my perturbation, anger and powerlessness. Perhaps he thought the experience was teaching me a lesson – was a form of karma, payback for my treatment of Mr Sargood.

A game would start and Randall, looking down at his own lap, would somehow see the board and the future there and be able to shape it. Defeat is always a mystery. If you knew how it happened it wouldn't have. But clearly this kid was smarter than I was at this game by a snail-versus-Beethoven type distance.

On the walk home in the dark Dad made jokes. 'You had him worried, Boyboy. He opened an eye during your second game. He might have even been awake for a moment.'

'Shut up, Dad.'

It made it a little harder to consider myself evolution's largest trophy when I was getting beaten by a Chinaman one week and a retard the next, while believing both to be inferior life forms. It took some explaining away.

These days I know more about autistic people and the Chinese than I did then, and think a lot better of them, and don't feel bad about being beaten by either of them at anything. But back then I had a pretty low opinion of both, which meant I was doubly down on myself for being manhandled by both.

I escaped from this mess by convincing myself chess was a pointless pastime for people who were either mentally sick or had undergone a program of eugenics targeted at making chess players and were thus nothing but board-game automatons who wouldn't know how to steal, fight, vandalise or set a paling fence on fire with a magnifying glass.

'Dad, I don't want to go to chess anymore. I don't like it. It's stupid.'

'Is that right, Boyboy? It's not just because of Bernard and Randall?'

'Who? No.'

Debbie looked up from the *Dolly* magazine she was sneering at. 'Maybe you'd be better off playing Twister against quadriplegics. You might be a Grandmaster at that.'

I told myself that Dad taking delight in me being walloped at various activities by flawed minorities must have meant he had faith in me to be really good at something else . . . something important.

\*   \*   \*

In 1969, while I was still amazed by coloured pencils, small-bore rifles and confectionary, mankind landed on the moon. There'd been a lot of talk leading up to the day. By men, mostly. Men with the veins on their foreheads standing proud and their voices dropped basso profundo and their hands opened flat and sweeping across the heavens beseeching us kids to rise up for a moment from our infantile bemusements and behold an epochal wonder. The Yanks, these men told us. The bloody Yanks are going to the moon.

I tried to find this as amazing as the men did. But when you're eight it makes perfect sense to care more about a mother's mood or the tensile strength of a new bubble gum than about a moonshot. And Black Cat bubble gum had recently been launched, so I was pretty maxed on mankind's latest and greatest accomplishments. The Black Cat was licorice-flavoured bubble gum that stuck to your face like tar when a bubble burst, disfiguring you and making women paw and fuss over you as if you were a returned soldier.

When the day of the moon landing came they led the whole school, class by class, into the school hall, a booming room of raw wooden floorboards with a corrugated-iron roof. We sat on rows of benches pointed at a black-and-white TV in the distance high atop a spindly steel frame. It was winter but the room was hot and we couldn't keep still, but had to poke our neighbours and whisper and eat lollies and pull the hair of the kids in front.

The whole moon thing took ages. From what I could see halfway back in the hall a sort of water tank with ears was lowered inch by inch onto an ash heap. Slowly decoding the information given off by my new seventeen-jewel Timex wristwatch I worked out this took forty-five hours. During which every third kid had to wriggle and writhe and whimper and put up their hand and yell out, 'Please, Mrs Roberts,' to be allowed to go to the dunny. Except the prep graders who were too dumb and just wet themselves splashily right onto the parched boards and took to bawling amid concentric rings of hilarity.

Then this Armstrong fellow – who all the boys had been pretending to be in the playground for weeks leading up to this day, and had imagined as a Marvel Comics figure, bull-muscular in a skin-tight costume – he appears in a fat suit gargling and joshing in a silly robotic voice and gamboling around as slow as a sloth in syrup. This Armstrong was no heroic figure, no Hulk, no Flash, no Green Lantern, no showman. Then he compounds the insult of his fatness and slowness by trying to talk up his dreary act, saying, 'That's one small step for a man. But a giant leap for a mankind.' No way was it a giant anything. It was a small, slow step, no matter what you said about it. A sluggish descent of a small ladder. No more exciting than a home movie of a groundsman fetching a cricket ball from a roof gutter. The mood in the school hall was pretty flat. The whole day stunk of anticlimax with an aftertaste of piss.

This wasn't the first time NASA had disappointed us. There had been other overhyped adventures in which their rockets hung in space as perfectly immobile as the plastic Spitfires and Hurricanes that hung on fishing line from my bedroom ceiling; not blowing up, not exuding pointy-eared spacemen in silvery suits holding ray guns, not crashing into Africa and setting fire to a village. NASA was always doing boring stuff like this.

As we filed from the hall we were exhausted, hungry, feeling flat about being bullshitted by our parents and teachers. 'This was their worst show ever,' I said to Newmo.

'Whose worst show?'

'NASA's. I'm sick of them.'

'Me too. Nothing happened.'

'Nothing.'

'I like Disney. With Disney, stuff happens. Rats get whacked and there's treasure and bombs and princes and it always ends in a big ending. How did that end? Armstrong just hanging round like Humphrey Bear with a big plastic head . . . not saying anything . . . same as Humphrey Bear . . . a show for babies.'

'Yeah, and they're telling us, "It's a triumph. It's a triumph," and that's it, it's over. And I couldn't work out who was who. Both the Armstrong and the Buzz Ordren dressed in the same white fat suits. That's a silly mistake, dressing everyone the same.'

'It was shithouse.'

'If they do it again I'm not watching.'

'Me neither. I'm not watching any more NASA shows. They're a waste of time. I'm going to go to sick bay and read comics and chew Black Cats if they do it again.'

'Me too. Neil Armstrong's a boring fart.'

'I'm sorry I even pretended to be him.'

'I never did.'

'You did so.'

'Not anymore. I'm going to be the Human Torch from now on. I wouldn't even want to see the Torch fight Neil Armstrong. It would be sad.'

\* \* \*

For boys the schoolyard was a seasonal war waged with marbles in summer and yo-yos in winter and occasionally these were laid down so two boys could fight. The girls carried long elastics that they hooked around their legs making geometric mazes for other girls to hop and jump through. When that season of elastic-calisthenics came to its end they took up chalk and drew hopscotch squares on the bitumen and numbered them and hopped from square to square, writhing and clawing the air for balance, before bending to retrieve the small tokens they had thrown.

After this there would be a brief season of swap cards. These were playing cards with pictures of kittens and fairies and lakes and puppies on them and the girls bartered them to and fro among themselves, each trying to best the other and end up with the largest and most treasurable collection of puppies and pixies. Some toted collections of cards as large as bricks. Swap-card season was a rising hum of covetousness, during which each girl slowly took on a miserly, slit-eyed, hunched deportment from guarding her own stash while trying to swindle cards from her friends.

The season ended in a campus-wide rolling rut of scrag fights. Negotiations over a card with a picture of a cartoon Princess would come asunder and an origami shitstorm of swap cards would explode into the air and two girls would go for each other, both taking a hank of the other's hair and beginning to whirl as if about to throw the hammer. 'Ya mole.' 'Ya scrag.' We would begin to chant at the top of our voices, 'Scrag fight. Scrag fight. Scrag fight.' Until the entire student body had gathered into a tight ring around the combatants ensuring they could neither disengage nor escape.

141

'Scrag fight. Scrag fight.' What a happy clarion. During rare wonderful combats buttons might be popped or torn away and a training bra revealed. If the fight went to ground underwear was sure to be sighted.

Friends of the fighting girls would swoop on the flotsam of swap cards, pretending to be collecting for one combatant or another. For Jenny (nine years old and currently in a headlock and being called the town bike) or Grub (again, nine, her ponytail in Jenny's teeth and Jenny snarling through it that Grub is a slack mole). But the friends, while feigning good intentions, were usually thieves. They squirrelled the prized cards away in their pinafores – Dalmatian puppies and incorrigibly cute kittens surrounded by golden nimbus like mediaeval saints were smuggled off campus hidden in knickers and admired secretly in small rooms in the Housing Commission.

The two girls who got into a scrag fight would be robbed blind while they fought. The friends of each would accuse the friends of the other of stealing all the cards that had been lost. This could lead to new scrag fights. Swap cards erupting into the blue sky like geysers as a contagion of violence and a redistribution of wealth swept the schoolyard. A Siamese kitten fetchingly tangled in pink ribbon might change hands half-a-dozen times in a day, leaving a trail of bedraggled and bruised girls pouting in its wake.

The girls at North Shepp, like the boys, had an established ranking as fighters. Cherry Baker was the best in the school. Followed by Julie Britain, who could punch like a boy, and then Debbie Carlos, who had nails like an aardvark. But these were unusual girls with a rare gift for combat. Scrag fights were designed for stalemate, pinching, hair-pulling, face-slapping affairs in which no decisive blow was ever landed. They would go on with the girls getting closer and closer, almost becoming one, until they were locked together in a hyperventilating confusion, their insults become winded whispers, 'Fkn mo . . .' 'Fkn scra . . .'

The fight would be ended by a teacher bursting through the chanting ring of students and taking hold of the exhausted girls and pulling them apart and demanding to know what on earth was going on. Our teachers always appeared astounded by girls at fisticuffs, though they broke up scrag fights as a matter of routine. When they were asked what on earth was going on one girl usually burst into tears and the other, a Scott, or a Knight, or a Baker, would reply, 'Mole was askin' for it.' A mole was always asking for it, if you were a Scott, or a Knight, or a Baker.

Fighting was infectious. When a fight ended it left residual aggression in the air, which would be inhaled by hair-trigger types. The hair on our backs was up. Boys with grudges would call out other boys. Boys who wanted to climb the ladder of toughness would front boys above them on that ladder and put out their chin and ask, 'You wanna go?'

The other boy would ask, 'You pickin'?'

'Yeah, I'm pickin'.'

'I'll job ya.'

'You couldn't job me sister.' And the fight would begin. We had twenty-nine fully-fledged rumbles in one day via this martial infection. I was involved in two. The first was with Phillip Marshall, who I picked. This began as a good and graceful fight for me. Mainly because he was too scared

143

of me to punch me back. Once I cottoned on to his catatonia I danced around him punching him in the face with jabs and hooks, an uppercut to the guts, putting together three-punch combinations while my friends urged me on. But after a while I gave up, not feeling too good about his lack of response and the fact he was crying as I punched him.

Half-an-hour later Johnnie Dale picked me. He shouldn't have done it. He had no right to. He didn't have the rank to call me out, and I was pretty angry about it. Unspoken rules of station said you couldn't just pick anyone. What was he thinking? He was a year younger than me and much smaller. But he was a blackfella. And I hadn't met one who couldn't blue.

Fighting was serious, stomach-churning stuff. You didn't do it lightly. You could get your nose broken or eye blackened. But, far worse, your whole carefully earnt and nurtured status could be ruined by defeat at the hands of a lesser boy. Great social demotion could come from losing a fight. But blackfellas fought with laughter in their eyes as if it was the least earnest part of their day. It was just another type of game, and they'd learnt it earlier and more fully than we had.

A chanting ring of boys formed. Rumble, rumble, rumble. I hoped this chant might bring a teacher before something went seriously wrong. Before I took a blow I couldn't talk my way out of.

The first thing every fighter learns is that to throw a punch is to open yourself to a punch. So most fights start with an arm's-length pas de deux and each fighter taunting the other, 'Come on. Have a go. What's up with you?' The ring of spectators, getting tighter, baying, blood high as Coliseum clientele, begins to taunt both fighters. 'Get into it, you weak pricks.' 'Come on, Camo. Knock the little mongrel out.' 'Flatten 'im, Johnnie.' Until someone becomes bored and shoves one or the other fighter in the back and sends him reeling toward his opponent.

Someone shoved me. And as I lurched forward I dropped my hands, opened my arms for balance, and Johnnie Dale must have seen my head served up like a Christmas turkey on a silver salver. He punched me in the mouth with a crisp left hand. I saw stars and went deaf and I grabbed at him so I didn't fall and we went Greco-Roman for a few moments as I hung on until the world stopped yawing and pitching and the baying of the spectators came back to me. I slipped an arm up around his neck and got him in a headlock and dropped to ground, leaning forward as I did so to wham his face into the bitumen.

From there the fight degenerated into a wrestle with me slowly choking Johnnie. But choking had no value as a spectacle, so boys kindly stepped in and pulled us apart and stood us facing each other so we could punch each other again. My mouth was full of blood, so I was comforted to see Johnnie had gravel embedded in his forehead and skin off his nose. Blood would count for much when the story of the fight was told.

Over the next few minutes, and each minute is a deep cul-de-sac filled with demons when you're fighting, Johnnie and I stood facing each other, fists high as our eyes and resting on our cheekbones, ribs flaring for breath, punching each other when we could. But the dream of precision as witnessed on *TV Ringside*, the dream of consecutive blows landed from opposing angles, of dancing combinations, that glorious vision of being able to taunt a defeated but still standing opponent like Ali did, that dream was gone.

We both wanted a way out. I could see it in his eyes and I knew he could see it in mine. But there was no way out. We were exhausted and our moves had become a clumsy mime of combat. Single, looping, heavy-armed punches easily blocked, then a grapple and a shove. The connoisseurs watching knew all hope of an entertaining Armageddon had ebbed from the fight, there was no chance now of a knockout, no chance of an upending or a surrender, no big result coming. The event had tailed off, like they mostly did.

The bell for class rang and boys began to drift away. Johnnie and I fought on, with a couple of close friends watching. All were disappointed their man hadn't jobbed the other outright. They were hardly even barracking now.

It ended when some spectator, one of his fans or mine, tired of watching our docile hostilities, and looking around at the deserted schoolyard and knowing we'd all be in trouble for being late to class, asked, 'Are you guys done?'

'Maybe,' I gasped.

'Yeah, maybe,' Johnnie said.

'Yeah, then. If he is,' I figured.

'Okay, yeah, if he says so,' he agreed.

We stood there staring at each other sucking air and running ideas through our heads to work out what this grey status quo meant. Most fights between boys don't have a clear winner. The lust for annihilation is rarely fulfilled. A fight is the physical version of a quiz, a series of rapid-fire questions barked with the clock ticking and you firing back clumsy answers you conjured in a moment. The answers are never right. To have the right answers would be choreography, or adulthood.

Boy fights end in confusion. And a skilful storyteller can take this confusion, these unnarrated moments, and shape them into a tale of personal victory. Boy history doesn't belong to the victor. It belongs to whichever liar is quick enough to write it before counter truths take wing.

And that's how I beat Johnnie Dale to a pulp. By lying well enough about the fight in its aftermath; fibbing into the dust and hyperventilation, until my lies became the thing itself.

I looked at Johnnie's bleeding forehead. 'You better get that gravel scrubbed out. It's bitumen. Bitumen's got gangrene.'

'Bullshit. What grangene is, anyway?'

'Gangrene's poison. It rots you. You can even smell the stink of yourself. My brother had it and he stunk like a polecat. He nearly died.'

'Only a bit of bark off.' Johnnie touched his forehead and looked at his bloody fingertips. He was starting to look worried. 'Ain't nothing, eh.'

'Well . . . okay. But if you wind up in hospital you tell 'em you did it falling off a monkey bar or a bike. I don't want to be blamed. I don't want to go to jail.'

'Blamed? Jail what for?'

'Gangrene. For whatever might . . .'

'I could go the sick bay . . . If I want.' His nonchalance sounded brittle. 'Might not, too.' He spat drily. 'Graangeene,' he mocked the disease and laughed. 'Fuck graangeene, eh.'

But Johnnie's mates could see adventure in a visit to the sick bay with a gangrenous friend. 'Come on, Johnnie. Don't be a idiot. Let the sister get on that gangrene.'

'You don't wanna rot, Johnnie. 'N' stink like a polecat. Or any cat either.'

'Come on, Johnnie. I smell something bad.'

Johnnie sniffed, shook his head and tried to smile. But he'd smelt something bad too, something festering on the backlot of his imagination that made his smile collapse. He and his mates walked away and before they'd gone twenty steps each had taken one of his elbows, promoted themselves to medics in the service of a diseased comrade. Johnnie suddenly felt the importance of his role, gangrenous and giving off a deathly reek as he was. His head sank down and he began to shuffle as though he might keel over at any step. Psychosomatic gangrene was spreading through his tiny frame.

The fact my stomp-arse, iron-fisted fighting skills had sent Johnnie Dale to the sick bay made me a clear winner of the fight. Even boys who had been part of the ring of spectators yelling rumble *ad almost infinitum* and had seen that the fight was no better than a draw for me started telling the tale of how I'd sent Johnnie Dale to the sick bay with either gangrene or grangene, depending who you listened to, and saying it was a blessing for me the kid didn't die because I'd have been sent to Turana Boys Home with the school-burners and the other killers. I was a budding propagandist, and the Johnnie Dale fight, and his near death of gangrene, was a great lesson to me. I lost no status from fighting Johnnie Dale to an inglorious draw, though he was younger and smaller.

At sick bay the sister laughed at Johnnie and washed his forehead and told him to go to class. So he naturally enough snuck out of school and went down to the Raymond West

Pool to swim while a rumour I started ran through the students at North Shepp that Johnnie's body had been smuggled out of the school and was lying right now on a slab with his family around it squealing and moaning and pointing the bone at me.

*   *   *

Summer was ending and the first footballs were out. During afternoon recess we played kick-to-kick, a recreation where two packs of boys kicked a football to each other and tried to take speccies and then wrestled for the crumbs until someone had legitimate possession of it and could kick it back to the other pack so they could fight over it in their turn. Some kids would 'wax', which meant forming a partnership with another kid and taking alternate kicks when they won the ball. When waxing it was wise to choose a partner better than yourself. Not hard for me. We scragged each other and pulled each other by the shirts so everyone lost buttons and felt grand as soldiers with our gaping, ruined clothes. Each pack smelt of sweaty, unwashed boys.

Being no good at footy, and not getting many kicks on my own, I usually chose a good partner to wax with and kept up a loud smart-arse commentary that made me seem an integral part of the combat.

But this afternoon I had an excuse for my ineptitude. Every time I was beaten for the ball I groaned a small groan that I hoped sounded like a brave suppression of a much larger groan, and I took a few wobbly steps so all the boys knew I was under attack by blackfella magic. The bone had been pointed, but I was soldiering on, weighed down by the voodoo but still determined to live my life, still smiling, clamping down on the involuntary groans.

Strangely, before long I was taking mark after mark. Space cleared for me as other, stronger boys fell away. My judgement was perfect. For a change no other boy was at the fall of the ball before me. I was suddenly faster than everyone else and could cut through the pack with a swallow's fast broken flight. Baulking, taunting other boys, showing them the ball before kicking it away. I had become a champion. 'Cameron takes another speccie! How good is this young Shepparton lad?' I began to commentate my success.

If you asked these boys about the power of blackfella magic they would have scoffed and laughed. But that afternoon no one wanted to risk getting too close to me. The bone had been pointed. (Well . . . it hadn't. But I'd told them it had.) And while they didn't believe in curses and bone-pointing, they all stood back and gave me space in case lightning came from the blue sky, gripping me and shaking me back and forth in a vast wattage and x-raying me transparent, my skeleton blinking neon as the skeleton of a cartoon cat with its claw in a socket, then dropping me black and smoking to the earth. When I realised why I had all this space, that the other boys expected I'd be exploded by Dreamtime death-weapons momentarily, I began to feel frightened too. And I knew Johnnie Dale had gone swimming.

* * *

My world was way bigger than the world of any other kid I knew because I was a bookworm. Guy and Debbie and Vicki continually told me I was a bookworm and not only would I be blind before I was ten, I would deserve my blindness. If you were going to go reading books all the time you deserved the bubonic plague and a foot in the arse, besides.

I read when other kids played footy. I read when other kids watched TV. I read when other kids slept. And I read when they went to Sunday school and boy scouts. I read in bed until my eyes ached. Then I read illegally under the sheets with a torch until books bled into my dreams.

This was the edge I had on almost all the other kids; I came to school equipped with gangrene. And mustard gas, and time travel, and sarcasm, and a sense of honour, and sacrifice and nobility. I could mimic the sounds of Madame la Guillotine at seven. And came to school knowing Lew Wetzel had finally seen Wingenund through the sights of his rifle but, most wondrously, let him live. Through Rikki-Tikki-Tavi I knew how a mongoose waged a cold war on a cobra. As well, having read of James James Morrison Morrison Weatherby George Dupree's troubles, I knew mothers had to be watched – if you scratched the surface they were wanton, and given a chance would get coked to the gills and wander away into a life of sin and dancing, never to be heard of again. I came to school with visions of the Geebung Boys and the Cuff and Collar Team playing to an honourable draw / death, and the Drover's Wife gazing long at the shimmering horizon in her infinite loneliness. I had heard Stonewall Jackson shout at his troops – when they were heckled by Barbara Fritchie – 'Who touches a hair on yon grey head dies like a dog. March on.' I shouted that line around town at various old people who looked back at me with lopsided grins, shaking their yon grey heads while my chest swelled with munificence.

Other kids' minds weren't coloured by these tremendous events and rousing stories. Their families had neither money nor use for books and they were suspicious of them. They turned up at school in the morning with the work-day curses of blue-collar fathers ringing in their ears and no idea that Tom Sawyer had suckered his friends into painting a fence by telling them they couldn't. I came to school armed with the many worlds and ways that bloomed in books. I had galaxies and heroes in my head. Ideas and alibis plagiarised from masters, famous plots and surprise endings lifted from classics, I knew how to die properly, and could live in a palace, among its protocols and plots, at a moment's notice if required. Having read so many stories that no one else had read made me seem wise, full of new ideas and brilliant schemes.

Reading not only gave me the many worlds contained in books, because famously and easily it does that, it also gave my thinking the impetus of narrative. I began to think in stories. An understanding grew invisibly in me that life's moments and events fitted into a continuum, were linked, were related and interactive, and every now and then some Rosetta Stone moment remembered from a book led to the translation of life as it was happening now – it gave me the inside running on the day's events and the family's troubles. It made me, relatively, wise.

I was a bookworm. A bookworm, hooked on the gobsmackingly multifarious life found in books. A boy as addicted to Princes and Lost Girls and Wounded Soldiers and intercontinentally faithful Labradors as Darwin was to his beetles and his finches. And a bookworm, in a village of the avowedly anti-literate, is as powerful as Jehovah. A bookworm has superfluous worlds at his inky little fingertips and is omniscient compared to the boys and girls who do not read and are thus imprisoned in the few adjacent streets and joys and fears of childhood. So I had advantages.

\* \* \*

When very young it was my habit to try and sort out the many mysteries each day threw up by tapping Guy's knowledge of the world as we lay in bed at night. If I was five he was twelve. If I was six he was thirteen. I couldn't seem to catch him. And this enormous gulf naturally meant he was Hercules and Davy Crockett to me. He was a posse of wild enthusiasms that frequently needed reining in by parents and police. An owner of many deadly firearms and traps and bayonets and knives and clubs and poisons and theories. He owned all the country between boyhood and manhood that, to a young boy, is a region much more exciting and heroic than the land where a fully adult man lives tamed and sensible. And he was mine, a fact I constantly lorded over my friends. I have a cowboy big brother likely to burn your shed down or blow a hole in your fence if I give him the nod.

But, like almost anyone, when you flattered him by assuming he had wisdom he got stuck being wise and couldn't be anything else even if he couldn't be wise. He began to puff up and pontificate and lay it on like he was

Solomon himself. He hid a lot of ignorance that way. And he hid most of it behind the phrase, 'That all depends.'

My bed was near the door and above the foot of it I had a poster of Raquel Welch in a fur bikini that was a great distraction to Dad when he read me stories at night. Guy's bed was across the room in shadow. He had a fox skin above his head on the wall. Lying in the dark with the truck brakes on the highway whining through miles of bush and possums on the roof outside breathing as ragged as robbers, I would puzzle over the stuff of my day while watching occasional chips of reflected car light moving across Raquel, hoping to divert their trajectory with concentrated desire so they might light the valley of her cleavage for a moment.

'What's hotter, a red-hot poker or a coal?' I'd ask.

He'd weigh the question a moment, then answer, 'That all depends.' It was an expression that bewildered me and led me, reluctantly, on.

Every night I had a brace of philosophical stumpers for him. Who was worse out of Hitler and the devil? Could Dad belt up a VFL footballer? Who would win a fight between a wolf and a bear? Would a Spitfire shoot down a Messerschmitt or the other way? Who was the fastest draw out of the Sundance Kid, the Cisco Kid and John Wayne?

Guy would let me wait awhile in the dark ogling Raquel's dim silhouette, until my hope grew and I knew he was going to come up with a good, satisfying answer. This time he would set the question to rest with a definitive truth. A bear. A Spitfire. John Wayne.

But in the moonlight I'd see him put his hands behind his head and his eiderdown rise as he sucked a big contemplative breath and I'd know he was getting ready to be wise and I was sunk. Then he'd say 'Hmmm . . . well, that all depends.' And 'that all depends' was an infinitely long tunnel. If I said, 'That all depends on what?', he'd answer, 'That all depends on if Cisco is at the height of his powers and using his preferred Navy Colt, or is he in his declining years and using that fancy light-framed silver revolver given to him by the Countess Valverdé for saving her ranch from low-life greasers.'

'He's at the height. Using the Navy one.'

'Well, then that all depends if Sundance is drunk or not.'

'Sundance isn't drunk.'

'Well, then that all depends if he's horny and distracted by women.'

'He's what? He's not . . . There are no women. It's a gunfight.'

'Well, then that all depends on who's in the right. Who's got justice on their side.'

'Justice? It doesn't matter. I'm going to sleep.'

I knew there was some sort of grown-up profundity behind 'that all depends' and it made me scared of growing up and losing the certainties I owned now behind an adult fog of deeper considerations.

Once, at school, after Guy had stonewalled me the night before with upwards of twenty-five 'that all depends' when I asked him if it was better to be a lawyer or a doctor, Miss Stoddard singled me out of our routinely dumbfounded class and asked, 'Anson, what is three times five?' And I told her, 'Hmmm . . . that all depends, Miss Stoddard.' In its ignorance the class laughed at this, thinking it idiocy rather than a prelude to adult rumination. Miss Stoddard held herself expressionless through the uproar and when it died she asked me, 'All depends on what, Anson?'

'On whether a doctor gets to make women strip off so he can see them nude.' The class went wild enough for Mr Smith to rush in from the adjacent room to see that the roof hadn't collapsed and to frown at Miss Stoddard awhile about her lack of control.

'Mr Schatz?' I asked her. And she nodded slowly with a sorrowful look like she was becoming doubtful about punishing me because, really, what type of riot played in my head?

* * *

But I didn't mind being strapped by Schatz. I would rather Mr Schatz strap me a hundred times than Mr Deasey whip me once. In grade three I had Mr Deasey for a teacher and he had me to despise. He was a Seventh Day Adventist or a Jehovah's Witness and frequently whipped me. Chewing gum in class, backchat, pinching girls, oinking like a boar, fencing with imaginary enemies . . . I never worked my way through the full list of whippable offences, and it seems to me I never could. I think the list was being written on the fly to answer my hijinks. I was often surprised by what turned out to be whip-worthy, though. Hiccups? Hiccups, Mr Deasey? Surely you're not going to whip me for hiccups. Oh, hiccups flagrantly amplified. That's okay, then. Flail away.

I'd stand out front of the hushed class and pull my sleeve up above my elbow, presenting the full length of my bare wrist. Every other teacher who ever whipped me used a flat piece of leather across the hand. A strap. They strapped me. The strap stung and made a blood-curdling thwack in the hollow of the palm that echoed like a gunshot – but it pushed air before it and bounced on a thin pneumatic cushion and didn't bite muscle and vein. The skin-deep welt left by a strap was a trophy that had to be shown fast, because it faded by day's end.

Mr Deasey didn't favour the flat strap. He used a rounded piece of leather as thick as a child's finger, like a skipping rope . . . or a whip. He used a whip. And he didn't go across the hand. He went right up the full length of the wrist. He'd swing at me with his whole arm, bringing the whip from behind himself over the top in an arc with his face grit like an axeman making sure of his Boleyn. The sound of the whip tearing air made the class wince. If I moved and Mr Deasey missed, and was made to look foolish, the number of strokes doubled.

When it landed it didn't make a sound that could be heard above my whimper. It bit hard and stuck, momentarily embedded, him and me conjoined, tyrant and vassal, executioner and doomed. Then that moment fell away into pain and the fight with my jaw and lips and eyes not to cry.

After school I'd go home and watch *Hogan's Heroes*, a TV show where two Germans named Schultz and Klink ran a POW camp during WWII. They were such smiling jovial dolts, one chubby, one bald, both caught in foul circumstance and serially upended by the show's American hero, stung by his witticisms and confounded by his schemes. Colonel Hogan was a good-looking cool cat, and he reminded me of myself.

So next day I'd go back to school and, leering and leaning like an American wise-guy who had his own TV series, I'd try a few of his barbs and tactics on Mr Deasey. By morning playtime there'd be a range of purple blood blisters the size of Christmas beetles along my wrist. It was a confusing time – our German was so much nastier than the Nazis.

*　*　*

Only in hindsight can I make the black kids black. They were just kids, then. To me, anyway. And to all of us kids, I think. But maybe, without me knowing it, those kids, those black kids, had heavy knowledge of their blackness in that white place.

In class, aged eight, a Yorta Yorta kid named Ronnie Scott sat alongside me while Miss Robertson taught us that Captain Cook discovered Australia. On the blackboard she had drawn kangaroos and spindle-legged natives spooked by his landfall and helter-skeltering with fear-whitened eyes into the bush. There it was laid out in coloured chalk. Honour and bravery and gold buttons arriving on our island continent and our proud country born in this moment, thanks to this hero with the braid and white girly plaits.

We were asked to draw our own versions of the landing. Ronnie and I copied her picture of kangaroos and blackfellas stampeding into the scrub. The brown pencil with which Ronnie coloured those folk in could have been a sixth finger on his right hand so closely did it match him for shade. Being easily tempted and having itchy trigger fingers we added glorious gouts of flame leaping from the muzzleloaders of Cook's commandos as they spooked the blackfellas into the bush. Australia had to be created. So with delight we drew blooms of blood on the blackfellas and kangaroos.

There might have been four Yorta Yorta kids in the class. And in truth I can't remember too much about Miss Robertson apart from the remarkably detailed pictures she drew on the blackboard before class, which made every morning a visit to a gallery where some new masterpiece was unveiled. She was young and likely a Melbourne girl straight out of teachers' college waving a new degree and unlucky enough to be given the far-flung nowheresville of Shepparton as her first posting by the Department of Education.

The history she taught was given to her from on high and couldn't be questioned. But it must have seemed to her a strange truth to be telling, that the world had begun with a triumph of British navigation and the people who lost out, by a hairsbreadth, were the French. Particularly with four Yorta Yorta kids blinking happily at her. And a strange thing to be conducting us while we sat at our desks, twenty small whitefellas and four small blackfellas, our arms out straight and our hands folded neatly one into the other on the desk in front of us, while we sang 'God Save the Queen' to celebrate Cook's discovery.

They would be running a long time yet, those natives who had just taken flight in our drawings. Running back off a frontier of farmers with firearms, leaving behind Ronnie and his brother Moody and their sister Sherry in the new world that had come.

If the blackfella kids in the class knew the startled natives Miss Robertson had drawn on the blackboard could be placed ten rows above them in a family tree then it was a secret they kept, while laughing along with the rest of us at the white of their panicky eyes. None of us linked those first-contact natives on the board with our friends. Ronnie and Moody and Sherry were part of the here and now with no hint of the past.

Did they know it was them being chased into the scrub by Cook? Did they know that for a long time there was another world that had been swept away for this one? I didn't know I was white. And I don't know what consciousness of loss the Yorta Yorta kids brought to school from their homes. We were kids, and the world was born when we were born and all of this Cook and First Fleet business was a bunch of colourful stories to sit alongside Red Riding Hood and *A Christmas Carol*.

If Moody and Ronnie and Johnnie Dale and the Bambletts and the Atkinsons and Briggs knew that the rascals Cook's men were firing at in the drawings on our classroom blackboards were, essentially, them, wouldn't they have trudged the grounds sullen and aggrieved?

They didn't. They weren't that way at all. The Yorta Yorta kids were anything but deadened to the sparking and sparkling moments of a kid's day. They were shy with adults, but lively away from them. Always breaking out into offbeat ideas and making wild suggestions. Like me they were slightly tipsy with humour and likely to erupt into laughter any time at all. They had a capacity, an itch and an urge, to break from po-faced actuality to a place where everything was coloured hilarious. I could laugh like few other people. I found jokes in the patterns of tree bark or the gait of a minor official. I considered myself a brave laugher. But I couldn't laugh as well as the blackfellas. I could only stand back and envy them when they got right down to binging on life's absurdity. They claimed that glorious luxury as theirs.

This lesson, Cook On The Beach, was the only point at which I remember blackfellas ever touching our learning at North Shepp. We studied of England and her kings and queens and wars and explorations mostly. When we learnt of ourselves we met bushrangers like Ned Kelly, or the explorers Burke and Wills and Sturt and Stuart and sundry other misanthropes. No women. Hume and Hovell, the first men to discover our district. MacGuire who set up a punt on the Goulburn River which became the start of Shepparton. The only blackfellas we met in our lessons at school were those startled few who ran away from Cook's party at first contact. They must have run a mighty long way, because we never saw hide nor hair of them again.

*   *   *

Ronnie and I were best friends for a year. If I had no money for lollies we would sit on the oval and eat yam-yams, a small seed pod of a wiry grass. They were sweet and crunchy and if the Bellboy and the Metro Gum and Sherbet Bomb hadn't been invented, yam-yams would have been a passable delicacy. But an array of wondrous confectionaries, for which I pilfered Mum's golf money from a small pewter trophy, had made the yam-yam a sweet of last resort.

As we sat on the oval nibbling them I told Ronnie that soon I would be leaving this place and going away to a proper school and I would live there and have my own bed to sleep in. A big famous school called Geelong Grammar made of red-brick castles with a high tower, a place where princes were taught.

Ronnie stared at me, blinking like a small owl. Then he nodded. He knew all about it. He was going there too. He'd see me there. We'd still be friends, us, at this royal court for specially chosen boys.

I was excited at the thought of a friend being there with me. But I was disappointed too, that such an illustrious school would accept a poor boy like Ronnie. It lowered the tone of the fabulous institute I had built in my head, where I had been expecting to befriend a cast of minor royals and hyphenated surnames. When I told Mum that Ronnie was going to Geelong Grammar and at least I would have one friend she said, 'Well, we'll see, Boyboy. Ronnie might be confused about going away.'

His big brother Peter, known as Moody, had a name as a fighter and boys were scared of him. He was called in to settle disputes. We went at it one day and I ended up on top with him flat on the ground beneath me, his arms up beside his head and me holding his wrists. I had him pinned. Total control. But I was as trapped as he was. I was riding a tiger wondering how the hell I was going to get off. I wouldn't get this lucky twice. He'd kill me if I let him up. Boys had gathered and he had lost face and I'd have to get a good belting for him to get it back.

Usually when a boy had another boy pinned beneath him he would hang spit from his mouth over his captive's face in a long pendulous drip before slurping it back up into his mouth, allowing it to emerge again and letting it hang, lower this time, almost to breaking point, the tension frightful, before sucking it elastically back. This torture would go on for many minutes while the boy beneath writhed for release and made threats of revenge or offered bribes. Until the boy on top let the slag stalactite hang too far and it snapped and its bulbous, quivering payload landed on the captive's face, most effectively in his mouth or eye.

We spat on each other a lot. There were different methods of spitting and different viscosities of saliva and some boys gained reputations as ballistic virtuosi who could summon pinpoint oral cannonades such as an orca might drench you with at Marine World.

Spitting was, as often as not, a reply to a casual question asked of one friend to another. I would ask Stowey if he was going to the pool after school and he would turn around and spit point-blank in my face. Everyone would laugh and I would wrestle him to the ground and spit close up in his ear, that mucosal payload accompanied by a fearsome pneumatic roar that would make his eardrum ring for hours. All the rougher boys smelt of rancid saliva by day's end.

Moody and I stayed on the ground a long time. Threatening, bargaining, repeating the snippets of script boys remember from TV stand-offs. My exhaustion got deeper and deeper until I had to let him up or collapse on top of him. I released him and we stood, me tensed to fight or run, and he smiled and put his hand out and we shook. Moody was a good kid. I don't know what the country Captain Cook discovered offered him as an adult. I don't suppose it was much.

\* \* \*

A year later, in the small shaded asphalt playground before the shelter sheds, I finally found real love. Two girls held a rope while a third, with the kind of perfectly straight blonde hair I admired, skipped at its centre as nimbly as a cat. The rope swingers sang:

> Down in the valley where the green grass grows,
> There sat Debby pretty as a rose.
> Up came Nuttsy and kissed
> Her on the cheek,
> How many kisses did she get this week?

Then the rope swingers began to count the kisses, one kiss to each cycle of the rope, 'One . . . two . . . three . . .', getting faster with each rotation.

Debby Neeld's pretty face focused harder and harder as the rope orbited her faster and faster. Despite the concentrated effort she was graceful. Her red-and-white checked dress flounced at the hem each time she landed, mesmerising me with staccato flashes of her brown knees. But each skip was another kiss from Nuttsy. 'Seven . . . eight . . . nine . . .' Each time she successfully avoided the rope a piece of my heart died.

It is likely I was standing so close by the time she glanced at me, and looking so wan, so flagrantly moribund, that she got a fright that broke her rhythm. But to me it seemed when our eyes met she instantly renounced the kisses of Nuttsy by letting the rope whip her on the ankles and its transparent oval orbit shatter and fall around her like a scorned world, freeing herself for me.

I said 'hello' and meant it more than I ever had. And she said 'hello' back in an evocative way, and love's intuitive treaty was thereby signed and within minutes she was skipping again, her friends making my heart sing by singing

Down in the valley where the green grass grows,
There sat Debby pretty as a rose.
Up came Ansy and kissed
Her on the cheek,
How many kisses did she get this week?

Twenty-three. On her first attempt. Hovering like a hummingbird in that cage made of moving rope. Twenty-three fictional kisses from that new Romeo in the skipping song. Her swayed back squared her shoulders and made her bottom jut prettily, giving her a strong, athletic air. A gymnast with straight blonde hair.

Nuttsy, otherwise known as Norm Almond, was a friend of mine. And though I'd never noticed Debby Neeld before, I was astounded to find him kissing her in song behind my back and hated him for it. I picked a fight with him at lunchtime and jobbed him. Ended up on top of him punching an ear. I didn't tell him why because that would have blown the fact I was head-over-heels in love. I told him I'd seen one of my pencils in his desk.

I couldn't stop thinking of her. I'd drift toward her at recess and lunchtime moving my friends with me until they mingled with hers and we became a mess of refracting romances. We began to play kiss chasey. When I was 'it' the more cumbersome girls were invisible to me. I'd take off after Debby, peripheral figures moving in grey slow-mo around us as I chased her, red, white and blonde, through the school, down the centre aisle, across the main oval, round the shelter shed, ducking and weaving through the monkey bars. Glancing back over her shoulder now and then, she squealed with laughter and burst away. She could run like no other girl. I couldn't catch her. But, sensing the danger of not being caught, she'd slow with a subtle grace that feigned fatigue and, finally, I'd tag her . . . and thus she'd owe me a kiss.

Kissing a girl was a risky manoeuvre. It was known to be a dishonourable and effeminate thing to do. But like a drag on a smoke or a gulp of beer, it gave off a blurry hint of some distant but possible buzz. Behind the shelter shed I struck at her like a taipan with its lips puckered. The deed was done. Her downy cheek brutally caressed. We were lovers and pledged for marriage and children of our own.

For a few days we lived happily in thrall to each other. Sitting side-by-side every playtime and lunchtime, I fed her jelly babies and spearmint leaves and she gave me a stainless steel cupboard catch. We swung our legs back and forth and thought of things to say.

Despite the weight of the steel cupboard catch in my shirt pocket reminding me of love's validity, my mind ran. Across the grounds I could see boys climbing trees, and throwing stones at boys who were up trees. I could hear a game of British Bulldog on the small oval and the shouts and roars of this combat made me itch and writhe.

Neither was Debby so faithful. I saw her stealing glances across the playground at groups of girls forming new skipping allegiances, trying out new rhythms with the ropes, singing new songs, attempting new tricks, setting new records. Her less-gifted rivals were getting uppity now that love had taken her out of the game.

We were secretly nettled that love and our obligations to each other had shrunk our worlds so small. I was a warrior who constantly heard the bugle and she was a hummingbird that only came to life in a rope cage. And as the brutal wars and grand ballets of the playground were fought and danced, our love bound us to this bench seat behind the shelter shed and made us swing our legs and had me ask silly questions like: 'Do you like coconut ice?'

And had her tip her head this way and that before answering, 'Sort of.'

'My sister can make it. Next time she makes some you can have some.'

'All right.'

By Thursday of the week after the kiss I was back playing British Bulldog, running flat out and leaping knees up at the surprised faces of boys who had thought me moved on from violence to the world of romance. And Debby was skipping again, floating weightlessly inside her shadowy ellipsis of rope as her friends sang

Down in the valley where the green grass grows,
There sat Debby pretty as a rose.
Up came Darryl and kissed
Her on the cheek,
How many kisses did she get this week?

And they sang it loud. There seemed to be no place in the schoolyard I could go and not hear them. Forty-six is the answer to the question in the song. An impossible number of consecutive skips. I had a vision of Debby and her friends sitting on the bench behind the shelter shed cupping their hands around their mouths and shouting the song at the air and giggling while they counted slowly to that improbable number. Maybe she wasn't skipping at all. Maybe it was a fraudulent forty-six, a myth made in song.

But I didn't believe that. I knew she skipped forty-six consecutive skips to grant herself forty-six fictional kisses from this Darryl. Whether to make me jealous, because she still loved me, or for love of him . . .? That was the question. And who was this Darryl? There were too many tough Darryls at school for me to take revenge on. Again, I retreated from flesh-and-blood girls to find love among the pretty housewives laying their hands atop tumble dryers in magazines, those steadfast beauties who stared at you smiling no matter what face you pulled or what appendage you showed them.

Not long after the death of love, Beckwith came riding past my place. When I think of Beckwith I bite my lip and nearly feel regret. Beckwith, lying there, is further proof of my nature. Beckwith explains plenty. Beckwith was a boy so pure he whistled Prokofiev while riding his bike. His mother loved Prokofiev, and though he preferred Mahler, he whistled that Russian's tunes to please her. He was adept at long division and helped others navigate its degradations. On Sundays he sang in the Saint Augustine's choir, rising early to bake biscuits for his fellow falsettos. He invited all thirty-six of his classmates at school to his birthday party because he wasn't into exclusion. He had rosy cheeks and curly hair and . . . do you hate him yet? I did. Fucking Beckwith.

Beckwith was selling us out. The very notion of capriciousness, selfishness and hostility as core traits for boys was being refuted by Beckwith's goodness. The guy was wrecking our gig and rewriting the possibilities of boyhood in a way that was going to place nasty obligations on us all.

So when Beckwith came wobbling past the mouth of our crescent on his electric-blue Peugeot it never occurred to me not to fell him. That letting him ride happily into his future with phrases of *Peter and the Wolf* playing on his lips might be a thing to do. No. Look at the curly hair. Notice the unscabbed knees rising and falling provocatively as he tootles along. Beckwith must be crushed for the good of those for whom long division is a pipe dream and Prokofiev a snide adult negation of Suzi Quatro. You are mine, Beckwith. The falcon is no surer of the bilby than I am of you at this moment. Did I mention Beckwith's first name was Darryl?

I had a beautiful left arm from throwing hundreds of items a day. I only had to heft an object in my hand to have the kinesthetics innately sussed. I didn't need conscious thought – heft twice and the trajectory was set. I rarely threw balls. Normally rocks, clods and shards of masonry, at fragile or living things like windows or trees pretending to be Beckwiths.

There was a bin of rotten pears near our gate waiting for rubbish night. I grabbed one and threw it in a high parabola with a preordained pay-off. Somewhere down the road Beckwith would find himself on the other end of this arc and he would be changed forever.

I felt a primal thrill of biomechanical perfection as it landed on top of his head. In the language used to describe burns victims: he sustained third-degree rotten pear to ninety-five per cent of his body. He squealed and his hands, for some stupid reason, went to his ears. His front wheel naturally jackknifed and he went over the handlebars to the bitumen.

He had a most surprised look on his face as he hit the bitumen. Why? If you don't want to be knocked sprawling onto the road, why, in the name of God, steal my girlfriend and then ride past my house whistling Prokofiev?

As I squatted behind our low brick fence wracked by Chaplinesque hysterics, Beckwith lay glistening, reeking of fructose, attracting wasps. There was blood too. But the blood wasn't as instructive as the pear-mash, so let's forget the blood.

The pear-mash was important as first proof of evil. After a while Beckwith sat up and touched a finger to his shirt and tasted it and shook his head sadly and lay back in the gutter staring up at a suddenly curdled universe. Someone had definitely thrown a rotten pear at him while he was riding his bike. A new darkness had entered his rosy little life; the devil was loose in his garden.

Sitting there ten minutes later with my laughter thinning I thought to myself that some day, some way future day, when I'm fifty maybe, and writing of myself as a boy, I will have to confront the kid who knocked Beckwith flat into the tar. I suppose that kid will disgust me, I thought. And I was disgusted at the future man for being disgusted at that kid. How many selves are there, I asked myself. Through the course of a lifetime? How many?

Darryl Beckwith, meanwhile, was being hauled up from the gutter by a young couple with a toddler at foot and a baby in a pram. The toddler was holding his nose and pointing at Beckwith and shouting, 'Poopoopoo . . .' Would it be wrong to bombard a young family with rotten pears? Could they tell where they were coming from?

When we went into the CBD of Shepparton, only a short walk from our house, we were 'going down the street'. The centre of town with its grid of streets lined with shops set in the shade of verandahs was 'down the street'. Larrikins, idlers, sharpies, fruit pickers down from Queensland, gangs of tough kids from other schools, big women lugging wicker baskets . . . down the street was a pose-off, a dance, guys leaned on parking meters claiming a slice of street as their own. Look down as you walk, count the lines in the footpath. Don't give 'em cause to shout out at you.

Saturday morning, loaded with twenty cents of pocket money, we kids would arrange an expedition. Little fish heading out among groupers.

From Talinga Crescent I'd set out with Pigsy and Langdo. Langdo was Vicki's age, three years older than me, and one older than Pigsy. He was a thoughtful kid, often asking adults questions he knew they couldn't answer, just for the joy of watching them perplexed. Some of his questions couldn't be answered by adults on grounds of propriety, and some on grounds of ignorance. Being endlessly cheeky, he enjoyed both types of non-answers, both methods of stymying an adult. But his favourite way of snaring one of these giants inside a minute of confusion and embarrassment was by ambushing them in a pincer movement made of rosy innocence and explosive vulgarity. He would blink and twist his lips and a look of loud puzzlement would come onto his face and he'd ask, 'Mrs Pigott, can I ask you a medical question?'

'Of course, Langdo. Go ahead.' She'd be thinking tinea, or cramp.

'Have you ever had anal sex?' He had a thousand variations on this theme and adults were wary of him.

He was an inventor. His father was an electrician with a shed that smelt of grease and was full of electrical gear and tools, nuts and bolts and fuses and naked women on tyre calendars. Langdo was always out there winding something into the vice, crimping wires together, soldering, or unscrewing the backs off radios for parts and cannibalising blenders to make robots that performed no more robotics than a clod of earth.

For one of my superhero personas he filled a backpack with batteries and ran some nasty amps down a line into a pair of rubber-handled barbecue tongs so I could take a pinch of whatever archenemy was currently threatening mankind and lay that son of a bitch low, squirming in a straitjacket of voltage and despair.

173

To test this weapon I sauntered up to the Langdons' Siamese cat Hex who looked a little, if you squinted your eyes and said, 'Hey, Catwoman,' like Catwoman. I brandished the wondertongs above my head silently to give her full warning justice was nigh, then grabbed her by the tail. She meowed as if trying to lighten herself of her lifetime supply of meows in one go and lit out for heaven using the freeway of a nearby liquid amber, bursting out the top of the tree and scratching at blue air. When she hit the ground she re-enacted the perpendicular launch horizontally, a honey-coloured smear of cowardice. She forsook her family. That's cats for you. There's a traitor in every one, only awaiting concentrated voltage to bring it out.

So the wondertongs apparently worked on dozing cat-sized fiends. But would they work on life-sized villains, opponents with a heftier biomass? Would they fry lizard-featured humanoids?

Langdo's mum wasn't a lizard-featured humanoid. She was quite pretty, malingering there in her small kitchen at an endless chain of minute tasks. She'd taken the pre-sliced, processed cheese from the fridge and unwrapped the white bread from its waxed paper to delight the husband and sons of the house with grilled cheese on toast for lunch. Again.

These staples lay on the table, their status as food so dubious there was no need for a fly net. In my experience grilled cheese on toast was the only foodstuff ever prepared in this kitchen. The Langdons only ever ate grilled cheese on toast or large tin buckets of ice cream so white it looked like snow. And despite my mother blackmailing me into eating every bitter absurdity in the whole food pyramid, the Langdons seemed no less healthy than me. I loved their grilled cheese on toast. It had all the blandness a boy needed.

Langdo's mum had turned to the sink and was washing dishes in an uninspired fashion. She seemed to be looking out the window at what might have been. At a life that wasn't. To me she had the look about her of a woman who, if given the opportunity, would embrace higher purpose. I saw the languor that cloaked her face as a form of silent yearning for greater responsibility. This woman hadn't been put on earth to wash dishes. She was, with her dull look, showing disgruntlement and begging to speed the course of scientific warfare against super-villains, offering herself up as the first human test pilot of the cat-launching wonder-tongs. But maybe I just saw her disenchantment with her lot in life because I needed to. 'Hello, Mrs Langdon.'

'Hello, Boyboy. Do you want some ice cream?'

'Maybe later . . . after the . . .'

'After what?'

'After nothing.' I sidled up behind her, stood there awhile eyeing her buttocks like a deli customer torn between small-goods. Or in this case rather big goods. The gypsy ham or the mortadella? The left buttock or right? They were dimpled as scoria, stretching her lemon-coloured rayon house pants beyond the maker's recommendation or imagination. Left or right? Eventually I went left, clasped a hefty tongful of that buttock and held on tight.

Mrs Langdon was generally a placid woman lost inside a halo of hair curlers, sheepishly shuffling room to room avoiding the rolling household wolf pack of male domi-nance. Who'd have thought she'd set up such a wailing and contrive such expressions of pain? Not me. I felt let down. This wasn't scientific. Better to make her observations on the wondertongs verbal, concise. 'Boyboy, the new instrument gives off a mighty zing. It started my pubes smoking.' Something like that. Factual, informative. But she offered nothing valuable, nothing I could take on board and integrate into the next generation of wondertong.

I think an electrician (and, remember, her husband, Roy, was one) might tell us the wattage of the wondertongs was amplified by her having her hands in a metal sink filled with water at the moment of application. More fool her for being trapped on a domestic treadmill. I can only imagine the havoc the wondertongs would have wrought on sea monsters if they hadn't been confiscated and I had got to grips with those sodden creeps.

Langdo's mum gurgled and headed for the linoleum as if bullets were cutting through the kitchen at hip height. Once there she convulsed and shuddered and set to screaming the same scream over and over. By the time she'd screamed three times Langdo was living in a share house with Lord Lucan and Ronnie Biggs. Goner than just gone. Miraculously gone.

So when Roy Langdon burst his normally sloth-slow arse through the kitchen door to find what variety of catastrophe was mauling his missus, he found her on the wood-patterned lino screaming that scream and me standing there, delighted by the wisps of smoke curling off the wondertongs, but also chagrined by his wife's refusal to answer, as I asked her, again and again, 'How did that feel?'

I was thrown out of the house and kicked in the arse all the way down the front path to the gate and from there shoved for home and told I was a dangerous idiot. Mr Langdon then decommissioned my wondertongs by helicoptering them over the fence into Mr Sargood's yard. It was not uncommon in Talinga Crescent to launch jerrybuilt devices packing unknown wattage over one fence or another, thereby making them some other sucker's problem. I guess they lay in Mr Sargood's hydrangeas hissing at his chooks until the batteries went dead. Super-villains everywhere flexed their biceps and smiled.

The wondertongs had fused Mrs Langdon's rayon house pants to her left buttock. And these unfashionable pantaloons had to be coerced off her haunch by her mother-in-law, Nanna, using tweezers and lanolin and, knowing that old bitch, gleeful roughness. I guess I was defamed by both parties during the whole process. It wasn't an era that valued scientific research.

Drugs sent Langdo to jail early. Vicki visited him there, which was like her. I didn't, which was like me. And while we were all still flexing our dispositions to see who and what we might be I heard he was dead.

\* \* \*

To go down the street with Langdo we would cut through his nanna's house which was out the back of his own. Her garden was dark with high greenery and we crept down her driveway hoping not to be caught, because she was a shrivelled widow in black with greasy grey ringlets, prone to pop up out of the ferns like a Viet Cong with bursts of angry, unanswerable questions. Our standard defence against her existence was to sneak around her or run from her. Langdo wasn't scared of her, though. Once she shouted at us, 'What are you children up to?' And he burst into loud song, 'And I wonder, I wah-wah-wah-wah-wonder . . .' This was a recent Del Shannon tune and his use of it in this moment seemed genius to me.

First stop was usually Halpin's Sports Store. It was a cave made of wood, dark with a wooden floor and a wooden counter and wood and glass display cases, all of which made the garishly chromed racing bikes that stood in ranks inside appear like UFOs that had come crashing through the roof of Shakespeare's Globe.

Behind the counter was a wall of dark wooden drawers and if I told old Bunger Halpin, the small and bald owner, that I was here to buy a Ferrari Matchbox car he would roll the wooden ladder along on tracks and in his long grey dust-coat climb to that drawer and pull it out and pluck from it a small yellow box sided with plastic windows in which sat an electro-red auto-morsel. He'd hold it between his thumb and forefinger, smiling like a miser with a widow's pacemaker, and before coming down the ladder he'd demand I lay out the forty cents I'd stolen from Mum's golf-change cup on the counter.

Boyish morals melt like ice in the fierce blaze off a red Ferrari. Every time I stole from her I made a pact with myself to repay the money once I'd saved enough. The Me that was promising to repay the money knew I was lying and the Me I was lying to knew I was lying but we both nodded our heads, or head, in rank complicity and affirmed it was a done deal, that the money would be paid back to Mum if it was the last thing I, we, did . . . which it still might be, I, we, suppose.

Once Matchbox cars lost their allure there were the cases of knives and guns and hunting bows and fishing gear. Sometimes Mum would leave me with my nose pressed to the glass of the knife cabinet while she went shopping. Like tying a terrier to a parking meter, she knew I would be there when she got back. You could track the greasy wanderings of my nose tip across the scratched glass countertop and know which knives I coveted most.

The nationalities and characters of the knives made the knife cabinet a geopolitical theatre. It was filled with villains and heroes, dark racial stereotypes and clean-lined saviours. All covetable in their own way. The folding Pumas with their Germanic geometries, the rustic English Barlows with handles of horn and antler, the futuristic American Gerbers made of hard steels and covered with space-age materials, sheath knives such as Tarzan wore, and Bowies large enough to kill grizzlies that made me lament Shepparton's lack of dangerous giants.

I often bought knives. But it wasn't easy. It was an excruciating deliberation. Only one could be mine, and to choose one was to unchoose ten others I wanted badly. Bunger Halpin, once I told him I was here to buy a knife, would go about his business, knowing I would prevaricate until right on closing time at midday, when he would say to me, 'Very well, young Cameron, come back on Monday. I'm closing up.' And I'd grimace and thrust my finger at a knife. 'I want the Puma Cadet with the green handle.' Every beautiful knife I ever owned, every killing trinket, was haunted by the ghosts of all those knives I rejected to own it.

One Saturday morning I ogled Bunger's knives so long

and got home so late Mum burst into tears as I walked in. She'd thought me kidnapped, run over and drowned.

Next stop was Darveniza's Newsagency, where fresh editions of Archie and Donald Duck and Phantom comics had to be handled and considered. Mr Darveniza knew me as an undecided shopper. 'Are you buying that? This isn't a library.' And the half-understood college humour of *Mad* magazine, which always left me feeling empowered and enriched by the half I got, and ripped off by the half I didn't.

Then, and I would break away from the friends for this, Every's Bookshop. Right next to Bunger Halpin's Sports Store in Fryers Street. Shepparton wasn't awash with bookworms then and a bibliophile in baggy shorts blowing fist-sized pink bubbles of Bellboy gum was a rarity. So they treated me kindly in Every's. I think they thought me a boy who, like the boy bibliophiles in books, was outcast from his generation and seeking comfort in fictional worlds.

In here was the ecclesiastical hush that accompanied reading, the vow of silence taken with each book, a sly whispering that suggested reading's secret getaway, the deft slip from this world into distant, compelling realms.

I knew Mum and Dad wouldn't object to expenditure on books, as they did when I splashed ridiculous gouts of cash on lollies, knives, fish and chips, arrows, ammunition and incense. I understood books were exempt from fiscal logic because they had a long-term unknowable but undeniable pay-off. You became a better boy if you read. And somewhere down the line when I became a lawyer or school principal or scientist, Mum and Dad could nod wisely about their policy of letting me go hog wild in Every's. It's also likely they recognised my every other enthusiasm was so venal, so wrong, so immoral, so likely to lead to jail or ruin, that they promoted my love of books in the manner believers cascade Bibles onto natives and infidels – to save them from Hell.

Anyway, I played havoc in this financial free state. We had an account in Every's Bookshop. We had accounts all over town and Guy was given to buying rope, lengths of chain, guns, and, once, a racehorse, by telling the sellers to put it on the account. The racehorse went back, Dad yelling down the phone, 'What type of moron sells a thoroughbred on credit to a clearly unstable boy of fourteen?'

I didn't often put things on the account. But I did in Every's. I had no idea what an account was apart from it meant I could sign for books rather than pay for them. I had a vague idea we were getting stuff free because we were Camerons. A sort of tribute paid to a sort of nobility. And, despite having no signature, I signed a showy splash of gobbledygook in front of shoppers who looked on in awe as if I was an antipodean Onassis, the type of gilded individual who could buy sports cars using just his face as capital.

Being the youngest of four I had access to hundreds of hand-me-down books. And the older three siblings being devout illiterates almost all of these books were new, most unopened. This gave me the whole series of Secret Seven adventures and the Famous Five. But the books that live unloved in your house are rarely the books you want to read.

In Every's the skin-prickling thrill of reading a catchy blurb on the back of a new book promising mystery and escapades, then flipping it over to eyeball the gunslinger or laughing boy or fighter ace on the front cover, this was how great adventures began. An unread story is the best ever written and my hands would shake as I turned a new book over and over. I'd lift it to my nose and inhale the inky vapours of a new place. Then I'd walk quickly to the counter and grandly tell Mr Every, as if he were a porter helping a great explorer cross a small stream into a new land, 'Put it on the account.'

Every's was all dark unpainted wooden shelves forested with book spines. A mezzanine balcony ran right around the shop and you could climb to it and browse more books up there while looking down on shoppers below. It was a private and cosy place, like a loved library it affirmed an endlessly interesting world.

Every's also sold fireworks, and in October, with Guy Fawkes Night approaching, the shop would fill with boys buying penny bungers and halfpenny bungers. All the pretty pyrotechnical hues, the Catherine wheels and rockets and roundels and starbursts and glittering concentric fires raised in the night sky over these few weeks were just tinsel on the gift of war to us. We admired explosives, percussion, concussion, destruction and the ballistic power that was a byproduct of detonation. We wanted crackers. Amid the smell of gunpowder and the rustle of red cellophane, boys with smirks hiding schemes for wild pyrotechnical vandalisms came and went.

But for the rest of the year I wouldn't meet many kids in Every's. And I was suspicious of those I did encounter. Readers were known to be effeminate and clumsy; mummy's boys retreating from sport, and girls who shot their hands up in class when a question was asked, huffing, 'Me ... me ... me ...' I read stuff that took me to wonderlands and badlands. They read How, When and Why texts because they were housebound by their own lack of sociability or because they were budding know-alls. They didn't read like I read.

Every's had to be monitored keenly. What new books had arrived? What favourite famous author had crept into town and humbly taken up his or her half inch of space on the shelves? What new adventure was standing quietly there leaning on older, known neighbours? Was Roald Dahl jousting with new giants there? Had Enid Blyton set up another two-hundred-page run of dominoes for me to knock down in slo-mo revelation? Had an undiscovered J. M. Barrie miraculously appeared?

In Every's, ogling the latest dun-coloured hardbacks in their garish dust jackets, I promised myself that when I grew up I wouldn't be one of those writers who turned their backs on real fiction by writing for adults. I would write for children my age, people whose minds were open to time shift and who knew a beach was a veneer of sand atop the bones of the brave and treasure chests bursting with rubies. I would write clear moods and honourable acts for a readership that believed in straight-up happy endings without all the obfuscations, justifications, considerations and Janus-faced sentences which were the grey atoms that made adult literature. I would, in my own books, find kelpies lost a hemisphere away, and save poor but pretty girls from arranged fates with deranged princes. I would never abandon the young to write for adults. In Every's, running my hand along the vivid spines of books written for people my age, I told myself I would never leave this children's section, this wondrous tumult of tales.

* * *

We sauntered through Coles and Fairleys, the large department stores, chiefly to steal. The things we wanted to steal – bubble gum, pocket knives, firecrackers, Matchbox cars, model planes, water pistols, cigarettes – were kept behind the counter or under glass. This left us having to steal stuff we neither wanted nor needed. Which was all right because we stole so we could be thieves – for the bravura of shady doings, for the status of saying to each other, 'I hooked some superglue this morning. If anyone wants to glue something.' 'Superglue . . . okay, cool. I hooked a whole pack of paper clips, if anyone wants to . . .' The loot was worthless but the thrill of shoplifting was addictive.

In Coles I sauntered blatantly, casing the joint like a pro, before subtly sliding a screwdriver down the front of my underpants. I had no need of a screwdriver but had calculated, correctly, that it would fit comfortably in my underpants.

'You put that back. You put that back right now or I'm taking you to the store detective.' In the aisle watching me was a little woman, tense and angry with having to confront a thief. I saw a long wreckage stretch before me . . . a shoplifter, shamed family and ruined schooling, and a prodigy sentenced to a lifetime on a production line.

It was all right for Langdo or Pigsy to get caught shoplifting. But I had family status that might be undermined and brought down by this sort of scandal. I was vulnerable because of my name. Slowly I pulled the screwdriver from my underpants and put it back on the shelf. Not knowing what came next I just looked at the small woman sheepishly. She didn't know what came next either, so she just looked at me angrily. After a while I turned slowly and walked away, cringing that she might call the law.

\* \* \*

Just up Fryers Street, in an arcade branching off to the south, acting as a vortex for long-hairs, ne'er-do-wells, itinerants, dole bludgers and other shifty types, was the Star Bowl. Standing on the roof over the mouth of the arcade was a box-light sign spangled with box-light stars that read 'STAR BOWL', topped by a box-light pin and ball. The Star Bowl. Even now a thrill of truancy attends the name. It was a place for the town's ill-fated young to loiter harbouring an incommunicable intent to turn out differently to their parents. We were forbidden to go there.

So we went there. When I was seven Mum and Dad travelled to the Mornington Peninsula to play golf for the weekend and left us in the charge of a waddling babysitter named Mrs Flanagan who smelt of camphor and unwashed rodents. (I had a white mouse named 'Hey' who smelt sweet as pie when washed regularly, but gave off a spoor like Mrs Flanagan when not.) They told this large woman not to let us go down the street and certainly, under no circumstances, to let us go to the Star Bowl. The Star Bowl, all adults understood, was a place where children might be set on a path they shouldn't be set on by people they shouldn't even meet.

Mum and Dad left on Friday night. Come Saturday morning Debbie began womanly preparations upstairs in her room. She donned her tightest purple t-shirt and a pair of arse-hugging bell-bottoms and raided Mum's beauty case, and though the beau she was trying to fascinate went more for the reek of engine oil and Camel Turkish & Domestic Blend cigarettes, she sprayed on a flowery scent and pocketed a lipstick.

Then she came downstairs and brought forth a week-old chicken carcass from our round-shouldered Frigidaire and laid it before Mrs Flanagan who was sitting at the kitchen bench giggling with her ear up to the radio. The wreckage of the bird bedazzled the woman and the aforesaid parental guidelines came all asunder in its gravity. She corralled the thing inside the fleshy parenthesis of her arms and was leaning close, sniffing and studying to ascertain what type of assault to launch on it, when Debbie mentioned she was going down the street to buy Mum a birthday present.

Tapping the pooled jelly in the dish with her little finger and leering at it as it wobbled, Mrs Flanagan said that buying a present was all right but stay away from the Star Bowl.

'Ya . . . uck,' Debbie said. 'What type of girl do you think I am?'

We might have been much younger, but Vicki and I were onto her. Mum's lipstick was silhouetted against her arse-cheek in her bell-bottoms. A dead giveaway. We caught her in the garden. 'You're going to the Star Bowl, aren't you?' I asked her.

'No. I'm going to buy Mum a birthday present.'

'You smell pretty good.'

'Just let us come,' Vicki begged. 'We won't get in the way.'

'Piss off.'

'I'm dobbing to Mum and Dad if you don't take us,' I said. 'But if you take us I can't dob, 'cause I'd be in trouble too.'

'Jesus, you shit me, Anson.' This was the declaration with which Debbie invited me on many of her little adventures. 'Okay. But don't hang around me when we get there. Piss off and play the pinnies, okay?' Vicki and I agreed. We loved the Star Bowl; the rattle of the balls busting through the pins, the tolling of pinball machines, the serial asphyxiations of the cappuccino machine, the harassed woman on the loudspeaker telling lane three their time was up, and the shouts of the teenagers telling her to stick lane three up her arse. The Star Bowl was a small piece of a big city smuggled into town.

Outside the Star Bowl Debbie ran Mum's lipstick around her mouth, making herself a woman. She was fourteen, and as set to burn herself on a boy as any girl ever was. Seeing her, red-mouthed, a woman, I knew this was a serious day and wondered if I could close my eyes, go back to sleep, open them and start again.

She gave us money to play the pinnies and told us not to bug her and walked over to lane ten, the furthest lane, in the shadow against the far wall. She stood near a small posse of long-haired teenagers, wearing denim flares and western shirts run through with tinsel. They were years older than her. Youths. They were youths. Their arms tattooed with skulls, dice, flames and pythons.

One of them left the group and walked over to Debbie and flicked his head at her. I could see only a narrow slice of his face between two curtains of hair. To look at him you felt like you were spying into someone's house from their garden. But I knew who he was. Everybody did. She smiled at him, held her hands out wide to show herself, to be appraised. He nodded and the curtains hiding his face shimmied. She took a smoke from him and he held a gold lighter up and they both leaned at the flame with a cigarette, sucking and then basking in each other's exhalations.

Vicki and I began to play the pinnies. All around tough kids from the tech schools drank milkshakes and smoked and made strange noises that could only be understood by their friends. Wallster, a friend of mine happily freed from parental control by them becoming couch-bound alcoholics, was playing a machine, slapping its glass face and thrusting his hips at it, forefingers on the flippers cajoling it into hours of servitude. Wallster was good enough that, using a piece of wire, he only had to winkle one coin from one parking meter and he could play all morning racking up bonus balls and letting his mates take a turn now and then, until the score needed boosting for a free game and he'd take over and keep the silver ball aloft, like Bradman with a cricket ball and a stump, until the machine gave off the gavel-rap that signalled a bonus play.

You had to work the pinnies a lot to be as good as Wallster. I couldn't keep the silver ball in play. I kept looking across to lane ten where Debbie and the known guy with the tattoos and the vertical stripe of face were holding hands. 'Look. She's holding hands with him.'

'I know. Shut up. Don't look,' Vicki said. But she was watching them too. Her contortions at the Batman machine were merely cover for a wide-eyed surveillance, her fight with the silver ball a pantomime.

In the semi-circular booth of lane ten where the bowling balls appeared magically from a chute and the low-life slung them back down at the pins and catcalled and laughed at each other's ineptitude, they sat side-by-side. He put his arm around her. 'Look, Vicki. He's got her. He's hanging onto her.'

'Shut up. I can see. They're just hugging.'

'Hugging? He's her boyfriend then. Oh . . .' A hollowness, a despair, came over me that Debbie had fallen this far, into this group, this fellow's tattooed arms. Had renounced goodness and gone off hugging notorious scum. Where was help? Mum and Dad had motored away golfing with high-tone friends while I fought a class war for the family's honour.

I thought of the behemoth babysitter back at our house spinning a carcass in her hands like a corn cob with an eagle eye for some dried skerrick of flesh. Should I run back and get her? Tell her Debbie was embracing low and dangerous men? No. She was three blocks away and slow as the moon. Debbie would be gone the way of all young female adventurers, down the moral vortex of lane ten, before Mrs Flanagan hefted herself for rescue.

Soon they were kissing, their faces hidden in a meeting of hair. This was wincingly fascinating. It had all the emotional push-and-pull of watching a dog you dislike wander onto a busy road. 'This is why she sprayed perfume. And the lipstick,' I told Vicki. 'I want to go home.'

'We're not going home. We just got here. Play the pinnies.'

'I hate the pinnies. I hate the Star Bowl.' I went closer and sat in the booth at the end of lane five, watching them. She sat in his lap. They kissed, head pivoting against head on a fulcrum of lip. I waited for police sirens. I waited for God to bring down the ceiling. I waited for the harried woman on the loudspeaker to speak out against this. 'Will the couple in lane ten, the goon headed for Hell and the girl from a good family, stop kissing right now. Lane ten, your time is up . . .' Tears came to my eyes. I knew there was no way back from this. That innocence, like Humpty Dumpty, once shattered was beyond the reparative guile of all the King's horses and men and Mum and Dad.

Absorbed and disgusted by the horror of their kissing I focused my disapproval right at them. Pale and pouting and with my eyes wet I became a moral beacon. I beamed censure until my face ached. The young couple bowling in lane six looked at me, looked at what I was looking at, and back at me. Then the boy burst out laughing and was slapped on the arm by his girl and told not to be so mean.

Before long one of the group of lane-ten hoods nudged my sister and she and her hooligan broke apart and looked over at me, he through the gap in his hair and her radiating anger. He bucked her off his lap and began to walk my way.

Even a violent criminal couldn't just punch a kid in the face in a public place. I knew that. And then I didn't know that. I blinked my eyes, trying to make the tears go. Time to be tough now. I made my mouth mean.

He squatted down in front of me, a pack of Camel tight in his Miller shirt pocket right at my eye level, and 'Jane' tattooed on his wrist. 'Anson, right?'

'Yeah.'

'How ya goin'? Benny.' He held his hand out for me to shake. The hand attached to the wrist with 'Jane' on it. Debbie's middle name was Jane. Had this man tattooed my sister's name on his arm? She would have to go away, live in England with an English aunt, surrounded by tweed and peonies.

The only kind of fame available to a young male in Shepparton was infamy. And Benny Zambrano had infamy . . . and was reaching out to shake my hand. I put my hand out and he shook it softly. I was in this too now. I felt as if I'd joined a gang.

Wallster was watching from the pinball machines, his own machine oddly silent, his fingers raised off the flippers, letting the silver ball ricochet dead without a fight. I knew Wallster would tell the town. Camo shook the hand of Benny Zambrano. I tried not to smile at the thought of all that might come of it. Camo knows Benny Zambrano. Don't mess with Camo, Benny Zambrano's going with his sister.

'You want a milkshake, Tiger? And a Crunchie?' I barely nodded. It seemed outrageous to accept gifts from such a person. 'What flavour?'

'Chocolate.'

'What about your sister there?'

'Strawberry.'

His hand was surprisingly soft for a thug. He had called me 'Tiger.' He came back with milkshakes for Vicki and me. 'Thanks, Benny.' It seemed a wildly intimate thing, to thank this infamous teenager for what amounted to a bribe. But I wanted those two words to mean a lot, I wanted them to mean, 'I don't care what the cops or my olds say, Benny. I'm on your side. Even in gunplay or truancy, I'm on your side. Us. Outlaws forever.' When a desperado befriends you it is a far greater patronage than when a plain old nice person does. This twisted sharpie has come down out of an habitually dark mood to be agreeable to me. Has made the gruelling pilgrimage into niceness – for me.

Having bought himself some time he went back to kissing Debbie. I sucked on my shake and fondled my Crunchie. The chocolate bar was a dilemma. Crunchies were a favourite of mine. But if I ate it I no longer had it to show off to my friends and to casually mention it was given to me by Benny Zambrano to pay me for unbuttoning my big sister's bellbottoms. Trying to have my Crunchie and eat it too, I ate half of it and tied a knot in the wrapper, before realising this would be too obvious a prop, too clumsy a way to start a conversation about my notorious new friend. So I bit through the knot and ate the second half.

Benny Zambrano delivered Vicki and me gifts from the kiosk regularly over the next few hours. By now I was talking to him easily, eagerly. 'Hey, Benny, what's it like to get a tattoo? I'm going to get a tattoo.' 'Hey, Benny, have you ever stolen a car? I've shoplifted heaps of shit.'

'I never stole nothin', Tiger,' he winked. What sly insolence. A denial of vast crimes overlaid by a simultaneous secret admission to those very crimes. Wow. This guy had all the wiles of a major bandit. A Great Train Robber. Right here in the Star Bowl he denied a life of crime while admitting to it for those of us smart enough to get what the wink meant. And it raised all sorts of bank heists and hold-ups in my mind.

192

He went back to kissing Debbie and I practised my wink. I could only do it with my left eye and had to screw my mouth sideways showing teeth, but told myself the mouth thing emphasised the irony of the wink. I began to wink at Vicki and Wallster after everything I said. 'You guys want some Twisties?' Screw-mouthed wink. 'What are you doing this arvo?' Screw-mouthed wink. Until Vicki told me, 'You can't wink at everything, Boyboy. It doesn't make sense.'

By mid-afternoon I'd watched Benny put his hand up Debbie's t-shirt, undo the top button of her bell-bottoms, snake his tongue into her ear and flay it on her braces, then stand her up against the wall of lane ten and try to grind her through the brickwork into the clear light of day. I was a fan of the show too. I'd been paid well. And I was thrilled to know a criminal who dealt in irony via deft winks. I was barracking for him to use her in whatever way he could think. But after three hours they were played out in this theatre, nothing more could be done. And both Vicki and I had bellyaches from his bribes.

As we were leaving the bowl he lifted me up and put me on his shoulders and carried me down the front steps. It near broke my heart that nobody of note was there to witness this. Debbie was right to kiss him. Benny was cool. A good guy misunderstood and forced to live under a town's heavy prejudice. 'See you soon, Benny. Thanks for all the stuff.' He put a finger to his lips to make me promise silence, then he leant his head to the left so the hair fell away from the left side of his face and winked that revealed eye. I would go to war for this guy. This guy stood tall in the rankings of the town's most magnificent people. How had Debbie attracted a cool, winking major criminal like this?

When we got home the bones of the Frigidaire chicken lay in a splintered monorail around the lip of the bathroom basin and around the lip of the bath itself. Each had been sucked for marrow. Mrs Flanagan had evidently invited a pack of famished wolverines into our family home. Mum would be hearing about this.

Our sated sitter sat in her favourite armchair, her lower face glazed with the piquant marrow of Frigidaire poultry, watching tractor ads on GMV-6 while she waited for the Matinee Movie to light up and take her away from the here and now. The TV guide in the *Shepparton News* had advertised a tale in which a talking mule named Francis joined the United States Marine Corps and she drew our collective promise there would be no chatter during this treat.

She had no inkling that under her care my sister had been defiled by one of the town's premier hoodlums. Had been pressed against the wall of lane ten and dry humped in her bell-bottoms by a tattooed long-hair. And looking at her making rolling motions at the TV with her forefinger to hurry the tractor ads past and usher forth the wondrously droll mule, I doubted she would have cared. A dangerously neglectful babysitter, I decided. I would sort her out.

Three days later détente between Debbie and myself was shattered, as it usually was, by Debbie being a bitch. I had wanted to borrow her bike for Pigsy, because his had a flat tyre. We were going to ride over the back of the levee and shout abuse at people sating illegal lust with the cramped cross-denominational sex practised in borrowed Holdens. But she caught us riding out the gate and slapped Pigsy across the nose off the bike onto his back into the white gravel of our driveway. As he lay there blinking, she called him a thieving little dick and told him to go home.

Pigsy, bleeding from both elbows, was angry with me because he was scared of Debbie and it'd taken me half an hour to convince him she'd said he could borrow her bike. Which he should have known she would never do.

As he walked across the vacant block that separated our houses, first cradling his right arm in his left and then his left in his right, he called to me that I was a liar and he wasn't going to play with me anymore. 'She said you could use it,' I shouted back. 'Then she changed her mind. That's sheilas.' But it wasn't sheilas. It was Debbie. She'd broken my best friendship and probably bones in my best friend and she was going to get hers.

When Dad got home from work he changed out of his suit and opened a can of beer and got Mum a whisky and soda and then he ate some cheese and biscuits. I challenged him to wrestle and he said not tonight and I called him a chicken, so he said okay, but only two bouts. He got down on his hands and knees on the rug in front of the TV and I charged at him, feinting so he lunged clumsily and I got him in a headlock. His hair smelt of lavender pomade and he gurgled. I always won. I knew a lot of holds from watching Tarzan on crocodiles and neat little chops from watching Smart on KAOS. My strength was such that the man gave off zoological wails of pain. First I flipped him on his stomach and put his arm up his back until he hooted like a monkey's ghost and yelled, 'I give in. Don't bust my arm.' In the second bout I knocked him out cold with an elbow to his ribs.

He went down on his back with a hoomph, eyes glazed, then flickering shut. This gave me the feeling I'd reached life's one and only summit, this moment of glory, this proof of my worth was so undeniable that from here nothing would ever be so valid again, and nor would it need to, after this miraculous thing I'd done. I felt like this about once a week.

As he lay there unconscious I leaned in close to his face to check for signs of life and to surreptitiously smell his breath made of beer and cheese, the beautiful scent of Dad wrestling. As I was leaning in, only a hand's breadth from his face, he opened his eyes and said, 'Righto, Boyboy. I'm going to watch the news now. Go and help Mum set the table.'

Since Guy had left home we remaining five ate dinner in the kitchen at the Formica-topped table. I'd beg Dad to do the fork trick and if I promised to finish my whole meal he'd spread his hand on the tabletop and stab his fork into the gaps in his fingers, bang, bang, bang, fast back and forward never touching flesh. He had scads of daredevilry like this.

Mum was a good cook with a global range of dishes and cuisines – unheard of in the Anglo world we inhabited where people were getting just flat out aspirational and uppity if they wanted more than lamb chops and mashed spuds and a salad of lettuce and tomato and, occasionally, the cosmopolitan foray of spaghetti Bolognese. Often Langdo or Pigsy would be stopped by an exotic smell in our kitchen, a bubbling French cassoulet, a steaming Spanish paella, beef Stroganoff. They'd wrinkle their noses at the new scent, mystified. Was it a good smell or a bad smell? 'What's that smell?'

'Dinner.' They'd grab at their throats and make choking noises. 'How come your dinners smell so weird?'

'I dunno. Mum uses ingredients.'

'Our mums use ingredients too.'

'What sort?'

'Chops.'

'That's why your dinners smell like chops.'

When the others were out Mum and I would cook together. She would be chopping or mixing or sifting and I would be pushing green beans through the bean slicer, a handle that had an aperture on one end with blades inside. Push the beans in and they came out sliced. I would stand on the yellow pouf so I could reach the bench. Our heads would bend together, just cooking, her hands quick, mine slow, me questions, she answers, until we got the job done.

Mum was lonely, I think. Women didn't get to choose their own friends in those days. They became friends of the wives of their husband's friends. So their friendships were served up to them as a fait accompli and must have been, at times, shallow and perfunctory, and as a consequence Mum must have felt she wasn't really reaching anyone. There was nothing wrong with Mum's friends. But they probably weren't the women she would have chosen for herself.

I had planned a tit-for-tat payback for Debbie. She had broken my friendship with Pigsy by slapping him onto the gravel. And even though this friendship broke irretrievably about once a fortnight, this break seemed more irretrievable than usual. So, a commensurate revenge was required. I would ruin her love life.

Let's say it was a pot roast. Pot roast was a dish Mum did perfectly and one of Debbie's favourites and will serve well enough as her condemned love life's last meal. We sat at the table, Dad at one end, Mum at the other, Debbie on one side, Vicki and I on the other. Easy questions about our day from Mum and Dad. Habitual evasions and lies from us. Did you get a star for spelling? How was softball training? What did Mrs Benson say about the length of your dress? Gorging potatoes, nibbling cautiously on meat, hiding carrots in my shirt pocket and balancing French beans under the table's rim where generations of desiccated beans lay like Frenchmen in a catacomb. Waiting for the right moment.

'Did you pass your seven times table, Boyboy?' Dad asked.

'No. No I didn't, Tiger.' I stopped chewing and looked at him and winked, which meant twisting my mouth and revealing some half-chewed carrot I was storing in my cheek chipmonk-wise to spit into my top pocket when no one was looking. A shade of shock passed over his face before he laughed.

'Why not?' Mum asked. 'What happened?'

'You don't need to know what seven times seven equals to steal cars, Tiger.' I winked a flash of carrot mulch at her too.

Dad wasn't laughing now. 'What's this winking and "Tiger" business? And stealing cars?'

Debbie was staring at me, radiating warning. Her eyes and mouth had gone thin and her lips lost colour. She was trying to head me off. 'Benny taught me to wink,' I said. Debbie lowered her face. 'He's going to teach me to hook cars too.'

'Who is this Benny?' Dad asked.

'Benny Zambrano.' I said it matter of factly, as if I didn't know I was making a foul revelation, as if he was just another

198

teenage boy in a line of teenage boys. And if I didn't know I was revealing a crime, then I couldn't be accused of dobbing, could I.

Mum laid her cutlery down hard and put one hand to her mouth.

'Benny . . .? Where have you seen Benny Zambrano?' Dad asked.

'At the Star Bowl. Where else? He gives me lollies so he can feel Debbie up.'

I had never, until now, looked at it from their perspective. Their first little girl, made of ribbons and mispronunciations, fallen now among lascivious low-life. Feel up. Felt up . . . that expression fairly spits gynaecological implications.

'You go to your room right now,' Dad said.

'But I . . .'

'Don't say a word. You know full well what you've done. I'll speak to you later.'

Vicki was sent to bed as well. We listened from the landing on the stairway. From there a window looked down into the kitchen. They began to question Debbie, and then to accuse her of lies.

I had no idea that a young woman's identity was so invaluable and vulnerable. Apparently the whole reality of Debbie could be snuffed out and reincarnated in demonic negative by spending half an hour alone with Benny Zambrano. What she had risked was a kind of death. I had the sudden, unworthy thought that with so much on the line, with Benny being the vector of an incurable shame, he should have been paying me higher bribes to let him unhook my sister's bra. Milkshakes and Crunchies were a rip-off. Roller skates and an air gun would have been a more fitting payment. After all, my sister's life was apparently at stake. If Vicki ever straightened her curly hair and got attractive enough that hoodlums wanted to feel her up I would ask for more.

The main fight turned out to be between Mum and Debbie. The Benny Zambrano liaison hurt Mum more than it hurt Dad, it seemed. It was a direct assault on her teachings and ways. She understood how easily a girl could be taken down. Mum began shouting accusations at Debbie about her clothes and habits and where she was heading and what she was likely to become and what she was doing to the family. Dad took up defending her. Told Mum, all right, all right, go easy. Mum called her a hussy, which I made a mental note to call her myself when next we got into an argument, and Dad told Mum not to say it, just don't say it again because it's not true. From there it became a fight between Mum and Dad, vicious, with tense silences. On the landing Vicki stared at me, pouting, tears leaking from her eyes.

It became an epochal dispute, during which I realised my family was mortal, had a lifespan, would end, and was, in fact, fleeting. I suddenly knew the fragility of my world. And I felt the hollowness of freefall in my gut as that world began to drop away with the adults and teenage girl in the kitchen yelling and crying. My parents are only together because they agree, every day, to be together, I realised. Maybe I had brought this agreement undone. I began to wonder if I'd broken the family.

I waited, staring long hours at darkness, and listening as they all went to bed. The creaking of footsteps, the plumbing banging in the walls, the flushing of toilets, the brushing of teeth, the putting out of dogs, the doors slamming. Dad didn't come to my room. He never spoke to me about my part in the bust-up.

Our family stayed tense, the many bright refractions of ease and trust within it doused. Within two months Debbie was sent away to The Hermitage, an exclusive boarding school in Geelong. A fortnight after leaving, a parcel was posted home containing her tight purple t-shirt and her bell-bottoms with a note from the headmistress explaining they contravened the dress code.

It should have felt like I had won. Slain the tyrant who had kept me under all these years. But it didn't. I missed her. Who did I have now to play new records and tell me of new bands and brands and show me new fashions and dances and, most of all, to turn a sneer like a laser onto other kids who thought they were as cool as us?

And Benny? Briefly erotic, briefly heroic, and briefly demonic to various Camerons. Benny didn't become much more than the tattooed hoodlum and gentle handshake he was that day at the Star Bowl. The following year he brought a brown paper bag containing a hank of his own hair into Cameron and Cameron and took that hank out and laid it on my father's partner Johnno's desk as proof of police brutality and demanded that Johnno, as his lawyer, do some-thing about it. Johnno skewered it on the end of a black-lead pencil and dropped it in his waste paper basket and told him, 'That's not proof, Benny. That's hair. Don't bring hair in here.'

Not long after, Benny was tooling along in his Charger with the cops in pursuit when a young dead-eye fresh out of the academy leaned out the passenger window with a .38 and popped his tyres, rolling the Charger into a tree and torching him young. Kids my age took this as the naturally miraculous dexterity of justice. The kind of comeuppance delivered by James Bond. Further proof that physics was morally grounded and a good guy working for justice could gun down a baddy from over the horizon with his eyes closed. We brought Benny's death into conversations as often as we could for a while, just to weigh it up to see what it meant. There was something glorious about cops killing baddies.

And something not. I could still see him wink and that wink involved a smile and that smile was mine to keep . . . even now. I could smell the tobacco smoke on his breath as he called me 'Tiger'. Maybe by talking it back and forward one of us would stumble on the sense, the lesson, which surely lay behind wild teenagers and young death. We rode by the tree and pointed out the scars on the bark to kids who didn't know. 'He was going to teach me how to steal cars,' I told them.

It couldn't have been true. The cop with the .38. Shooting that good. It's likely Benny just took the corner too fast. Drunk? High? Scared, certainly. Cops in pursuit, his soft hands gripping the wheel. Anyway, he died in a roll-over fireball without ever seeing the world from any place near as lofty as respectability or adulthood. And you couldn't speak about him in front of Debbie without her jaw shaking and her eyes filling with tears. I'd look away and just let her cry before I caught it myself. If she was going to bawl over Benny Zambrano, well, that was the girl she was.

\* \* \*

Langdo was dinking me out to the golf club on his bike to hunt for the eggs of the rainbow bee-eater for my collection. A lot of the local kids raided bird nests and collected eggs and traded and bartered their way to fine collections. Mine was famed above others. Held in trays under glass in squared-off sections on cotton wool were the eggs of over a hundred species of birds, ranging in size from emu and wedge-tailed eagle, to the pardalote and the welcome swallow, eggs as small as pearls.

Only old Mr Vagg's collection was better, and he had been collecting for eighty years. My eggs were mostly collected by Guy and bequeathed to me when he went away to boarding school. He had been a daredevil, thief and black-market trader in the pursuit of exotic eggs. He would ride further from town than other kids, climb higher trees, scale cliffs, and even break into houses and extract rare jewels from other collections. It wasn't uncommon to see him up a tree clinging to a limb at dizzying heights, ducking as he was swooped by a hawk as he raided its nest, his sisters and me standing beneath, our opinions divided on whether death or miraculous resurrection awaited if he fell.

Despite his wily and fearless accumulation, we still didn't have a rainbow bee-eater egg. They were a rare bird, beautifully coloured, masterful aviators – they appeared from the north in spring and were gone by winter. Over summer they lived out in the sandhills by the Shepparton Golf Club, digging tunnels for their nests in the sand cliffs there. We would hollow out footholds and climb the cliffs and press flat-bellied against the sand and reach down the tunnels, hoping to find a clutch of tiny eggs rather than a coiled tiger snake full of tiny eggs.

I was a heavy-handed kid. It was impossible for me to make a hole in each end of a marble-sized egg and blow out its liquid innards without crushing the shell. But Langdo was nimble of finger, a maker of things, while I was a wrecker. I was already forming my arguments that he blow the eggs and hand them over to me. It made sense that such a rare and beautiful egg be in my avian reliquary, rather than in his paltry shoebox as part of his mundane collection.

If we got a few eggs and Langdo successfully blew them we could trade with other boys for eggs we didn't have. They were tiny, but being rare had enormous currency. A rainbow bee-eater's egg was worth two magpies and a kookaburra, or a spur-winged plover and a white-barred honeyeater, a dollar bird and a mudlark. We could, if things went well today, enrich ourselves.

We pedalled along under a blue sky, the Goulburn River and her gums on our left and the red sandhills in the distance getting bigger. Out on those sandhills was also the town cemetery. Easy digging in the sand and above the regular river floods. My people, immigrants from the British Isles, lay there under unadorned basalt headstones, just names and dates and family connections and every now and then one rose into the melodramatic heights to mention the deceased had been DEARLY BELOVED. These were the monumental incarnations of a puritan aesthetic. I'd go there and stare at them. They weren't much. They must have been small, shy people.

Then I'd wander into the newer areas of the cemetery and find the Italians and Greeks shouting at God through megaphonic family crypts made of shiny black marble and decorated with cherubim and seraphim and saints and alabaster Jesus and busty Virgins Mary in legion. They were patterned in gold, and some had photos of the pop-eyed deceased on them, fading beneath beautiful bubbles of glass. They were awe-inspiring. Each grave, each mausoleum, was a work of art and a thundering demand on God's time and attention.

When Dad took us out there, to those lovely sandhills with their peppercorn trees, he'd point out this or that relative who'd been gathered in by their creator, and I'd feel ashamed and wonder how on Earth my people were going to get heard by God while surrounded by this Mediterranean crescendo of architectural splendour?

I'd just shake my head. My great aunts and uncles and great-grandparents and theirs must all be still queuing in purgatory like the sorriest peasants trying to get to see an opera while Greeks and Italians who set out for the show way after they did whizz past flashing season tickets. The Mediterranean immigrants were the only people in our valley spending on public art.

Most Sundays, about mid-afternoon, Dad would announce, 'Righto, we're going for a Sunday Drive.' As though a Sunday Drive was a known and legitimate activity performed by all happy families. But I didn't know anyone else who went for a Sunday Drive or anyone who even knew what one was. Sometimes we were busy and truly didn't want to go, and sometimes we did want to go, but by duty we always complained and whined. 'Do we have to?' 'Why?' 'It's a waste of petrol.' 'It's a waste of time.' 'There's nothing to see.'

We owned a Galaxie 500, a coffee-coloured car hauled by a five-litre V8 that rumbled like a bootlegger's getaway. Dad would drive and Mum would sit in the front and Debbie and Vicki and I would spread ourselves across the rear bench seat. You could sit seven or eight kids across that seat and sometimes we took our friends. At first they didn't want to go. They couldn't see the point of driving around without a destination. But after they'd been once they queued up and begged to be able to come. Langdo and his sister Leanne and Pigsy would pile in the car with us, because the Cameron Sunday Drive included a dark thrill that dare not speak its name, a secret raison d'etre never mentioned, a slightly off-colour side to the trip that, if spoken out loud, would have seemed wrong.

Dad would drive a circuitous route through the inner streets of Shepparton pointing out this and that to us kids. And making provocatively banal observations, keeping us waiting, while we tried to be patient, to ride out the masquerade. He and Mum made coded remarks to each other, 'Hmmm . . . Clarry's VW outside the Thomson place again.' 'Oh, just look at the Higgins' lawn.' These were observations about adultery and drunkenness, if you knew what you were listening for. We would crawl through the Housing Commission estates and blackfella slums, noses on the glass to see how all the worst kind of people lived.

The Sunday Drive turned out to be a most explorative and expansive experience, rich with gossip, culture and landscape. No one flew anywhere, then. France was found in a book. Indonesia wasn't. The Sunday Drive was our Grand Tour.

We would cruise the town. But everyone knew where we were heading. And soon Langdo, bubbling with his usual impatience, would burst out, 'Come on, Mr Cameron. What about the wogs' eagles?'

'Immigrants, Langdo,' Dad would correct him. 'Not "wogs".' And he'd point the Galaxie toward the edge of town, to the orchards where the eagles and lions waited. Out there, in acres of fruit trees, monetarily-emancipated Medi-terraneans had built brick palaces and surrounded them with cement critters: vultures, stallions, lions atop gateposts, eagles perched on pillars . . .

Inside every Italian was a Medici who, freed by pear money, became a patron to a Michelangelo working in cement and cliché. Thus each Varapodio or Villani was soon keeper of his own stone menagerie, a job lot of noble beasts frozen in the act of defending a small orchard.

For us the pay-off of an otherwise boring Sunday Drive was ogling and guffawing at this cut-rate Renaissance. We'd motor from one palace to the next as Dad pointed out fresh affronts. 'Balboni's added two lions. He's got Nelson covered now.' 'Good God. Is that a rug rat mauling a mastiff, or Romulus having lunch?' As with Picasso, this art brought more pleasure to its delighted detractors than its defenders.

We Cameron children being an amalgam of unpretentious peoples – Scot, Paddy and Pom, a cocktail of dour bloods running in our veins – nothing in our world and nothing in our knowledge of the wider world and nothing in our imaginations was as racially hubristic, civically antagonistic, tastelessly ostentatious, or just plain un-Australian, as a cement eagle with its wings unfurled and given a lick of gold paint. These Italians, these Greeks, these Albanians . . . what type of crazy people were they? If their statues symbolised rich histories, then we didn't know it.

We would roll about on the Galaxie's back seat in stitches, Langdo's laughter flipping him like a landed carp. But as we drove back to town our jibes and hilarity died out into silence and a hollow mood. How could people be so wrong? Why would God persist with such eccentric folk? Why didn't he straighten them out?

We began to feel shame for these crazy immigrants, even sorry for them. Dad enjoyed our eventual confusion as much as our initial hilarity. He never wanted life's paradoxes cleared up.

'Mr Cameron . . .' Langdo would ask quietly, 'why do they do it?'

'One man's meat is another man's poison, Langdo.'

'But, no, Mr Cameron, them wogs . . .'

'Immigrants, Langdo.'

'Them immigrants, Mr Cameron . . . is Walt Disney their King?'

\* \* \*

Riding out for the rainbow bee-eater, on top of another sandhill ahead of us an old Turk lived by himself in a colossal wooden wreck-house. Mr Suleiman was a brown-skinned little man who grew the best spinach and silverbeet in the district.

He was the only Turk in our world, as far as I knew. It must have been hard being the sole agent of your race and culture. If you sin you blacken your people. But Mr Sooly's spinach was faultless and he enjoyed as much respect as faultless spinach can deliver. And as little respect as a gatherer of excrement deserves.

For Mr Sooly, world's only Turk, spinach magician and sand-hill genie, was also a collector of dung, regularly seen behind the livestock of neighbouring farmers with a scoop and a smile. Once, when Ashton's Circus was in town, I saw him wheeling home a barrow holding a stacked pyramid of cantaloupe-sized elephant droppings. This exotic treasure was freshly taken, and Mr Sooly was wreathed in aromatic steam, whistling and shaking his head at his luck as he trundled along, imagining the magic this mammoth muck would work on his garden.

I liked Mr Sooly. He came to our back door every week smelling of old sweat and newly turned earth and carrying boxes of sandy greens keeping his eyes lowered in the presence of my handsome mother and flashing me a broken smile.

But then, when I was eight, with Anzac Day looming, our teacher Miss Robertson foisted a potted Gallipoli on us, and it was revealed Mr Sooly had defeated us while we were trying to invade him for his own good. Miss Robertson showed us sepia photos of the wounded disembarking in Sydney. Shit. That little creep Sooly. Hadn't we praised his silverbeet and allowed him free rein with the faeces of our quadrupeds? I was gobsmacked at his treachery: *he accepts our elephant turd with a smile and gives us The Nek in payment*.

It was not uncommon then, and it is not now, for the children of veterans to pursue dead wars locally. And we couldn't forgive this Gallipoli thing. So on Anzac eve a posse of boys set out for revenge. We left our houses via windows and met in town and crept out of town and up the moonlit sandhill through the weeds past scarecrows Frankensteined from our own fathers' fashion faux pas.

When we got amongst Mr Sooly's veggies we stomped his spinach, kicking hanks of it high against the stars. We whipped his silverbeet with wire. Then, looking at the house, I saw Mr Sooly's moonlit face at a windowpane. He was not angry, frightened, amazed or sad. He was quietly watching, blank faced, as five small vandals mangled his crop. It was as if he had expected the slaughter. Positively known it was coming. Perhaps this happened every Anzac Day. Maybe he raised a sacrificial harvest each autumn so kids could use it to avenge Gallipoli.

I would rather he loosed a couple of barrels of quail shot at us than bear witness like this. It would have made more sense for a desperate war criminal to go for the gun and maim brave children than to surrender so meekly.

I went home fast through the moon-bright back alleys, up the grapevine and across the slatted roof and in through the flywire to bed, where I stared at Mr Sooly's staring face for hours.

What makes a man migrate to the land of his enemy? Perhaps he was a variety of Turk not getting a fair shake at home. Maybe he admired what he saw of those men down there in their slouch hats as he rained Hell on them at Gallipoli. Maybe some convoluted strain of guilt led him to feed us greens, to heal us after he'd wounded us. Or . . . maybe he wasn't even a Turk.

I was always deep in the house invisible when he delivered our veggies after that. I'd hear Mum talking to him, his politeness bordering on chivalry, 'Missus Camern, I not agree such lady carry such. Is big heavy. No, no. Lady is Lady. Sooly put box on kitchen table.'

From then on I thought of Mr Sooly around Anzac Day every year. Albanian? Pole? Bulgarian? I imagined, like any farmer sensing the cold coming on, he made preparations. Noting the town kids getting a little meaner and seeing schemes starting to bubble behind their eyes, he'd know the day was coming and he'd dig in manure and mosey up and down the rows with his great riveted watering can until he had a bumper crop for us to take our revenge on. I figured it was a tithe he paid annually to a freshly raised army of children. After this crop, for the rest of the year, all the greenery he could grow was his. Australia must have seemed a beautiful place then.

This day, this day of the rainbow bee-eater, heading past Sooly's tumbledown house, I turned my face away – one more site of shame. As I perched side-saddle on the crossbar of Langdo's bike, I took shots with my shanghai at cars as they overtook us.

The stones cracked against them and whined away sweetly as ricochets in a Western. The people in the cars were mostly old lawn bowlers heading out to their club for the Saturday afternoon pennant. Sometimes a driver and his wife would pull over to see what had happened. Stout and slow and dressed in white they'd walk around their cars, him scratching his head and crouching and squinting at the duco here and there. She'd be telling him the engine had exploded because he was driving too fast, or the steering had buckled because of his waggling it side to side incessantly like he thought he was Jack Brabham. 'The engine didn't explode, Jeannie. I think a stone flicked up.'

With the shanghai hidden up the front of my shirt we'd ride past smiling and say something nonsensical like, 'Beware the seven heberpants.'

'What did he say? What did that boy say?'

It was the type of workaday malfeasance that kept us amused on a long bike ride. A balancing act and an exhibition of mobile marksmanship and mischief visited on vulnerable civilians. I saw us as a couple of Comanches on a war pony firing arrows from beneath its belly at pilgrims in covered wagons.

The cars, coming from behind, couldn't see the shanghai, nor could I see them until they passed. A car roared up alongside and you just had to blast it before it was out of range. You had to shoot into the space it was going to be before you even identified it.

This is how I hit the metallic green HR Holden with P plates and a fox tail tied on the aerial and louvre blinds on the back window, driven by a sharpie with a blond mullet, high-rolled sleeves and an unlikely law-and-order outlook. Given time to consider, it was a dangerously young, hotted-up ride. But things happened fast. The HR swooped past us and I shot reflexively into the space it was heading and the pebble described a white tracer through the blue day and hit its side mirror and ricocheted inside and hit the driver. I saw his head lurch sideways like he was miming a presidential assassination.

Langdo was incredulous. 'An HR with a fox tail?' he whispered. Why the hell had I shot an HR with a fox tail? Here we were amusing ourselves frightening lawn bowlers, inflicting a modicum of vehicular damage and an afternoon of lingering confusion upon geriatrics, the sort of harmless fun that couldn't really bring us to grief . . . and I'd gone and attacked a sharpie.

The HR slewed onto the road shoulder throwing gravel and boiling dust and the sharpie jumped out. He was toweringly young and strong and he ran at us with his elbows high and grabbed the bike by the handlebars with both hands as if he were bulldogging a steer. Then he rubbed at a red welt on his neck. Langdo steadied us with his feet on the ground and said, 'Hey.' I was still perched on the crossbar, hunched to hide the shanghai. The sharpie lifted my shirt and pulled it out. 'You shot me.' He shook the bike and I fell off the crossbar onto my back on the bitumen without making a sound.

To this vengeful sharpie I must have looked like any other eight year old. He was going to teach me a lesson I'd never forget. A major lesson in picking the wrong guy, or doing the wrong thing. Maybe both. 'What are your names?' He let go the bike and grabbed a handful of Langdo's t-shirt. 'Steven Newman.' 'Norm Almond.' They were friends from school. We gave their names to enraged authorities routinely. They were probably being pinched shoplifting at that moment and giving ours.

I thought of bolting, but this guy was taut and primed and out here with no cover he would run me down. I was spastic with fear anyway and maybe I couldn't get my legs started and would just convulse a few steps before collapsing in a cowardly heap, having compounded my sins by trying to escape.

'I'll tell you what, you little yobs, you've shot my car with a shanghai. That's a dangerous act of vandalism. And you're going to pay for it.' Strangely, he wasn't fired up like a sharpie P-plater should be. He was speaking coolly, like someone a lot older, like a parent or a teacher, laying out a fully realised adult repercussion rather than making a wild threat. I would have preferred he swore at us and gave us each a thick ear and kicked our arses and be done with it. He was about twenty years old, sporting all the accoutrements of rebellion, and it would have made sense for him to belt us. We could tell our parents we'd been attacked by random drunks. Italians who sprang from behind trees. But this bloke was talking about police. This was way beyond normal consequence for an eight year old. Langdo's old man was an electrician, but my father frequently cross-examined and made public mincemeat of the cops of this town. This would play badly for me.

'We didn't . . .'

'Shut up.' He slapped Langdo across the face with the rubber tendrils of the shanghai. Langdo was three years older than me, and I was shocked to see him start to cry. It gave me licence to cry as well, but looking at Langdo, big wet tears and scrunched face like he was begging, I found myself hardening against the idea.

'What you're going to do is, you're going to go to the police station and tell them what you've done. You're going to confess. I'm going to follow you the whole way. I'll be watching, so don't try to get away.' He pointed back to town.

'Turn around. Go. And tell them everything. I'm following to make sure you do.'

'We're sorry,' I said. 'We shouldn't have done it. We were aiming at a magpie.'

This contradictory nonsense cut no ice with the vengeful sharpie. 'You will be sorry . . . attacking a motor vehicle. The police regard that very, very seriously. You might well get a custodial sentence. Turana Boys Home is full of kids who shot drivers.'

Turana was a mythical prison for children in the faraway Gomorrah of Melbourne. Boys who had turned too bad for Shepparton to contain went there. Boys who had stolen cars or started fires or perpetrated lurid acts with their near relatives disappeared to Turana and reappeared only in brief rumours of Dickensian torment. Brett Sewell, who set fire to our school three times, was in Turana, being burnt daily by the other boys. 'You like to burn things, do you, Brett? Try this then.' And they'd stub their cigarettes on his arms and stomach and neck. Garry Wilson had visited him and came back saying he was all motley and welted pink and had begun to stutter hopelessly.

We started pedalling back to town with visions of our imprisonment in our heads and the vengeful sharpie behind us in his HR. Then he disappeared. 'Let's go down here.' Langdo began to steer down a side street. The electric-green HR was sitting there, with its driver glaring at us. We chucked a U-ey and got back on course.

Discussing our options we were terrified. Maybe we go in there and pretend the shot had slipped and the guy was making a big thing of nothing. Or that we didn't even fire a

215

shot, the guy was confused by a stone off his own tyres. You couldn't send a boy to prison because a stone flicked up off a car tyre.

None of this sounded like anything cops would go for. Then Langdo came up with a pretty good plan; we'd go into the cop shop and ask if shanghais were legal, because we were thinking of making one, but we wouldn't make one if it was against the law. No mention of shooting the vengeful sharpie's car at all. If the vengeful sharpie didn't come inside the cop shop with us, how would he ever know what we told the cops? That wasn't such a bad plan. And I let Langdo think it was what we were going to do. But I didn't trust the cops to go along with it. And I wasn't going to go to Turana and be burnt alive by criminal boys.

The vengeful sharpie shepherded us the whole way to the police station, appearing out of side streets, coming up behind, overtaking and waiting as Langdo pedalled us slowly south to our doom. When we got there I got off the bike and Langdo laid it down and we looked around for a last-minute escape. Maybe the guy had been bluffing. Maybe he was wanted by the police and wouldn't come near the station. But he drove up and parked right outside the twin glass doors and pointed us inside.

How had a young man, probably still a teenager, dreamt up this punishment? Self-confession was a tool right out of the Education Department playbook. Schoolteachers and parents used it to make you consider, in a deeper, more meaningful way, the crime you had committed. And how did this young guy think this would pan out for him? I gave him a little wave as we went inside. Look. Here is us. Here is us about to go inside and face justice. He nodded slowly, right-eously. This was evidently panning out just like he thought it would.

At the front counter we rang the bell with vivid humility and a cop sauntered out of a back room. Before I could speak Langdo freaked out, lost his nerve and dobbed us in. He started honking tears and blurted, 'We shot that man's car with a shanghai. We're sorry. I can't go to Turana. I do a paper round.' He pointed at the electric-green HR parked out front. So much for his plan to enquire about making a shanghai.

'You did?' The cop, a self-important young man with a hook nose and a shaving rash, rested his arms on the counter. He slumped theatrically, made limp by Langdo's blurted skerrick of wrongdoing. He made a shocked 'O' of his mouth and put his eight fingertips to his lower lip like Little Miss Muffet seeing a spider. It took me a moment or two to realise he was mocking the triviality of our crime spree. When I did realise it, I took it upon myself to sharpen his interest.

'I shot his car because he showed us his thing.'

'He what?' The cop dropped his hands from his face and his eyebrows arched like cats offered an ultimatum.

'Showed us his thing.'

'He flashed himself? That bloke out there in the green HR?'

'He's followed us all the way here from the golf club showing . . . flashing it. It was shiny. And he was yelling rude stuff about it.'

'Sh . . . shiny?!' The cop's voice choked. His eyes glittered darkly. Ambition's crescendo played in his head. The more degenerate the crime, the more famous the arrest, and the guy smugly idling out there in the metallic-green HR was a sicko of the first rank. Maybe the cop thought he'd get a citation for removing a degenerate from our streets. Congratulations and a front-page handshake from the Commissioner.

He bent low over the counter to get a good look outside at the creep. The vengeful sharpie met his gaze and nodded, and did a double thumbs-up, essentially saying, I suppose, 'You and I represent a telling lesson to these kids. You don't need to thank me for the time and trouble I've gone to in bringing them in and making them confess. It was the right thing to do and will pay off by them becoming better people.'

But I guess to the cop, who knew what he knew about the guy, that blond mullet and that self-satisfied grin and that double thumbs-up said something more along the lines of, 'I get off flashing my dick at kids and I don't think it's wrong and I'm not in the least scared of you.'

There was a skittering for traction that reminded me of a terrier sighting a kitchen rat, and when the cop got around to our side of the counter he'd turned red and blown up to twice the size he had been when Langdo was confessing to his paltry spree. He was a different cop now, for a different crime.

He went out the door fast and the look on the vengeful sharpie's face began to ask why a policeman was running at his car. The cop wrenched his door open and reached in and pulled him out by his blond rat-tails and we heard the vengeful sharpie screaming, 'Whatwhatwhat . . .' like a pump starting up.

I said softly to Langdo, 'Let's fuck off.' We went out the door and he jumped on his bike and rode one way and I ran another. Nothing is as fast across suburban terrain as a boy lit by fear.

When I reached the corner I looked back. The flasher and the cop were rolling around on the road wrestling and punching each other. One of them was yelling, 'Fuck.' The other was yelling, 'Jonesy.' I can make a case for either man yelling either word.

The Shepp Show came every year with the start of summer. One of the quartet of annual highpoints that made the long year endurable; the other three being my birthday, Easter and Christmas. On Saturday morning we would dress up. Guy and I in knee-length shorts and ironed shirts buttoned to the throat, and the girls in white dresses with gathered waists and white sandals. We would swallow toast throat-raspingly fast and suck down cold milk head-achingly fast and then mime the brushing of teeth and be out in the garage sitting in the station wagon by nine.

By nine-thirty I would be chewing on the red plastic upholstery of the seat back and calling Mum the worst words I knew. Guy would be sitting back coolly, all showy patience, playing the adults at their own game. Debbie would be teasing Vicki and telling her her friends were ugly and dumb, and Vicki, in order to work toward a truce, would be conceding her friends' stupidity but saying they weren't so ugly when set alongside some other people who were even uglier. She would begin to name these unfortunate girls, 'Mardi Hopkins, Gabby Taylor . . .' 'No. Diane Matthews is uglier than Mardi Hopkins and Fiona Smith is uglier than Gabby Taylor. Your friends are uglier than everyone.'

Dad would emerge, actually sniffing actual roses on his way to the car, and stopping to mime a couple of chip shots, waggling his imaginary club back and forth while we screamed at him through the windscreen to come on and get in and he smiled slyly. He'd take his place behind the wheel, enjoying our impatience, and, I get the impression, using his slowly-slowly shtick to cover for Mum, trying to take the heat off her.

She was unreachable in her interminable dawdle, in a bubble of great protocol and theatre. She always kept us waiting. Perhaps as proof she was the cornerstone of the family. Or maybe it took her time to summon up the courage to go to public events. Many minutes later, as we whined and urged her on and asked Dad what was going on, he'd shrug and say, 'You're pretty thick kids if Mum hasn't taught you how to wait by now with all the lessons she's given you.'

Eventually Mum would glide out of the house with her hair in a green-and-white silk scarf and her eyelashes black as a senorita's and lips tinted silvery-red. No other woman at the Shepparton Show would look this chic or lovely. She would be photographed for the *Shepparton News*, no doubt. And on Monday Mr Maclean, my fourth grade teacher, would have a copy of that newspaper opened on his desk and be slumped in close appreciation of her and he'd say to me, 'Wow, eh, Camo. Your mum any relation to Princess Grace?'

'I don't think so,' I'd tell him. 'Who's that?'

He would make comments about her all through the morning.

The streets around the showground were lined with parked cars and the footpaths filled with people walking toward the show, kids hauling parents by the arms, their steps made urgent by the screams of girls already hurtling in deformed orbits on rides painted with alpine scenes piebald with rust.

The air was hot and the braided smells of various animal dungs drifted from the showgrounds. Once you got inside this cloud you discovered within it banks of oily fog where foods were frying and sweet reeks of hot liquefied sugar, and, most pleasantly, each open-air bar gave off a cool estuarine smell of beer and mud, which became, in my young mind, the whiff of hilarity and bad language.

People were making their way to the front gate from every direction. Overhead, carved into the gate's arch, 'Shepparton Agricultural Society Est 1877'. And down each pillar a list of past Show Committee venerables. My Dad, Atticus-like, had to nod and chat with a lot of passing men and women off small farms wearing rare, senseless clothes in a panicked sartorial stab at formal festivity. He helped shape these people's private affairs and they were nervous around him as you would be around someone who knew you supported a secret daughter from a previous marriage that your current wife didn't know about.

In the centre of the grounds was a wooden pavilion overlooking a grassy arena where equestrian events were held and bulls as big as rhinos were led single file to be judged and bedecked with satin sashes of royal blue and gold. Beneath this pavilion women would be awarded wooden plaques set with many small engraved silver shields for baking and preserving and crocheting and needlepoint. Fire trucks passed beneath the pavilion with their sirens blaring while amateur firefighters waved at their families and gave the finger to their mates. I once saw a firefighter jump from a truck and pinch the first-prize-winning baker of the pineapple upside-down cake on her bottom during the presentation of her plaque as she was posing for the local news photographer. He jumped back on the truck as the crowd roared laughter and heckled and she reddened and held the plaque up and hid behind it. I was appalled at this outrageous assault.

Down a thoroughfare to the south, the way your parents led you, were arrays of agricultural machinery, ploughs and windrowers and the newest irrigation pumps lifting azure water from low pools to high tanks all day long. And corrugated-iron sheds, one loud with the territorial spruiking of outrageously plumed poultry, and the next flinching with harried and nervous sheep. Startling as they were, we got through these sheds as quickly as we could. We paid due, but speedy, homage to the machines and animals that Dad wanted us to know were the filaments of our economy, reaching out, each connecting with the other and forming a vast agri-web that held us all aloft.

And these things were interesting, in their way. It is always rewarding to see a chicken bred to sport a headdress worthy of one of Napoleon's hussars, or a duck with a hairdo flagrantly plagiarised from Elvis. And if they'd come to town on any other weekend we'd have stared bug-eyed, firing endless questions of the 'but why?' sort at Dad.

Not now, though. This morning these exotic critters got up in their unnaturally selected glad rags were keeping us from the crux of the day – the gaudy, dangerous, semi-criminal wonderment of sideshow alley.

But before sideshow alley was the woodchop. The wood-chop is one of the few things that, upon adult reflection, is as miraculous as you thought it was as a child. A daredevil's ballet performed by brawny men in Dunlop Volleys and white trousers and white singlets. A fierce agrarian contest that showed men from the backblocks were artisans who shaped the rude world into weatherboard democracy. A PR tableau for a dying industry.

Their axe heads were as silver and sharp as scalpels. They would each stand on a short log as thick as a beer keg and an announcer in a suit and tie and felt hat would call, 'Axemen . . . are you ready? One, two, three . . .' The slowest axeman would start. The announcer would keep counting. Maybe on ten the next axeman would begin to chop, on fifteen the next and so on. It was headshakingly unreal how fast these men could chop wood.

The last to start was the backmarker, the champ, silver hair slicked with Brylcreem and ropey-armed, his axe head carrying the October sun on its edge, he stood waiting with a tycoon's smile while the young colts whaled away at their logs, and chips of wood large as slices of bread flew at the crowd. '. . . twenty-two . . .' The backmarker would begin.

Unhurried and clean. He could never catch the others. One had already cut a deep V in his log and turned and begun chopping from the opposite side. Another turned. The backmarker was done for. 'Dad, the old guy's a goner.'

'Never write off a champ, Boyboy.'

'No. He's a goner this time.'

The backmarker, sinews proud in his forearms, lips flared back off smoke-yellowed teeth, turned on his log. He hadn't blurred with urgency as the younger men had. He was using fewer strokes. But those strokes were landing like laser beams and woodchips large as Bibles were leaping from his log. Maybe he could catch the others. He might even be going past them. As his log broke in two, ends falling away, he stepped gracefully off them and gave a slight nod to the crowd. The fight ebbed from the younger men, then. They continued to chop at half pace. One by one their logs broke apart and they stepped down, each shooting sly glances at the backmarker's log and at the backmarker. Was he sweating? Red in the face? Perturbed at all? How many blows had he rained on the thing?

For the next event they were to chop at logs that stood upright in a row, like power poles. Trees stripped of their canopy and bark and pulled from the forest and raised here for this high-wire battle.

'Axemen, are you ready . . . one, two . . .' The axemen cut a notch in the trunk about chest height and inserted a plank, sticking straight out like a spoke from a wheel hub. Then they leapt onto this plank, balancing more planks on it, and began chopping another notch at chest height. Insert another plank into this second notch, jump up onto it and cut another notch . . .

This skill came from the days when they were cutting mountain ash out of the high gullies of Victoria. These great trees flared at the base to a circumference that might reach fifteen metres. But if you climbed ten metres that circumference had dwindled to only five metres. You saved days of work if you felled them above their wide base.

The axemen rose swiftly on their precarious ladders, until, balancing on a plank they had just notched into the tree trunk ten metres above the ground, they began the race to chop through the trunk itself. Watching these men high against the sun pivoting on the balls of their feet on a board, attacking their tree to the limit of their balance, was like seeing a medi-aeval battle fought on a cliff top.

Death was a byproduct of the working day in timber cutting then, and looked so likely in this sporty simulacrum that our fascination was never for the contest. We didn't care who won. We were aghast at the house-of-cards architecture of the event, the slashing blades and high-wire nonchalance of the axemen. It was a swordfight in the rigging. Swash-bucklers in singlets with small pot bellies. Who would die?

As soon as the woodchop had finished we made a pact with Mum and Dad to meet them at a certain hour, at the Main Pavilion to watch some ponderous parade of giant horses, or people dressed as pioneers in bonnets and hats re-enacting something that wasn't, quite frankly, so distant or fascinating that it required re-enactment. 'Okay, okay, three o'clock. But I won't have time to do hardly anything.' We would never honour this rendezvous. Some painted booth selling some fresh ghoul, a Bearded Lady or a Half-Man-Half-Woman,

226

always prevented it. We would always be in trouble for not turning up at the appointed hour. But parental rage was a price happily paid for a day in the sour-smelling freak show of the alley.

The pact to meet at three made, fraudulently on my part, Mum and Dad would enter the pavilion, where cool drinks flowed among Shepparton's select. Shepparton had a select. Australia isn't as egalitarian as advertised. There is a class system here. But not one where the lower class feels inferior. It's a happy peculiarity of this country that both the gentry and the proles feel superior to each other. The gentry have two or three generations of property ownership to boast of and someone in the family has made good at something and they are educated and visit the rellies o/s and spend the summer down the coast.

The 'working people' have a battler's pride. A battler's vanity. They have fought the class war and the marketers and demagogues of socialism have told them they are worthy, proud warriors, who know ennobling pain and have tasted real things that the middle class, the leeches who live above, haven't known or tasted. They might not have beach houses, but they are real people. Everyone's happy.

And we would blast away from the pavilion, into the crowd of battlers that stunk thrillingly of sweat and sugar, toward sideshow alley. I'd undo my top three buttons and untuck my shirt and break my hair from the undignified combed moulding Mum preferred. Within minutes I'd find a posse of mates and we'd brandish our money at one another and begin to boast of the things we were about to do. How we were going to gyp the simple-minded travelling sideshow people and ride their rides and shoot their ducks and win their prizes.

Hard rock songs were played at each attraction along side-show alley and they clashed and interwove into a demented multi-level bray of pompous power riffs – The Kinks and Slade and Led Zep and the Stones and the Easybeats. Now and then, we'd hear a piece of a tune we knew and lean back at the waist and jut our chins and play an air-guitar riff on our shirtfronts, caught in the sensory overload of the alley.

The Octopus was first. An eight-armed ride that gyrated in a wavering ellipsis and at the end of each arm spun a metal booth holding six unrestrained, screaming people. Anyone who'd paid the surly man besmirched with blue-blurred tattoos to ride the Octopus was soon caught in a vicious small orbit working at the end of, and powered by, a larger yawing orbit, and after five minutes these two revolutions jangled the inner ear of the rider and made his lips go numb and his jaw ache.

It's probably worth noting that these rides were bolted together by toothless itinerant alcoholics suffering delirium tremens and working below minimum wage who didn't give a pharaoh's fart for the life of a future National Living Treasure whose forthcoming worth to the country was, presently, disguised by maniacal face-daubings of fairy floss and dirt. That is, when I stepped up to the ticket booth of the Octopus and laid down my dollar note and, playing smart arse for my friends (you can, by now, just assume that when I'm with friends I'm packing my own portable audience and it is thus dictating my behaviour), told the toothless Joe who ran it, 'Make it hum, Mister. I rode this one last year and kept nodding off.' My friends laughed. He looked at me with muted delight and said, 'You go to sleep today I'll give you a full refund, dickhead.'

You will have noticed in this memoir that I have a predilection for . . . mouthing off. And noticed that very early in life I decided that the splash-back of adult vengeance was a price I was prepared to pay for the laughs I got from my mates. But here, in essence, I'd just taunted an amoral drunkard who almost certainly beat his women, before climbing aboard the derelict death jalopy he was piloting. The zenith of stupidity or the nadir of common sense? And it was only mid-morning.

Each ride on the Octopus lasted about five minutes, in which time you travelled the larger orbit about thirty times and the smaller orbit about one-eighty. By which time you'd closed your eyes on the blurring world but the maelstrom of g-forces continued to snatch at you and nauseated you and stretched and warped your balance, and dizziness had grown from a titillation to a major assault. Your lips and fingers were numb and a pre-nauseated ache in your jaw was making you waggle it side to side.

After that ride I was hyperventilating but smiling. I'd made it. It wasn't so bad. I waved at my mates. The toothless Joe smiled blackly up at me. You think this is over, kid? One by one he stopped the other seven tentacles at the disembarkation platform and released their payload of captors, who then stepped down and tottered drunkenly across the dirt mouthing relieved blasphemies to their families. He filled each tentacle with new riders. He didn't unload our tentacle. He started the ride again.

Another one-eighty fizzing orbits wrapped inside the yawing thirty. Shepparton and its surrounding orchards torn and smeared and lifted and tossed. My stomach queasier now. But, again, I survived. He stopped the ride and unloaded the other seven tentacles and shouted up at me and the other five white-faced collateral victims alongside me who were shouting down weak protests, 'You sleepy yet?'

'Sleepy? Did he ask if we were sleepy?' a young woman who was teetering on the edge of tears asked. And around we went again.

I held on until the fourth ride. Buzz Aldrin would've thrown his hands up and wrecked his career by soiling his pants during the third. I had earlier hogged down two sticks of fairy floss and the vomit rained pinkly across the crowd in pretty epitrochoidic patterns as a swathe of earthbound show-goers that corresponded to my overhead transit reached up Mexican-wavelike to pat their hair or their baldness or wipe their arms and faces and then began taking off their glasses to stare in wonder at the lenses spotted . . . pinkly. Pinkly? They began to dab their fingertips in the pink stuff and edge their noses toward their wetted fingertips to check out what this was and after this they began to swear and cast about for the villain who had carpet-bombed them with rosy bile.

I had finished vomiting by the time the hundred or so people I'd spattered figured out what had happened and started staring moodily skyward looking for the culprit.

The toothless Joe was baring his gums happily when he landed our tentacle at the disembarkation platform and opened the little tin door of our booth to let us stagger forth.

Several of the people I rode with swore at him. He ignored them and grabbed me by the collar and shoved me this way and that and shouted at the crowd, ''Ere 'e is. Ere's the little dickhead that spewed on youse all.'

Maybe in Bendigo a lynch mob of sorts could have been got up. Maybe in Seymour. But a rain of vomit in Shepparton, with her many grand corner hotels skirted by first-floor verandahs, was a relative banality. Vomit was just another form of weather in Shepparton. Rain, hail and vomit. Baptised once more by the downpouring upchuck of a fellow citizen, people shrugged, smeared it into their skin, and moved on to the ghost train or the dodgem cars.

Using guy ropes to support myself I staggered down an alley made by two marquees and lay out back in the dust hyperventilating at the blue sky with the thumping mélange of rock riffs and the screams of the riders fading.

Ten minutes later I was right to go again. Think of a honey badger bitten by a black mamba. A quick nap and I stood and shook my head and dusted myself off, flattened my hair, and checked my funds. I had had four rides for only a dollar. Sideshow folk were about as dumb as fence lizards and it was no wonder they limped from town to town in sinful cohabitation with freaks and dwarves immersed in laughable gap-toothed poverty. Four rides at twenty-five cents a ride. I'd stung that toothless Joe for three dollars.

I nosed my way out between the marquees back into the crowd. And the first friend I bumped into was Stowey.

I had thought I might keep Stowey out of these memoirs, but like a circus banned from town for its past excesses, he sets up camp on the outskirts and we can hear his lions roar and blaring horns and barkers hollering through bullhorns and snippets of his archive of idiocy and mishap drift in on the breeze. Better to include him, let him have his romp and then go away and grow up to become a disappointment.

Stowey. Okay . . . Stowey, if we must. It is said of some people that 'they won't die wondering', that is, they'll give anything a try to see what it's like and thereby appease the craving to know. But 'wondering' is too grand a term for what Stowey did. He was more in the mode of one of those hunting terriers that have been bred to a point of perpetual mental frisson where they'll bung their head in any hole, no matter if it looks like it harbours Beelzebub's sourest brother. It wasn't anything as grand or thoughtful as 'wonder' that made him drive a golf ball at a speeding VW Beetle, or punch a large Russian in the ear. As often as not it was me betting him he wouldn't.

Stowey was a sportsman of note. He could play any game well. Far better than I could. But if we squared off at twenty paces in a rock fight, which we did often, I would hit him between the eyes with a chunk of scoria every time and lay him out while his first rocks were still airborne, zinging wide, ricocheting off houses and cars. I had a concentrated excellence at bringing pain to others, or preventing my own, which is the same thing if you live in a combat zone.

But if I was swooping on a cricket ball to effect a run-out by throwing down the stumps, the scorer, without waiting to see the outcome, would casually lower his black-lead and add four overthrows to the batsman's score. Before the ball had left my hand the runs were recorded, so predictable was my ineptitude and so fatalist my teammates. Once I saw our team's scorer draw a tiny bathtub-type duck against my name in the scorebook as I was preparing to walk out to bat against Tatura State Primary. I stood there leaning on my bat while their fieldsmen heckled and I made our scorer upend the pencil and bring the eraser into play, expunging the duck and thereby reinstating the possibility I might plunder infinite runs.

I think it was the scorer's lack of faith, his heavily pencilled duck, like a stigmata of preordination, erased but still indented in the scorebook, that froze me at the crease. He only had to reverse the pencil once more and run its tip around that indented silhouette like a slot car along its track to bring the scoresheet up to date. And that about sums up my sporting endeavours; everyone knew I would fail, and I knew I would too, except sometimes, occasionally, usually in spring with the first pulse of strengthening sun, I got a brave notion I might not . . . but did anyway.

Now Stowey. At the Shepparton Agricultural Show. 'Hey, fucknuts.'

'Hey, dickbrain.'

'What you been on?'

'I rode the Octopus for an hour. Conned the dill who runs it out of three rides.'

'Fair dinkum?

'Fair dinkum.'

'We should go back. Suck him in again.'

'Umm . . . nah. I'm over the Octopus. It's boring. How long you got?'

'Got to meet the olds at four.'

'Me too. Where'll we go next?'

Modern Science's Most Terrible Wonder . . . The Headless Lady lay in a brocaded silk dress from another age, a garment Anne Boleyn herself might have worn proudly to the broadsword. A small paid-up crowd stood inside the marquee above the shallow, felt-lined sarcophagus in which she lay. A blurb on its side said her name was Ursula and she came from Romania and was beheaded in a 'Revolution Threshing Machine' there. Some wag had crossed out 'Revolution' and inked in 'Threshing Machine'. Sans head she would never see that country's beautiful capital, Sofia, again, nor hear the cries of its street vendors, nor smell nor taste its renowned cheeses. This blurb had me believe Sofia was the capital of Romania for a decade and that its cheeses were above the normal ruck of Eastern European stodge. Neither is true.

The end of the sarcophagus where her head should have been was roped off, so we couldn't see how her neck ended, but her head was definitely missing. A large laboratory beaker stood on a table nearby with tubes of bright green liquid going in and out of the stiff collar of her dress. Below that the dress opened and I could see her cleavage rise and fall, but figured this may have been some intricate bellows device rigged up inside a mannequin by a smarty pants. I guess similar doubt was rising throughout the crowd. Until she felt an itch – and her right hand flinched and lifted and crossed her body, ghostly slow, and her fingers scratched her left wrist just as deftly as yours or mine would. She was real. With no head. No hearing, no speech, no power of smell, nor of sight, nor, come to think of it, thought . . . How did she itch? How did she scratch?

Stowey – being Stowey – ducked beneath the rope and stepped to the end of the sarcophagus to peer down the lady's neck and debunk the mystery. What he saw there made him freeze and his eyes widen and whiten. The crowd, watching him, went silent, needing to know what he'd seen.

'A fuckin' wog . . . eating a donut,' he said. We were all pretty amazed.

Some arrangement of slanted mirrors was making the lady's head show as pure pillow from where we were. But Stowey having got behind the rope and looked from another angle had seen, reflected in these mirrors behind himself in a canvas alcove, the impresario, a Mediterranean type sitting on a folding chair innocently enjoying a donut and astounded to be called a fucking wog at his own freak show by a kid with a pudding-bowl haircut. Stowey assumed it was a tiny fucking wog sitting on the Headless Lady's pillow, whereas it was a life-sized one hidden behind him.

The life-sized fucking wog appeared to us from his canvas alcove behind Stowey, who was still watching him in the mirror thinking he was striding mousily across the Headless Woman's pillow. The life-sized fucking wog put his donut in the Headless Lady's hand. I saw her grip it. Only think how galling to be taunted with the reminiscent touch of a sugary donut when you have no head with which to ogle, chew and taste it.

Stowey looked aghast at the man, now frighteningly full scale and standing beside him. How did this happen? How had a Barbie-sized bloke he'd felt safe to abuse for sitting on a lady's pillow where her head should have been grown so big, so angry? The life-sized fucking wog grabbed Stowey by the shirt front and hauled him outside and pitched him into the dust of sideshow alley.

He was still sitting in the dust, blinking, trying to figure out what had happened when I got outside. Sideshow alley was a place where magic was routinely performed, but Italians didn't recover from advanced miniaturisation and throw you about as a rule.

'That guy got big fast,' he said.

'It was probly mirrors,' I explained. 'She probly had a head.'

\* \* \*

There were a few intervening rides. There was the stand where you threw twenty-cent coins, trying to land them on packets of Wine Gums and Minties and sundry other delectables and if they stayed on top the pack was yours. But they always slid off and the bald man got to keep your money. Unless you spat copiously on the coin, making it land like a toad or a turd or a toad's turd. The stall holder would then pick up your money between thumb and forefinger and stare at it like the toad or turd it was, dripping saliva from our Queen's mouth, and he'd shout at you, 'Deesgoost leettle poonk,' and tell you, 'No win speet. Speet no win. Fook of you.' And that diatribe was well worth the money paid. Fook of you, too, with your unwinnable prizes, as we ricocheted off farmers and cannery workers into the depths of the crowd.

\* \* \*

The drum. The drumbeat. The very same bull-skinned echoes chosen by Rome to quicken blood in her citizens and conjure sweet gore in their minds to drag them to the Coliseum. The same set of endlessly adamant aural steps that reached into the dungeons and walked the gladiators red-visioned to glory . . . or death.

You could hear the drum from a long way off. Beneath the rock riffs and the cliff-jump squeals of the Matterhorn riders and the calls of the barkers to come see come see and the moans venting from the ghost house, it was the funereal heartbeat of sideshow alley. Jimmy Sharman's drum. Real war had come, for those that spoke its language.

Certain boys, and certain men, too, pretended not to hear the drum. Walked on by in a mask of calm, looking this way and that for the next thrill; perhaps a coconut shy or the dodgem cars. These were cowards. The drum, being so frightening to them, they heard it louder than we did, but would as soon admit to hearing it as slap a tyrannosaurus on the arse. These people didn't look up at the warriors as they hurried past Jimmy Sharman's.

The fighters stood on a running board above and facing the crowd, some in shorts and singlets and some in shiny robes. Behind them ran a long canvas mural on which were painted known champions wearing championship belts. These painted pros were dressed only in shorts and each crouched in his distinguishing fistic stance shaping up to some foolhardy invisible. Painted above them the boast: 'Products of Jimmy Sharman's Troupe'.

The men on the running board hadn't reached the pro circuit. The men on the running board were the level of fighter who could beat anyone in the crowd they were eyeing off, but no one on the painted canvas behind them. They didn't fight a talent in a big hall once every few months like the painted champions. They were shift workers in a square-roped abattoir, poleaxing drunks and maladroit hulks and dancing away from the vivid assaults of gifted wild-men every night of the week.

They glared down at the crowd. Half blackfellas and half whitefellas, they were hard, wiry men from low circumstance in far towns, from homes broken and institutions despised . . . the wrong side of the tracks. Well, in truth, no blackfella was born on the right side of the tracks. These fighters had biceps worth ten law degrees to me. Each year, after seeing them, I'd do twenty chin-ups for three days straight, then check myself in the bathroom mirror. Three whole days. But still those biceps didn't come. The trick was to train on a strict diet of kangaroo and overproof rum like Jimmy Sharman's boys did.

At one end of the line the drummer, also a fighter, with a bass drum hanging athwart his gut, its shiny red mother-of-pearl frame contrasting with its skins stained dark where the padded stick landed its profound blow calling men to come and fight, taunting them, each beat a dare, an invitation, or a pang of shame. This heavyweight beat the drum once every few seconds while the spruiker shouted down at the crowd through a conical piece of tin, 'A round or two for a pound or two . . . Who'll take a glove? Who'll take on the Maori Wonder? What about Jimmy Sands, the Cumregunja Marvel? A round or two for a pound or two . . . come on, you blokes, step up, they said you was a tough town. They said you was a serious town. They said this town had hard men. I'm starting to wonder if the men of bloomin' Albury aren't tougher than Shepp men. Who'll take a glove?'

Oh, we would fight, all right. Nothing could hold us back. We had all easily imagined the glory of being inside that tent in that ring with the crowd baying while we danced around an opponent making him look a cinematic oaf before chopping him to the floor with some snippet of pugilistic tango that could be enjoyed in memorised slo-mo by connoisseurs evermore.

The town had good fighters, young men, known men, who walked the streets with a bouncing gait so each step said 'boxer'. You could tell a fighter as clearly as you could tell a cripple, from a block away. Darcy Ritchie and Gary Austin were said to be future Australian champions, if they didn't fight the police too often to get a good run at a career.

Spectators paid two bob to get into the tent. Inside was a crush of beery, sweaty men laughing at nothing. Some were talking too fast and some were stony silent. Everyone was a little afraid of public defeat, of becoming a fallen gladiator, dragged from this arena behind mules. Who'll take a glove? Who'll take a glove? Dusty beams of sunlight angling through the tent gave it the feel of a collapsing temple.

Boys were used on the undercard to get the men fired up for battle. But Jimmy Sharman employed no boy boxers. The boy fights were local against local. Fighters got to keep half the money the spectators threw into the ring. Jimmy kept the other half. Jimmy's man swept up the change off the canvas and did the count. The better the fight the more money you made. If you went nuts and tried to kill someone the coins rained like gamma rays.

You only had to step forward with your hand raised to fight. The ref would call you up and then pluck another boy approximately your size from the crowd and the deal was set. 'Okay,' I told Stowey. 'Get up there.'

For a week leading up to the show we had planned this sting. We were going to put on a fake fight and rake in the dough. Every lunchtime at school we had told our other friends to clear off while we practised feints and pulled punches. We mimed killer combinations of crosses and uppercuts and winced feigned pain, and staggered under hammer blows, a playwright's rollercoaster battle, each of us alternately on the point of defeat and victory, until the men in our minds were hollering delight and we were knee-deep in coin.

It never occurred to us that men who made their living fighting, and other men who fought drunk with some frequency, might be able to pick a fix in a moment.

'No. You first,' he answered me.

'What, are you chicken?'

'No.'

'Go on, then. I'll put my hand up after you get in there.'

'Okay.' Stowey ducked between the men and rolled beneath the bottom rope onto the canvas and onto his feet and began shuffling backwards jabbing and smiling at some phantom in front of him. The crowd laughed and shouted approval at the kid's bravado. Look who thinks he's Lionel bloody Rose. Hearing their roar he grinned stupidly wide and began dancing side to side, bending his head this way and that, stretching his neck like he'd seen the big names do on *TV Ringside*. Unbelievably, he began hissing as he threw jabs at the invisible challenger in front of him. Sss . . . sss . . . sss . . . pneumatic stabs of sound such as the pros gave off.

I suddenly realised Stowey was a prima donna sent mentally awry by the adoration of massed fans. It was obvious he'd forgotten his role in the fix. He'd gone mad. I began to rethink the day. Was I going to fight some fool who whored himself out for the brief adulation of drunks and cannery workers? I was as good as my word, but . . . Stowey was veering dangerously off script. Should I honour my contract with a harebrained adventurer like this? No. No, I thought, perhaps not. The deal was off. If the fool was going for glory he could count me out.

As one of Sharman's men laced pendulous gloves to the ends of Stowey's unmuscled arms the ref cast about for a contender. 'Who'll take a glove?'

He bent and asked Stowey's name. 'Bruce.'

'Who'll take on Battling Bruce? Three rounds of fistic fury and half the gratuities to the fighters,' the ref shouted.

Well, I would have taken on Battling Bruce if he'd stuck to the plan and not got carried away by fame. But with him hissing like a flyweight taipan and waving at the crowd as if it had travelled miles to see him alone, as if he was some sort of star attraction, then, no. Drunk on the shouts and whistles of the crowd as he had clearly become, I thought he deserved a whipping. I could see the sense in letting the fight go ahead without me.

In the ring Stowey's eyes began to dart back and forth like mice do when they hear a certain frequency that precedes a nasty fuck-up. He looked this way and that. Where was I? I'd let the suspense build nicely. I'd let him shadow-box and show his style. It was time for me to enter the ring and show a few moves myself, and then for us to act out our epic. His eyes zigged and zagged across the cheering faces for mine. 'Camo?' he called in a stage whisper. 'Camo?'

By the time they had his gloves laced Stowey's eyes had stopped darting. The frightening frequency trilling in his ears had stopped. He knew.

The ref pointed into the crowd on the far side of the ring. 'Yes. That boy there. Lift him up here.' The crowd hoisted Carlin Grey over the ropes and landed him unsmiling in the ring. Carlin Grey was a tough kid from Rumbalara, the war-torn blackfella settlement on the outskirts of town. Carlin Grey had a reputation even in Rumbalara. Disagreements with Carlin ended in a fight and fights with Carlin ended with Carlin standing over you asking how fuckin' smart you felt now. There would be no fake fight with Carlin Grey. Still, regret is a wasted emotion, so I decided to feel none.

I figured that, looking on the bright side, and taking the long view, as a wise boy should, Stowey might use this beating as a campaign medal. If Carlin went on to become a famous fighter or criminal, and either or both was likely, then Stowey could, in years to come when news came on the TV that Carlin had KO'ed a Chechnyan middleweight or been arrested in a bank heist, and vision of Carlin wearing handcuffs or a championship belt was shown, then Stowey could puff his chest and casually mention to whoever he was currently loafing alongside that Carlin Grey beat the living shit out of him in Jimmy Sharman's tent one day. Momentarily, I envied Stowey this fame. I felt a glow of magnanimity that I had given him this lifelong gift. And I even conjectured that somewhere down the track he might be grateful to me. Though grateful wasn't his normal thing.

Carlin didn't dance and showboat. He didn't throw flashy jabs at thin air. He didn't hiss like a pro. He stood quietly while they laced on his gloves, watching Stowey with a grimace of mild confusion, as if asking himself what the hell the Stowe kid was doing here in this place of battle that rightly belonged to his end of town, to Rumbalara and his hardscrabble people. Or maybe he was wondering how long Stowey would last, or just where best to hit him and how many times.

A fighter in a satin robe spanked an upended tin bucket with a tyre lever and the stools were whisked away and the crowd went dead. Carlin Grey walked out with his hands at gut height, head and neck weaving a serpentine hypnosis. This snake-man act might have entranced and befuddled a sharper kid than Stowey. He remained clear-headed. He screamed and charged at Carlin Grey. He used the various quadrants of his skull, his teeth, his knees, his elbows . . . any point where the Stowe skeleton rose up to the surface of the Stowe corpus and suggested itself as a weapon was mashed against a vulnerable site on the puzzled reality of Carlin Grey.

Stowey had rightly guessed berserkness was his only safe exit from this ambush and he went so berserk even Sharman's fighters, connoisseurs of every type of malignant combat the male brain could conjure, stood back aghast. I was excited and would have barracked, but I was also slightly sad. If the painted champions on the canvas outside were 'Products of Jimmy Sharman's Troupe', then so was Stowey and his berserkness. Stowey had brought the House of Sharman, an institution with a history of courage and fair play, to this new place that smelt of barbarity and shame. At a certain point violence becomes unseemly. Who wants to watch a lunatic hack an albatross with a tomahawk?

Stowey had a big brother called Peter who walked about town with a large-boned swagger and who would go on to become heavyweight champ of the Victoria Police and earn a fearsome name around Melbourne's inner suburbs as a street-fighter. Peter once gave a detailed kerbside kicking to a man named Gangitano who people rated as a thug. Peter could 'go' as the saying was. To keep Peter at bay Stowey was occasionally forced to go berserk. And he had become well versed in berserkness, how you leapt in and out of it, its pay-off and its power, how its near unbelievability stunned people.

He was not at all embarrassed to wail and scream like a spaniel caught in a house fire. He beat Carlin Grey from every angle: roared in his ear, bit his arm, stomped on his calf, kicked him in the stomach and ground his forehead on Carlin's nose like a millstone on a grain of wheat. If his dick was hard I believe he would have thrashed Carlin Grey with that.

Every so often Carlin would slide a clean shot through Stowey's martial contortions and snap him sober. Stowey would pause, blink at his options, then shake his head, reject sanity and retreat back into his cocoon of rotor blades and madness.

The crowd, initially stunned, found voice and found bloodlust and began calling for the head of Carlin Grey. They wanted him to become roadkill on the canvas pronto, using whatever crazy methods Stowey had invented or learnt from maniacs. The crowd around me began to writhe, pushing and leaning and cocking elbows and weaving and ducking its hips this way and that. They were reaching into their pockets for change. Coins began to rain down into the ring and to bounce off the berserk boy and the bewildered boy and to roll in diminishing circles, maybe fifty at a time, and to lie there as a mural of blood-stained canvas and doubloons celebrating the scorched-earth fistic stylings of Battling Bruce Stowe.

Before the first round was over Carlin Grey fell down dead, possibly the most bamboozled corpse any of us had ever seen. Jesus, I told myself, Stowey's done it now. He's killed an indigenous kid using foul means. He will be hanged and his friends vilified and slapped. I began to shuffle toward the tent flap. The ref wrapped Stowey in a bear hug and walked him to his corner. Men who had been howling for this death stood mute, complicit, their colour draining.

One of Jimmy's fighters knelt over Carlin and lifted his head and waved something under his nose that brought him alive, blinking and scowling in inquiry. He had no idea what had just happened. The world had accelerated into a whirring feral nonsense that hurt to touch.

Stowey made three dollars sixty. And on the way out of the tent men who didn't know him laid hands on his shoulders and nodded at him and puckered their lips like he was something profound.

Outside he was angry. 'Shit. Where were you? Why didn't you put your hand up? Carlin Grey. Carlin Fucking Grey. I might have been killed.'

'Old man Trelfell was in there. He's a client of Dad's.'

'So what?'

'I can't afford it getting out I was fighting at Sharman's. How would that look?'

'What?'

'We're lawyers. We don't fight in tents.'

'Oh, right. I can get beat up because my old man has shops.'

I nodded. That was about it. When you were involved with the law you had to be careful of your reputation. It was a heavy responsibility for a kid, but it was mine, and I carried it without complaint.

As we wandered along sideshow alley I ventured a compliment to make up to him. 'Jesus, you jobbed him. You went . . . You flipped.' But Stowey didn't much want to talk about it. He was embarrassed about using his berserkness in a public place. Like Barbara Eden in *I Dream of Jeannie*, or Elizabeth Montgomery in *Bewitched*, certain magics were forbidden, were unfair, unethical. He thought the berserking of Carlin Grey might become known around town and people would treat him as some sort of hair-trigger froot loop and start baiting him to see him put on a show.

Five minutes later, standing staring at a canvas sign covered in painted snakes announcing the Pit of Death and daring us to watch the hideous sight of a man climb into a pit containing over a thousand deadly serpents I said, 'This looks good. Let's spend our fight money on this?' It would cost a buck fifty each. Virtually all his fight money.

'Yeah,' Stowey said. 'I hate snakes. We gotta see them.'

\* \* \*

Summer weekends we would load up the car and drive up to the Murray River. One Saturday morning I was asked to help pack the Fairlane by carrying a watermelon outside and putting it in the boot. Did I think I could manage that? Manage it! Look, I can hold it with one arm. I was a stringy little kid, but like the Tardis, much bigger on the inside than on the outside. That is, despite all evidence, I believed myself mightier than most men.

A watermelon was a newly arrived foodstuff; a piquant pioneer years ahead of avocados and mangos, it broke the dual stranglehold of apples and pears on our palates. Watermelons were rare and expensive. To arrive somewhere with a watermelon was to arrive with a plate of larks' tongues. I was proud to be chosen to carry ours to the car. I hefted it in one stingy arm, 'Look, Mum. It's not even heavy.' (The thing weighed a ton.) Who could know that from a height of one metre a watermelon would self-destruct like a Bond car? The thing hit the linoleum and fairly detonated. A crimson Himalaya of wet flesh bloomed across the kitchen floor. Suddenly stripped of the social glory of arriving with a watermelon, Mum howled.

And as the sisters came running inside to investigate the howl, to see what I'd stuffed up now, both skidded in the tasty scree and went sliding on their backs across the floor, nearly decapitating themselves under the open dishwasher.

The Cameron family arrived at the big river marinated in watermelon, reeking of watermelon, but bearing no watermelon. The other kids eyed us off angrily. They weren't fooled. We ponged of rare fruit. We had obviously pulled off the track just over the horizon and gorged the mythic melon before dabbing our lips clean and appearing with more mundane foodstuffs to share.

The Murray was a big river then. A wide, suede-coloured stream with its surface writhing with muscular currents and dotted with wavering vortices and each of these marked the grave of a boy like me who had got out of his depth and tried to fight the river instead of go with it. Don't panic. Go with the river, Dad told us. Don't ever fight the current. Climb out downstream and walk back. The Barmah Forest was an endless, unexplored wilderness and the gums along the river-banks stood on great tangles of exposed roots that looked like cages for monsters.

The Barmah Forest with the Murray winding intestinally through it was the edge of our known world and the cusp of a beguiling nothingness. It was the past. Here it was 1880 all day long. Knives were worn on the hip and guns lay within easy reach along this river. This was the wild world and it was ruled with sumptuous lawlessness by a few of Dad's war-veteran friends.

Dad left school in '44, just too late to fight in the war. He joined the RAAF and slept a year at the MCG being trained in how to stay warm at night using newspaper. But many of the men who came to be his friends had fought in the war. Barrel was one of these.

The Barrel shack was jigsawed together from found and bartered materials: cement sheet, wood, lino, various unre-lated windows, a massive iron stove that burnt wood. Stripy canvas butchers' blinds shaded its verandah. It stood on stilts a metre off the ground in close trees just back off its own

248

sandbar. You walked a raised plank path to the dunny out the back in the forest.

Periodically the whole thing flooded, water inside for weeks on end. But once the mud was sluiced out and the red-bellied black snakes were unwound from the pots and pans and shot out from under the gas fridge, the house was as before, damply wooden. Like a Russian dacha on an endless steppe, it stood alone through winter waiting to be filled with loud summer humans. Sometimes as it stood empty drunks fired bullets through it from passing boats. Bullet holes were easy to patch with wine corks.

\* \* \*

We rise before dawn. Barrel, Lucky, Dad, Guy and me. The pre-dawn is a time of no authority, no law. We cross the beach to Barrel's boat, fog pressed flat on the water in slow swirls and the kookaburras loosing preambles of laughter. The big Evinrude gurgles alive and the moving air goes cold on the skin. Barrel at the wheel. Barrel always captain, a leader of men. He fought the Japanese in PNG, was bombed and burnt, but recovered to become heavyweight champ of the army as the fleet sailed home.

I hunker down behind Dad out of the cold air as we cruise upstream to the first springer. Haul the line out dripping and icy on the hands and the carp is still alive, still swimming with a hook large as cutlery through its lip. No cod. 'Shit. This set looked sure fire, Lucky,' Lucky says.

Reverse out and motor upstream and we can see the next springer, a sapling cut and speared into mud and a line leading into the water. 'Sure fire. Bardi grubs. Sure fire,' Barrel says. He pulls alongside and I lean over the gunnel to the smoky cold water and pull out the line. A long white grub tied to a hook with a rubber band. 'Bastard. Maybe they're off the bite.'

Then to the net. A gill net. Highly illegal. Untie it from the bank and track its length slowly to the far end, feeding it into the boat hand over hand and with it turtles and yellowbelly and a cod, green and grey and as big as me. Like a dragon, this legendary thing, this fish that I listen to men speak of in low voices and wild surmises like they do about women. Lucky laughs out loud right up and down the river. For the ineluctable joy of this fish. He doesn't care about getting caught. 'Sure fire, Lucky. Square bait. Sure fire.'

We check about a dozen springers, until dawn is angling long golden beams through the trees and we can no longer be poachers and no longer be the only men on Earth. The magic diminishes as the light grows. It is Australia again. It is Saturday. It is 1969.

* * *

Lucky Simson treated authority as if it was a ghost. A once-living and legitimate force that had been killed in the war and was now a pale adumbration, lingering and calling, but not real. It had lost meaning for him. He couldn't believe in it if he'd wanted to. He had seen beneath the shroud of rank, grace and dignity inside which humanity clothed itself and found a vicious idiot. God and Man were both frauds. And this revelation was constantly ratified with laughter . . . at God and at Man.

In the Second War Lucky had fought in the Western Desert as part of a machine-gun crew. A knuckleboner, he called himself. Because he ground good men into knucklebones. When I was seven he told me he had once seen a troop of Italian cavalry crest a dune at sunrise with the light behind them, the ostrich plumes in their felt hats silhouette like a field of wheat vibrating against the new sun. Grandest sight he'd ever seen. And what did you do then, Lucky? I asked. Killed 'em all, Lucky. Turned 'em into knucklebones.

He was captured at the Fall of Singapore by the Japanese and used as a slave on the Burma Railway, where he had a pet monkey the guards liked to burn with cigarettes. This, for him, was one cruelty too many. It seemed unnecessary, when they owned thousands of men who needed brutalising daily, that they stub cigarettes on his monkey. Why burn the monkey, Lucky? He would ask me this when I was a boy as if I had an answer and was holding out. 'I don't know, Lucky.'

'Well, think about it, Lucky. "I don't know" is a lazy answer. Why burn the monkey?'

I knew why they burnt the monkey. They burnt the monkey to burn him. But I couldn't articulate this.

He didn't like the Japanese. They had taught him discipline, death, malice, meaninglessness and survival. But after the coercions of Bushido, a water bailiff counting clicks on a Dethridge wheel, or a Fisheries and Wildlife inspector asking to search your boat, or the police wanting you to blow into a bag or aghast at the chronic unroadworthiness of your ute, or a magistrate throwing a gavel because you were singing 'Goodnight Irene' in his court – these were children brandishing junk rules and the law was a board game.

He could shoot a shotgun beautifully and could hit airborne targets with a rifle. Dad would throw a bottle into the air high above the river and Lucky, leaning into a .22 in a rare moment of furrowed seriousness, would explode it at its wonky zenith, glass raining across the water like a Zero crash as I called out in cartoon Japanese, 'Aww, Aussies shoot me down. Aussies shoot me down. No good for me. Aussies shoot me down.' And the men laughed at my joke.

Dad could never work out where Lucky got his dough. He was an orchardist, but not with huge orchards. He had an unexplained source of income, it was said. If you ever asked him how he financed some new purchase, a car, a holiday, a swimming pool, he'd say, 'Uncle Sos, Lucky.' But no one believed this. We speculated he had some benefactor from the war. Some mate he'd helped survive the Burma Railway. Some son of Toorak he'd nursed through that Japanese dystopia.

I revered these friends of Dad because they had a DIY ethical dexterity that Dad didn't have and couldn't afford. They were rascals. He had gone to a private school, was now a lawyer, respecting the law and working at the mysterious and somewhat unmanly combat that took place in our local court that kept our fragile community from breaking out into the more honest hostilities a boy longed to see. Our economic future as a family depended on his having a good name. His place in the world made him step back from the madcap adventures of his war veteran friends. It was risky enough that he hung around with these eccentric characters, without joining them to shoot ducks off the sewage ponds on a Sunday. His competitors, the district's other lawyers, didn't have friends like these.

WW2 made my childhood a godless era. We didn't go to church. Few people did, after the war. It was a hard time to be a priest. The soldiers had been to the red centre of existence and none of them had come back extolling the Light of Jesus or confirming the Compassion of the Lord. Priests were no longer experts in the thing they were trying to sell. For a generation after any war priests ply their trade on the widows and scuttle light-stepped with shame away from the returned men.

The cops of the Goulburn Valley were too young to have gone to war. The magistrates and judges were lawyers during the war, essential citizens, so they didn't go away either. And these men, Lucky and Barrel and others, having tasted cordite and bonemeal, were expected to come back here and toe a line prescribed and enforced by wigged home-bodies and badged youths and scuttling widow-charmers. No. No. The life of these returned men was lived against the odds, was borrowed from their dead mates who took the bullet or the sword blow that might have been theirs. It was a precious gift from friends who would never be met again. And they would live it how they wanted. These returned men would frame their own morality. And that morality was deaf to priests, coppers, Fisheries and Wildlife inspectors and magistrates because they yapped provincial truths in a frequency the veterans could choose not to hear.

They seemed as free as children to me, a child. They laughed without weighing laughter's propriety. They drove Willys Jeeps and army DUKWs, they let off explosions to sort out small glitches in reticulation. They walked barefoot through the bush, over patches of devil's-heads, and picked

253

hot pans from campfires with their bare hands and drank beer from long-necked bottles. And they spoke without filter. The town knew they were owed a debt, these men who had returned from death. So the town cut them a lot of slack.

The summer I was seven Lucky bought a brand new cherry-red Mercedes-Benz. The Goulburn Valley was a plain of Holdens and Fords with a few old Humbers wheezing along. A beast as futuristic and red as this stood out like a unicorn at the sheep yards. There was wild speculation in Shepparton and Mooroopna. Did Lucky pay tax? Did he grow illicit crops for long-hairs under his pear trees? Was he supplying the embryonic counter-culture with Mary Jane? Running weed up the Hume to the big smoke?

The seats were cream leather and the Mercedes smelt so strongly of new car that I could sit in it and inhale and become a Jetson, see visions of myself zipping around a future city on a flying scooter.

Lucky was a rabid fisherman and shooter. A hunter always knee-deep in mud wearing Y-fronts. Like Huck Finn, who reasoned a stole watermelon tasted better than a bought one, Lucky found rare piquancy in illegally shot game and illegally caught fish. He was a tireless and inventive poacher. A week after Lucky bought the Mercedes, he and Barrel dragged Victoria Lake.

The lake is still there, right in town, a massive puddle left over when the flooded Goulburn River retreated. Dragnets were, and are, illegal. So they arrived in the last of the night with magpies carolling and, in their underpants, waded out and hauled the net through the lake. They felt it jerk and become heavy and they whispered across the water to each other that they were onto something. We're onto something here, Lucky.

The catch was massive. Yellowbelly, undercover of the local by-law that prevented fishing in the centre of town, had bred up to massive numbers. As Lucky and Barrel dragged them out onto the levee they realised they had a logistical problem: how to steal away with half a ton of illegal fish before dawn and discovery.

They began to put them in the boot of the Benz loose, alive. A well-fed yellowbelly is about the size of a badly-fed corgi. They filled the boot with them and then they began to throw them into the car itself until it was filled with flipping, gaping yellowbelly right up to the windowsills. They couldn't open the doors or the fish would pour out. So they climbed in the front windows and squirmed down through the depths of fish onto the seats. Lucky felt around with his bare feet until he located the accelerator and brake. Sitting in his new Mercedes up to his tits in live fish he reached out, swimming his hand through their slimy mass, and found the key and turned it. The car started. 'The Krauts, Lucky. The Krauts don't let you down.' They drove off dressed only in their underpants immersed in half a ton of live illegally netted fish.

And, by my reckoning, anyone who saw them, any early riser, the paperboy, the baker, the milkman, the garbos, the insomniacs and peeping Toms, would have thought to themselves, 'There goes Lucky, nude, in fish, in his Mercedes.' It would have been no especially peculiar thing, Barrel and his friend nude in illegal fish, and the early risers would have forgotten the sight by mid-morning.

The inside of the Merc was veneered with fish slime and scale and fish piss and mud that after a few summer days became an iridescent, almost pretty, shellac. Lucky's wife, Margie, was, and needed to be, the most forbearing woman in a shire of women who cut their post-war beaux plenty of slack. She must have known regular tides of despair as his schemes and affronts broke over the shire. But she was never angry, always kind, always able to accept in a minute some craziness she couldn't have imagined a minute ago. Her new car now stank like a prawn trawler.

A week later we were leaving Lucky's house to pick sweet-corn from a surprised Italian who leased some land from Lucky and was confounded to see Lucky striding out into the middle of his crop, again and again, and helping himself and his friends to all the corn they could pick. The terms of Lucky's leases were loose. Mediterranean types who leased his lands had become sharecroppers without knowing it. He constantly gave us baskets of tomatoes or sacks of broad beans he picked from the crops of his tenants.

Dad and Lucky got in the front of the Mercedes and I got in the back. The stink of fish on German leather turned out to pack the same nasal affront as an inflated roadside wombat. I gagged and tumbled out onto the ground sucking air. The smell inside the car was one Jonah would have known. 'Lucky, your car stinks.' I spat into the dirt. Lucky, red-faced, pot-bellied, looked at me on my hands and knees, a weird boy always reading books and asking strange questions, not quite in tune with his laudable rural escapades. Then he looked at Dad to let him know he thought the man had a problem on his hands.

'Fish don't stink, Lucky,' he told us. Dad sat alongside him, smiling. Enjoying my consternation. The Japanese had placed this man so far beyond normal cares he couldn't smell rotten fish and didn't think it wrong to use a brand new car as a dumpster. He lived in a happy place where material possessions had lost all value and wrecking a new Merc with fish made perfect sense.

If Charles Darwin, that chronic collector of whelks, beetles, finches, pigeons and dormice, had owned a Frigidaire it wouldn't have contained a fraction of the dead critters Lucky's did. In there were cigar tubes filled with dormant bardi grubs, jars of frogs, jars of spiders, jars of sparrows, wading birds cocooned in Glad Wrap, jars of sludge that turned out to be blends of finch and mouse, or huntsmen and yabbie, all atomised using Margie's Magimix into delectable pastes that could be frozen and strapped to hooks to catch the elusive Murray cod. Lucky's quest for the cod kept him awake at night.

The Simsons lived out of town among green orchards in humid air and lapping channels from which the water fanned out among the trees, each gallon counted by the shire using steel wheels called Dethridge wheels. Outside their big wooden house was the district's first private swimming pool. All water in the Goulburn Valley was brown. Even the Raymond West Pool, the town's public pool, had a sandy bottom and held brown water. Lucky's pool was filled with aqua water that people drove miles to see. It was like seeing a green sky or a turnip the size and shape of Harold Holt.

But that colour, that stupendous aqua, being Lucky's, and not adequately tended, soon faded and died. The second time we went out there to swim it wasn't quite so brilliant. I blinked at it to try and light it up. Maybe I'd become blasé. But within two years it was as brown as all other water in the valley, a live bait tank that had carp and frogs and yabbies living in it and water spiders skating across its surface in formation like Christmas Canadians. Shags dive-bombed this cube of corralled canapés and Lucky would sometimes shoot them out the open door while sitting on his sofa watching *Ironside* on TV without ever losing track of the intricate court-room drama or killing any member of his family. He was, I suppose, a multi-tasker.

All the riverine life forms living in Lucky's swimming pool were competing for scraps and concoctions launched at timed intervals across the water in pellet form from a small pneumatic cannon that had originally been used to serve tennis balls at a local pro but, since that athlete had done his knee and was off the circuit, was now firing Lucky's blended and desiccated gruels at confused aquatic critters who would usually sniff at them and maybe nibble them, before turning up their noses, if they had them. And if you think the gulf between species is so wide that homo sapiens in the form of a nine-year-old boy couldn't see flat out unadulterated disappointment flare in a yabbie's eyes, then you never saw how his airborne snacks were received by Lucky's incarcerated host of river life.

I was out at Lucky's place one Sunday afternoon doing jobs to pay for his rain gauge, which I had shot a hole in with an air rifle down so low it couldn't give a reading of any but the lightest shower. I sat down poolside and began to admire the food launcher, its parabolic grace, the way the fish flinched as Lucky's dried sludge bombarded them at ten-minute intervals. But I was soon bored with watching them rained on with foodstuffs that had no real ballistic bite. Donning my artilleryman's cap I emptied Lucky's foul fish-feed from the feeder magazine of his food launcher and replaced it with gravel and clods and pointed the barrel of the thing directly down at the water.

It blasted viciously into the pool and the water spiders raced this way and that like a school excursion being dive-bombed by Stukas and the fish panicked for the depths. Ten minutes later, by the time of the next bombardment, they had assumed a truce and risen innocently into the peaceable shallows – to be viciously strafed once more. They were serial suckers for a first strike.

But nothing was being killed. So I was upgrading my ammunition from clods to half bricks I found on a pile behind a shed, and telling myself that these half bricks were more-or-less atomic, the invention of Fat Man and Little Boy, and that these carp were entering a harsh nuclear reality, when I saw a black Rolls-Royce coming slowly up the Simsons' long drive. I dropped my half bricks and gave up my war. Here was something more fascinating than forcing carp to surrender in Japanese accents with their fins held high.

Margie had invited female acquaintances around to play bridge. The guest list suggests the occasion was an attempt at social advancement, a shot at rising up the community rankings. For Lady Frampton, matriarch of the retail family, had wended her way glacially from town in her Rolls-Royce ferrying unimpeachable matriarchs. Myrna Stuart of the meatworks Stuarts and Calm Furphy of the water-cart clan. Big, dynastic women who smelt like geraniums in a heatwave.

Lady Frampton was a fascinating piece of powdered aristocracy. I was always expecting her to die or insult someone. And she never died while I was watching. She was known for her rheumatism and this day she flashed her knobby finger joints beneath my nose as proof she had been singled out for excruciation *nonpareil* and said, 'Some of us are tested. Pray you aren't tested. Though,' she looked me up and down, 'I doubt you will be.' No. Why would the Lord bother testing me when he was guaranteed a fiasco?

Forgetting my chores, which, to be honest, I had already forgotten in preference to bombarding fish with bricks, I followed the ladies inside and hid behind a sofa and ceased to exist so I wouldn't cramp their far-ranging and bitter talk.

Given that Lady F was tested by the vicious strain of rheumatism the Lord usually reserved for royalty, Margie, though it was autumn and the day warm, had insisted Lucky light a fire. Preened and pearled the ladies took their places at the card table and sipped a sweet sherry before the pulsing hearth. The cards were played in wily fashion by the liver-spotted hands, and a tea cake was served and the lesser women of the district were having their shortcomings brought forth and magnified and cast in bronze by whiskered lips dotted with yellow crumbs when a rumbling was heard.

In later life I recognised it as the sound of a train coming at you through a tunnel when you're on a subway platform, pushing a tide of air before it. The bridge quartet went still as the chimney huffed a lungful of smoke into the room prior to disgorging what looked like the smoking, blackened head of a Roman centurion still wearing his helmet.

The thing splashed red coals across the rug and onto the ladies' shoes and rolled out among them with its mouth gaping a silent scream and oozing smoke rings and a drizzle of white smoke escaping from each blackened eyehole. The pandemonium of the aged ladies was a thing that would have done credit to much younger, slimmer, drunker women. In their adrenal high they shouted words plucked from the North Shepp playground that goose-bumped my flesh to hear from the lips of the district's dowagers. And they pulled at each other's hair and hauled on each other's pearls to be out the door and into Lady Frampton's Roller first. Lady Frampton, in her haste to get gone, left a mink stole behind, which Lucky later cut into swatches he wrapped around bardi grubs for cod lures. I remember him dejectedly ticking mink off his list of possible sure-fire cod baits a week or so later, saying, 'Mink's no better than fox, Lucky. Or cocker spaniel.'

The trio of social lionesses crammed into Lady Frampton's Roller and the two that weren't driving told her, Go, Lady F. Go. Gun this enormous status symbol for the Greater City of Shepparton where the citizens won't bowl the smouldering heads of dead centurions at us as if we were morticians, archeologists or ninepins. Lady F cut a tunnel through Margie's much-loved bamboo grove by way of short cut or by way of revenge as she turned the Roller for home.

Margie, a veteran of improbable events, a woman regularly sent sliding back down the social ladder by her husband's fantastic doings, stood her ground. She shovelled the red coals out of the black nests they'd made in her carpet

261

and back into the fire and then knelt before the smoking head with the cool eye of a crash scene investigator. Ogling and sniffing she soon came to the conclusion it was the head of a mighty fish. A Murray cod. It lay there gaping, giving off the same heartbreaking wisps of smoke as her social standing. 'Oh, Bruce,' I heard her whisper. Then I stood up from behind the sofa and said, 'One of those old ladies said, "Fuck".' This seemed to cheer her up. To know that one of these grand dames' deportment had slipped in the crisis, that one had something to answer for.

Lucky had caught the fish months before up on the Murray on a springer, an untended line left attached to a sapling and baited with a live carp. Illegal, needless to say. A monster hundred and forty pound cod. He'd lowered its head down the chimney on binder twine to smoke it and then been called away to other duties. The occasional hint of putrefaction descending into the living room in the following months hadn't reminded him of the cod's head. He thought George his German shorthaired pointer was sourly flatulent.

The binder twine caught alight just as Lady Frampton was beginning to roast one of my aunts in parable and the fish fell with the aunt only half cooked, just as Lady Frampton was saying that with Newcastle being such a large, blue-collar Gomorrah it was just possible my Aunty Liza may not have been the most devious trollop that ever issued from it . . . but she was unquestionably in the top half dozen.

Lady Frampton must have thought the fish's head was the head of the aunt currently being ranked among the infamous trollops of Newcastle, thinly disguised in blackface and wide-mouthed with a vengeful rage. Because on her way

out of the room as she made for her Roller with her rheuma-
tically dilapidated knees taking my sofa at a hurdle, I heard
her squeak a panicked apology to Liza and a retraction of
the Newcastle trollop stats and offer up an olive branch by
saying Aunty Liza was probably only just inside the top fifty.

*　　*　　*

He was arrested by sudden enthusiasms, Lucky. In one he
hired a water diviner to come out and find a subterranean
reservoir on his orchard. Bugger paying over the odds for the
meagre water allocations the shire served up. Those days are
over, Lucky. A guy in a faded Bedford truck rolled up. He
had the look of a late-blooming prophet about him, the look
of a bloke who'd failed at too many occupations, been found
wanting at a dispiriting number of minor, mundane tasks
and become known to family and friends as a worthless shit
kicker, until discovering a surprising superannuation selling
dreams of Eden to gullible cockies.

He climbed out of his truck in baggy shorts holding his
bent piece of wire like a piece of the true cross and insisted
we stand at some distance so as not to interfere with its 'direc-
tionals'. 'How far back do you want us?' Dad asked. 'Bearing
in mind the boy just drank a can of Fanta.' Dad loved nothing
better than to witness hokery like this. The diviner, without
any hint he knew he was being mocked, pointed at a place a
hundred yards away. 'Over by them palms should do. Never
find water near palms.' This flew in the face of everything I
knew about oases from reading of Arabian adventures. Dad
jabbed me in the ribs and winked at me. Pay close attention

to this shyster – and to Lucky. Both are in on this. One is the dupe and one the conman. Both willing, in their way. Water won't be found. Excuses will be given. At some point Lucky's belief will falter and he will turn into a sceptic, hands on his hips and leaning back with a sneer on his lips. This will be fun. Dad's rib jab readied me for the full arc of the play.

Harry the Diviner wandered around with his bent wire held out before him wincing and frowning like a widow at a séance with strong info teeming in from another sphere. He was pulled along by invisible currents of something or other beyond explaining. He'd take a series of rapid steps in one direction, then stalk slowly, high-kneed, in another as if coming up on a sleeping lake from behind. From time to time he would stop and kick the heel of his boot backward into the dirt making a divot and telling Lucky, 'Don't lose that spot. That's a hotspot that spot.'

'Righto, Lucky.' Lucky would hustle to his ute and get an empty longneck or a car jack and stand it upright in the divot to mark the hotspot. Lucky was, at this stage, a convert, with all the convert's slavish determination to please his new priest.

Mid-afternoon Harry the Diviner leaned up against his truck mudguard, dramatically exhausted from feeling the earth's pulse, or calling forth the traces of hydraulic energy, or just from playing the lead role in a farce. He huffed and puffed to show this wasn't kid's play, this remorseless stalking of timid reservoirs, this drawing of treasure maps to riches of water.

There were about a dozen items taken from Lucky's ute standing in heel divots around his orchard by now. He'd hired a drill and an operator from Tatura and the man sat high in his seat and set about auguring down through the topsoil to the water. He'd drilled eight holes to his deepest reach while we looked on and he'd been unrewarded with even a smear of mud on his drill.

And it was like Dad had said it would be, only it took longer to get that way. By evening there were pyramids of drilled red clay across Lucky's orchard and the driller was shaking his head and Harry the Diviner was scratching his head and pouting his lips in a practised way and Lucky was leaning back with his hands on his hips looking at Harry the Diviner with a sneer on his lips. 'Harry the Diviner?' he asked out loud into the evening's redness. 'Harry the Fuckin' Bullshit Artist,' he answered.

This was the denouement of another Simson farce. A day splendidly spent. 'Righto, Ans,' Dad whispered to me. 'Into the car, we'd better go.'

\*　\*　\*

Adrenaline was the problem. Lucky read about it in what he called a scientific journal but was probably nothing more than the barstool musings of a retired plumber. 'Adrenaline's the problem, Lucky. By the time a beast has been trucked to the saleyards and then the abattoir and finally got the bolt between the eyes the bastard's been scared witless about eight times and had eight tides of adrenaline flush through its system. It's adrenaline that toughens the meat. Killing a beast unawares, Lucky . . . that's the secret. Take it from a distance, like a sniper. Dead before it knows it, Lucky. A gentle death equals tender meat.'

To get around the scourge of adrenaline Lucky had bought a steer and let it loose in his orchard to feed among the pears. He'd arranged the death and organised a local bloke who advertised himself on the cork pin-up board of the local pub as Jack the Butcher to dismember the beast. Whereupon Lucky would parcel out the steaks and snags and roasts to whoever bought into the scheme. Those of us lucky enough to be involved were going to have five-star beef at a quarter its usual cost. Dad bought into the scheme. Not, I think, for tender meat, as much as for an interesting Saturday. If so, he was the only one who got what he paid for.

We assembled on a Saturday morning. Dad and Guy and I drove out to Ardmona where we met Barrel, who had his man Donny with him. Donny hung around as a sort of vassal who would pick up things Barrel dropped or go back for things Barrel forgot or agree with things Barrel said or get on his back on liquid-hot bitumen to look under Barrel's jeep when Barrel asked, 'What's that ticking noise, Donny?' on a January day. Barrel was, in a small-town sense, grand, and needed a valet or gofer. Donny currently filled the role. His gofers didn't last long – he worked them hard and they were pretty soon disfigured in a semi-industrial accident or disenchanted in a semi-permanent way.

There were also a couple of dark-skinned Italians on hand who had some arrangement with Lucky to be at his beck and call when he becked or called. No one knew their names because Lucky just called them 'Lucky' when talking to them individually or 'the Arabs' when referring to them collectively.

Lucky was a crack shot but didn't generally waste his rarefied marksmanship on his own livestock. He handed the .22 to Guy. 'Go on, Lucky. Walk up close and hit him in that hollow right behind the ear. He'll drop like a bag of shit.'

We all heard the bullet ricochet off the beast's horn stump and go whining through the pear trees. The steer shook its head and blinked as if it had heard something entirely incomprehensible, high calculus or foul gossip. Guy cranked the bolt and let another shot go and it hit the beast right in its reservoir of adrenaline, I guess, and the stuff flooded out and made a supercow. The thing became a grey bawling blur. Lucky snatched the rifle from Guy and shot it twice more as it disappeared among the trees, but you can shoot a supercow with a .22 a lot of times before it takes off the cape and becomes a Clark Kent cow again.

Dad had seen a lot of this type of thing. It was as if Lucky's schemes were an endless train of idiocy and the engine had jumped the tracks in the fifties ensuring all the carriages would follow, one by one, down the years. 'I'm a bloody fool,' he said to no one. Then shouted, 'I'll be waiting in my car, Lucky.'

Lucky understood that Dad was weighted by the terrible millstone of the law around his neck. 'Right you are, Lucky,' he called back. There followed a confusing hunt through the orchard, the occasional crackle of gunfire and swearing in Italian and English. Eventually the Italians began to call to us. 'The Arabs've got him cornered, Lucky,' Lucky shouted. We closed in stealthily. The beast had been brought to bay in a corner of a paddock up against a barbed-wire fence alongside a service station owned by Lucky but leased by Arabs (Greeks, I think, in this case) right on the Midland Highway. It was bleeding like a machine-gunned water tank and drooling white strings of foam and staring our way white-eyed as a Biblical prophet. You couldn't have crammed any more adrenaline into the animal with a hypodermic needle and a fire pump.

One of Lucky's Arabs had the gun now and he bounced a round off the thing's skull that you could track across the highway by its whine as it intersected the cars filled with mums and dads driving their kids to Saturday cricket and netball. He fired again and missed the beast altogether and this round hit the side of a passing truck, which stilled my mind momentarily and made me blink and wonder if I should be back in the ute with Dad. I too, had a future to consider. Geelong Grammar. Serious, important people who would surely look askance at the random slaughter of motorists on my CV.

Barrel calmly slapped the gun out of the Arab's hands and observed, 'You're a dangerous little bastard, aren't you.' Lucky picked it up and let the scene settle. The steer stood huffing in its carapace of gore, all its run gone, the coup de grâce was coming, expected, needed.

Lucky brought the gun up as gracefully as a man with a heart rate of a hummingbird and a looming custodial sentence can, and I watched his finger whiten on the trigger . . . but now a buzz, rising, rising, a throb, rising still, tending to a roar . . . a Hell's Angel came east along the Midland Highway and swooped into the servo alongside the petrol pump with the kinetic swagger of a pro surfer. The roar of his Harley brought a black fear back to the steer's eyes and it took off again and Lucky blew a fuse. As the Angel shut his bike down and swung his leg to the ground Lucky ran at him hollering, waving his gun above his head. The man in leather paused – is that pot-bellied guy in shorts and gumboots yelling at me . . . shaking that rifle at me?

Lucky fired a shot that skipped across the concrete pan of the servo and punctured the air hose people used to inflate their tyres, making it a live and angry viper that whipped the biker viciously at crotch height hammering his testicles. With an armed, pot-bellied fruitcake running at him, and being flogged in the privates by a rubber hose with a mind of its own, the Angel leapt aboard his Harley and accelerated toward Shepparton with the hounds of Hell riding pillion. I guess in hindsight he justified this to himself as a tactical retreat, and I suppose he explained his bruised gonads and welt-covered cock as a symptom of some orgy of over-eager barmaids and horny strippers.

They found the beast dead back among the trees. Lucky stood over it swearing about Hell's Angels as if that criminal clique had been responsible for ruining a perfectly good plan. 'Lucky?' I asked him. 'Is all that red stuff blood or adrenaline? If it's adrenaline I think we might be okay. I think we might have drained the beast.'

'Get fucked, Lucky.' I was young. But he knew me.

No one held out hopes for the meat now. But Jack the Butcher came and collected the steer and butchered it. When he told Lucky the cost over the phone Lucky shouted at him, 'Jack the Butcher? Jack the Fucking Robber!' So none of us got to eat the meat. Because, who was going to eat foodstuffs supplied by a bloke you'd insulted? As if he wouldn't have rubbed our T-bones all over some orifice.

Our only compensation, and it lasted for years, was imagining Jack the Butcher and Little Jack the Butcher Kid and Jill the Butcher Wife and Joy the Toothless Butcher Mother in Law trying to chew that meat marinated in adrenaline and made into indestructible supercow sirloin.

When I was ten, somehow, there was a new sister. It was casually mentioned to me, as I sipped my evening pint of chocolate milk from a pint pot stolen by Dad from the King's Head and Eight Bells when he was practising law in London, that there was happy news and that the happy news was Mum was with child. She wasn't. She was with an amorphous little gatecrasher who knew no better than to break into a settled domesticity squealing like a piglet on a roller-coaster and monopolise the parental delight that had once been mine.

What were they thinking? Guy was seventeen and had finally been expelled from Geelong Grammar for dangling a friend from the clock tower so he could paint 'BEGGARS' BANQUET' on its side. The sign was mocking a party the Masters were planning. The hardest thing about that piece of student activism was, he later said, teaching Rankin, who was swinging from a condemned rope ninety feet in the air, where to put the apostrophe. Guy was born bristling anti-authoritarian impulses and had finished school early, unrepentant, with those impulses intact.

Debbie and Vicki were discovering and flexing womanly appetites. So they came and went from the best private schools regularly, suspended and expelled for this or that debauchery. Some mornings I'd bump into Dad down at Guyatt's Garage filling up the Fairlane in the middle of the day when he should have been at the office. 'Off to Geelong, Dad?'

'Yes.'

'Which one?'

'Vicki.'

'What for?'

'None of your business.'

'See you tonight, Dad.'

I'd spend the next week trying to get Vicki to tell me what she'd done to get sent home this time. My parents paid years of boarding school fees for girls who were upstairs listening to Suzi Quatro and painting their nails.

It was clear Debbie and Vicki's school days were coming to an end and that nothing could be expected of them afterward but the type of lazy criminality thought up while plastered on Blue Nun moselle and sucking Alpine cigarettes so hard they crackled like cellophane.

I hadn't even left the preparatory playground of Shepparton for the real world of Geelong Grammar and my siblings were all returning, spurned by the greater life. I was, of course, cut from far finer cloth than they. That is . . . I had an unassailable sense of my own importance that I hoped fine schools and Australia's best-bred children warranted.

But it was obvious to me the family was nearly done. Nearly over. Everyone had new interests and everyone was making plans to move on. Mum and Dad were at a frosty distance, arguments flaring. And Justina Gaye was born into this on an evening I was making ginger beer. I was known for my ginger beer. I brewed it once a month just to hear the profound 'Ahhs' and the heartfelt 'Oohhoohoos' Dad would give off after he walked home for lunch on a hot day and swallowed a mouthful of it. To see the way he held up the half-empty glass, turning it in his hand as if it were the signature elixir of some famed magician, was to know you had a place in the world. My ginger beer saved his life about once a week judging by the things he said in its praise.

Gran and Grampy were out from England so she could be on hand to help with the new child. I didn't see what help she could be. She hated children. But she was a good lawn mower. The old trout could take summer heat. Sit her on a rider mower and she'd travel round and round soaking up the Australian sun and sucking on Rothmans cigarettes as if it were a holiday treat akin to skiing the French Alps. You couldn't burn the woman. Our lawns were just rough paspalum and they didn't grow in summer. But they grew in her head, so she mowed them on our mower.

Dad came to me while I was bottling the latest batch of ginger beer and told me I had a new sister called Justina Gaye. It seemed a stupid name even then. The sort of thing a poof would yell if he was having sex when his doorbell rang.

273

'Hang on a mo, I'm just in a gay.' Everyone else in the family was allowed to go visit Mum and her new toy at hospital, but I was, at a venerable ten, deemed too young. I had to stay home with Grampy.

His stories of aerial combat against the Hun in his Sopwith Camel usually enthralled me. He was an actual Englishman who had flown against actual Germans in the First War and duelled with the Red Baron, a sneering Kraut assassin I'd wanted to get to grips with myself for some years. This night, perhaps sensing a special need, he let me run my fingertips across the scar on his forehead where a member of the Red Baron's Flying Circus had grazed him with a machine-gun bullet. 'Two flying machines,' he told me. 'Move either of them an inch in another direction . . . not only would I be dead . . . so would your mum . . . so would you and Guy and Debbie and Vicki . . .'

'And so would Justina Gaye,' I said while smiling.

A few days later they brought the thing home and sang its praises into whatever moment wasn't taken up with more immediate tasks; how beautiful she was, how lost we'd be without her, what a gift, what a wonder. I checked them with sneaky glances when they thought I wasn't watching, just to see if they were kidding. But they were deadly serious. They'd flipped. And this stuff went on for years. 'Isn't she a wonder, Ans?' 'Where would we be without her?' 'No' and 'Right here but twice as happy' were my silent answers to these questions.

The treachery of Tina's arrival broke a long and loving bond between my mother and me. We were never the same after. And she was not rewarded for turning her adoration to the new toy. The child turned out to be an ingrate. As I knew it would after only one month's acquaintance when, trying to cram a sherbet bomb into its mouth to stop it squealing during *Get Smart*, it choked and went blue out of spite and had to be rushed to the doctor. My decade-long reign as the apple-of-every-easily-fooled-adult's eye was over.

* * *

Before Geelong Grammar there was high school in Shepp. With Tina a baby on her hip, Mum took me down the street to Lunn and Fordyce Menswear to buy a new school uniform and, most portentously, to try on long pants as part of that uniform. Long pants for the first time. The light mufti of childhood was being shucked off and I was donning the solemn, pleated tailorings of manhood. Long, grey slacks. Say goodbye to scabbed knees and other scars of the warrior. Say a happy goodbye to startled people staring at my inordinately skinny legs.

The school was huge. You couldn't know everyone. There were forbidden corridors and off-limits rooms, laboratories and gymnasia. In cul-de-sacs and forgotten triangles of space there were pimpled teens from surrounding towns smoking cigarettes and heavy-lidded long-hairs choofing dope. The school's oldest students were adults. The males wore beards and rock 'n' roll hair and baggy jeans, the females were as hipped and made-up as real women, wearing baggies and bangles.

You didn't confine your learning to one room here. Every hour, at the sound of a bell, classes fractured and the students dashed in monochromatic white and grey to other classes that studied specialised subjects. A bell would ring and off you'd hustle to Mlle Michailovich. This tactile young woman with a dark European face and rich brown eyes and full lips made me fall briefly in love by wantonly uttering patient reiterations of 'Un, deux, trois . . .' and speaking much other equally sex-laden French. But then, it wasn't uncommon for me to believe a young female teacher was in love with me, only held back from a whispered declaration and a kiss by strings of propriety pulled by heartless goons in the Education Department.

A second bell and you'd cross the campus for maths, into a portable classroom where enfilading sunlight made it impossible for the innumerate to hide. Mrs Cooney was Methuselah with a vagina. Presumably. A hag born of Dahl. Bent and warlike and known to be around at the invention of mathematics. There was a rumour Pythagoras had taken her virginity while she screamed the value of pi to the three hundredth decimal place. I started it.

She clearly hated the young, and took delight in maths as an instrument of legal torture with which she could gouge and scald them. And was particularly tickled by my excruciations with numbers.

I saw quickly that any mathematical solution was only a platform onto which she could unload another, more iniquitous problem . . . infinitely. Thus triumph was not only short lived and Sisyphean, the mathematical rock you had to push up the hill got bigger, more irredeemably foreign, each time. Mrs Cooney surveyed the class for a bamboozled face hungrily, the way a lioness eyes a flock of wildebeest for a gammy leg.

She lit on mine. 'Cameron, what is the square root of sixty-four?'

'Oh, Mrs Cooney, don't ask what is the square root of sixty-four. Better to ask, "Why is there a square root of sixty-four?" Why invent that type of root and then seek to know what it is for sixty-four? Why make such trouble? Why, Mrs Cooney? Why? Why?'

'You foul-minded little twerp. Haven't we just spent the last week learning square roots?'

'Again, Mrs Cooney, the clear thinker, the fair and reasonable citizen, wants to know why.'

'Answer my question or you'll have detention.'

Stowey, whose mind was mush in all other fields, was strangely mathematical. He was holding up eight surreptitious fingers. 'Eight,' I said.

'And what is eight squared?' She leaned toward me, her whiskery mouth gaping like a Venus flytrap threatening to clamp my head. Stowey wasn't showing any digits. He didn't have (I've since Googled the answer) sixty-four of anything.

'Eight squared, Mrs Cooney? But this is another question of the square-root type I've counselled you against. The fair and reasonable . . .'

'Five seconds to answer or you will complete chapter three of *Springer-Verlag on Mathematics* by start of class tomorrow.'

'Am I allowed to get it wrong? Is trying, sort of, like, nearly as good as being right?'

'This is mathematics, not some history written by victors. Two seconds.'

'Eight.' The laughter was pretty widespread. Rob Godden fell out of his desk.

'Are you telling the class your answer to eight squared is eight?'

'No. Not anymore. Fifteen.' More laughter.

'You are the stupidest student I've ever had in my class. And I taught your brother Guy and both your sisters.'

'Hey! Mrs Cooney, you can't say I'm stupider than Vicki.'

\* \* \*

The bell again and I ran for Mr Maynard's Australian history class. Mr Maynard knew less of Australian history than I did, but for some mysterious reason that may have approximated compassion, I couldn't press home this advantage.

He was a large man with short back and sides and a slow military bearing that would have made him a general in any war fought among sloths. He made me think of Big Bad John, a character in a song of the time who, at the cost of his own life, held up a collapsing mine so all his workmates could escape. This seemed to me the most likely way Mr Maynard would make good. Certainly his teaching of history wasn't going to get ballads composed in his honour. He talked with laboured precision, making a terrible, visible effort to keep grammatical error and mispronunciation at bay. He went red with the speed and predictability of a traffic light, and could be embarrassed, sidetracked, confused and flummoxed by even the least gifted reprobate.

His conception of Australian history was that the real fun began when Irish bushrangers took to gunning down cops from behind rocks. While he was giving us a lesson on the Kelly gang's shootout at Glenrowan, Sandy McCormack, a girl of lean Arabic beauty, asked him how Ned Kelly took a piss while wearing his armour. Mr Maynard blushed and turned away and wrapped his great shoulders around himself (oh, for a collapsing mine to hold up at this moment) and said huskily that that sort of thing wasn't history. Ned Kelly's toilet habits. That sort of thing wasn't anything to talk of in class and probably he walked off behind a tree and kept the procedure private like a man of dignity naturally would, and not even Dan Kelly or Steve Hart or Joe Byrne knew the true answer to that question and it was lost in the mists of time and he didn't want to hear any more about it and, gosh, the relevant thing about Ned Kelly was the injustices visited upon him by malicious English coppers for his Fenian pride and the crimes he understandably committed as a result of these injustices. Not . . . not the urinary problems that assailed a man decked out in amateur armour. He said all of this with his back to us because of the unmanly redness of his face.

I felt an unsettling compassion for Mr Maynard and decided I wasn't going to make his teaching life harder than it had to be. But other, less gifted anarchists stepped into the breach. Kids who were usually too afraid to speak to a teacher began to riff on him and backchat him. Stutterers and shy boys and goody-goodies began to heckle like inbred dukes at a puppy hunt. Front-of-class smilers who didn't know a joke from a fence lizard began to make him the butt of malformed, clichéd humour.

He was the red-faced bull's-eye of the mangiest jokes ever composed. Occasionally, as the class laughed and honked, Mr Maynard would give off a whimper of despair like a brontosaurus who'd cottoned on to the coming troubles.

Danny Caccavo was an uncool kid with a stutter, the blunt-minded son of a sharp Italian entrepreneur. A victim of much derision, he had finally, happily, found a victim for some derision of his own. His special subject was Mr Maynard's clothes. 'Mr Maynard, why are you wearing a yellow shirt? Only par . . . par . . . poofs wear yar . . .yar . . . yellow shirts.'

Poofter, poof, homo, this was our catch-all insult. If a kid showed timidity, weakness, hesitation, style, obedience, compassion, thoughtfulness or difference, he would be accused of, and taunted with, being a poof. A homosexual. The most venal ghoul in the whole cast of adulthood.

None of us knew a poofter; at least, none that were admitting to it. And none of us knew anything about them. Apart from their thoroughly deserved contaminated status. Which was a truth handed down to us and enhanced by us.

I secretly dreaded that I might have had the rank acorn of poofterism growing in me. I think we all feared this. How did one know? How did it show itself? Adults had recently told us that appetites were forming in us. Intense lusts and desires would soon be the elevator music that attended our maturation. What if these appetites zeroed in on another boy? How could you stop this? I didn't want to die. But you would surely have to kill yourself if you found you were a poofter.

For those that did detect that acorn of poofterism within, the blind hatred that was abroad for their true, unrevealed selves must have been a staccato torment. Because the accusation that someone was a poof was never more than a few minutes in the past or future at high school. Often as a careless jibe to a mate; less frequently, but more seriously, as an accusation to any effete or silent student. A gay kid at school would have been amazed to witness the terrible, inexorable metamorphosis of himself from a normal boy into a fiend over a few appalling years of puberty, such was the way we made our world.

So Cacca went at Mr Maynard with claims of poofterism. 'Mr Mar . . . Mar . . . Maynard, only par . . . par . . . poofs wear cardigans.' The jibes were always this light and pointless and a normal man would have been unaffected, but Mr Maynard had to blush and shuffle and roll his head this way and that in embarrassment and straighten creases from whatever article of clothing had been maligned as if to make that rag a little less reprehensible. Whenever Cacca publicly tagged an article of clothing as poofy, Mr Maynard presumably stowed it away in his wardrobe, because it never reappeared. By spring the big man was running out of shirts, ties and patience.

It was September, pollen in the air and Mr Maynard in long white socks and tight shorts. After two terms of being shot with blanks by tongue-tied teens the man was edgy and barely spoke in class anymore. He was stabbing at the blackboard with a stick of chalk, perpetrating there a calligraphy exclusive to epileptic giants, when Cacca launched his latest bar . . . bar... bon mot. 'Mr Maynard, only par . . . par . . . poofs wear war . . . war . . . white socks.' Our history teacher stepped slowly backward in among the desks and slapped Cacca on the side of the head and the class dropped from its habitual rude hubbub into silence.

My first feeling was regret that a great opportunity had been missed. It wasn't a man-killing blow, but it was going to bring the man down as surely as if he'd clubbed that pock-marked stutterer with a haymaker mid 'par . . . par . . . poof'.

And if this slow-moving giant had to go down I wished he'd gone down popping the kid's eardrum or blacking his eye.

Mr Maynard was the lion that, after endless taunting by its tamer, had taken a desultory swipe at him and pulled a golden thread from his brocaded jacket. This momentary lapse implied a larger, perhaps man-eating, appetite. Mr Maynard could no longer be in the circus.

He knew it too. He turned from us toward the blackboard and lay his chalk in the gutter that ran beneath it and without looking at us waved an apology, a goodbye, and walked from the room while Cacca stuttered about just who his father was and attempted, through his elocutionary jam, to describe the vengeance his father was going to bring down on the man. 'He'll kar . . . kar . . . He'll abs . . . abs . . . He'll fir . . . fir . . . fix you, you dog.'

We never saw Mr Maynard again. I hope he went on to a long career holding up collapsing mines for his comrades.

\* \* \*

That year we moved out of town to Kialla. Our house in Talinga Crescent, a castle when I was young, had shrunk and become shabby and my parents' marriage seemed to have gone stale and cantankerous in it. Or, perhaps, with the passing years I was becoming more observant. Though I doubt I could have missed a whole Cold War as a toddler.

In those days all professional couples aspired to build their own house. Lots of Mum and Dad's friends had done it. So Dad, dressed in his suit and gumboots, wandered around a straw-grass paddock on the riverbank a few kilometres out of town, looking at it from every angle. It had once been part of a dairy farm. I wasn't at all sure about living out here. How was I going to see my mates? There were no shops. No neighbours to spy on and vandalise and run secret missions and incursions against. A Blue Heaven milkshake was a three-mile bike ride away.

They built a tan-brick house with three wings carpeted in 1970s shag pile. Five acres of lawn that ended in a cliff that dropped to our own stretch of river. All around was bush. No blue heaven, but it was Eden and I was a hunter. I threw away my clothes and became a native. Stowey and, later, Sherm, and I wandered around in footy knicks carrying air rifles or bows, endlessly hunting snakes, hares, foxes, cats, rabbits, ducks and carp. I had a dinghy and when the river flooded we'd row out into the forest and hunt the snakes that were curled in trees. Enormous logs would come washing down from the hills and we'd strip off and ride them like submerged hippos for miles, walking back through the forest.

There was a wreck house on the outside of the river bend upstream from our new place. It was rumoured that Old Shaw had trip-wired the windows with loaded shotguns. He had put up hand-painted signs that read: 'TRESPASSERS SHOT. HOUSE BOOBY TRAPPED'. One Sunday when no other game was on offer Stowey and I shot out every window in the place. It took some doing, snipping off every fang of glass shot by shot. The bikies were blamed. The local cops somehow figured a bunch of Hell's Angels came out from town and spent a day prone in devil's heads laying siege to a deserted house. I think Dad implicated the bikies to throw the cops off the scent.

Flaring out west of the wreck house was a field of rusting junk. Car bodies and stock troughs and coils of wire and engine blocks and truck carcasses and ploughs and graders and sheets of iron and Ferguson tractors and horse-drawn buggies fallen to pieces and a Sunshine harvester and Furphy carts and swingletrees and drums marked with skull and bones, and water tanks holed by rifle fire and a mangle and the brightly silver innards of some freshly dead dairy.

I used to go there and sit in cars and trucks from my grandparents' time that had brittle leather seats through which springs erupted. Places small and private enough that they could be the world entire. Soon enough I would be a Great Train Robber on the run. Or I would grip the steering wheel of a ghost-Holden and become an air ace gunning for Krauts and Nips. I sometimes went there to get out of mowing the lawns and I sometimes went there to be Tsar of all Russia. And sometimes I just went there to be away. To be unfindable. The only boy left in a world that had died. To explore the goose bumps and haunted, hollow feeling of being deeply alone.

A Saturday, and I was zigzagging through Old Shaw's field of rotting machinery. I thought today I would be Tsar Nicholas II with Bolsheviks closing in. But I was stopped by the groan of a car door. I hunkered behind a little grey Fergie and watched as Robbie Brand stepped out of a car carcass and stretched his arms high, then opened his jeans and pissed rubbing his fingers on his face and combing them through his long hair. Emptied, he shook off the drops and zipped up and climbed back into the car and yanked the door closed and collapsed from view. It was like Keith Richards had come tumbling among the Corn Flakes into my bowl.

Robbie Brand, maybe nineteen years old, and the devil elect of every adult in town. He was the lead singer of a locally famed band. It was said he went shirtless on stage and became mesmerised by his own songs, locked in a shut-eyed trance with his head juddering and knees shaking. It was obvious to the adults there was some blue demon pulling the strings on this cat. Teenage girls who dreamed of throwing themselves from Parisian bridges screamed for Robbie Brand to point the way.

And here he was sleeping out in Old Shaw's field of junk. Whether he had taken up residence here because he was in flight from the law, or he had read in *Rolling Stone* that Roger Daltrey had spent six months sleeping in a Humber before The Who hit big, I can't say. Maybe some father of some screaming teeny-bopper who had subscribed to a bi-weekly delivery of Robbie's brilliant seed had vowed to make him pay. I climbed a red gum and watched the car, waiting for him to resurface.

Late afternoon a thin girl with long sandy hair wandered the dirt road from town wearing the unbuttoned shirt and tight jeans of a fan. She picked her way through Old Shaw's rust-brown field of extinct wonders and tapped her knuckles on the roof of the car carcass and Robbie Brand groaned the door open and got out shaking his head at her like she was a wonder too strong for easy thoughts and he took hold of her and they leaned against the car, their bodies pressing hard at one another, and they kissed while I said out loud, 'Wh-what now? Man, what now?' He broke from kissing and swept a chivalrous hand to the back seat and she climbed in and he climbed in overtop her and the split windscreen through which I watched flared yellow with setting sun.

I climbed down from my tree and crept forward through the dead machines and hid behind stacked spools of wire. Close enough to hear her urging a favourite to the post while Robbie Brand re-enacted the terrible sonics of a digger charging a Japanese trench. It had the ring of sacrilege to me. It sounded like noble soldierly energies being squandered on a low act. Him roaring fit to slay a Japanese with a bayonet . . . while smooching a girl. It made my heart sink. And soar.

After, when it was dark, they lit a fire beside the car and sat on blocks of wood naked holding each other, smoking, the flames orange on the car's rust and sparking on its chrome scraps. Downriver I could hear Dad calling me for dinner. The girl leaned on Robbie Brand and he kissed her flaming breasts at their tip. Just one kiss each. And I got no dinner but I got a vision to keep forever.

Such were the rewards of the private and abandoned places of our valley for a boy who crept around alone like a small Attenborough. We didn't have any TV that even tried to make sense of life. But we had this stuff everywhere. Homes were small and generations crammed together. Privacy was found out here in the bush, out here in these fields of broken things. People played out their ecstasies and treacheries amid rust and thistle while I slit my eyes and cocked my ears and tried to figure out what it all meant.

\* \* \*

By high school the blackfellas had vanished. They wouldn't be needing a tertiary education, so they'd gone to the tech schools to get fitted out with manual skills that might lead to apprenticeships in trades, if the other life didn't pull them down, as it was likely to do. Race came at high school. From above. From without. From within. From our widening consciousness, and our intensifying sensitivity to difference. Suddenly we were no longer an array of individuals, known for our wisecracking, or skill at pinball, or ability at concocting excuses, or our long blonde hair or pretty eyes or kindness or throwing arm. We were now just as much not something as we were something. We were not wogs. And we took this as a damned lucky escape.

Eighty per cent of the boys in my year were unaffected by the need to revel in their racial superiority and declare the tattered humanity of others. Two gangs formed from the remaining twenty per cent. The gang I belonged to was made up of the white and latterly successful imperialist races of the British Isles. We were workaday boreal blends of Scot, Celt and Anglo-Saxon.

It was our fathers who had first discovered Australia and tidied up a messy indigenous scene that was going nowhere. Our folk had built this place and we felt this should be frequently acknowledged. This place, Shepparton, was ours. And not just this place. Being adrift in historical ignorance made us easy owners of all the world, as it tends to for every grass-skirt tribe whittling sticks to spears.

The other gang was made up of Turks, Albanians, Greeks, Italians and even Russians. But really, why fidget with gradations of ignominy? They were just wogs. Chocolate frogs, dagos, wops, spaghetti-munchers.

Wogs were a type of freeloader who had latterly arrived to ride the gravy train now that the heavy lifting and frontier unpleasantness was done. Wogs were, in one sense, like poofters; in that we didn't know much about them, hadn't been to their homes, tasted their cuisines, talked to their parents, or kissed their sisters, so our ignorance enabled an unexaminable and almost flawless bigotry. Even Elvis was a wog, and I despised his greasy smugness beyond words.

The wogs called us 'skips'. A shortening of the name 'Skippy', a marsupial version of Rin Tin Tin then kicking baddies around on TV. When I found out they called us this I was outraged. Not at being likened to a serially heroic marsupial. Skippy was okay – smart, wry, able to keep a secret. It was the fact they had a name for us at all. We weren't some subset of humanity. We were the real, plain, proper people that humanity aspired to be. Others had to be categorised. Not us. We were normal.

Our loathing for wogs was made easy by us knowing nothing of the Classical world – of Ancient Greece or Rome, the Renaissance, or the Ottoman Empire. Because . . . these would have taken no little explaining away. But we would have done it. No one in our gang was prone to admire sculpture or theatre or art or architecture or democracy, so they could have been demolished as achievements if we'd known of them.

Wogs were from a clueless rural peasantry, never enlightened by the modernity of close, acrid suburbs born of an industrial revolution, as our people had been. Our people had lived in and fled fetid northern cities and thus loved the bush. Their people had lived in and fled rural vassalage under dukes, raising crops and herding goats, thus they took comfort in the novelty of suburbia and the futuristic promise of concrete. Green concrete as often as not.

As with the Sioux and the Apache, occasionally two warriors were chosen to represent the tribe at war and thereby save the tribe from war. So, each week nestled in the valleys between the furthest portable classrooms that stood empty and shattered, resembling the abandoned barracks of a defeated army, a wog fought a skip. Stowey took on the statuesque Nik Nostromo, and punched holes in him. Hearts, the leader of our gang, stocky and as muscled as a working man, especially fearsome because one of his eyes was sewn permanently shut, fought a disappointing draw with their boor-faced leader Camel (Kemal, I realised in later years). Rob Godden fought a small and, when unburdened by the obligations of race war, friendly Italian named Varapodio who wore a bullet around his neck on a leather thong. (And who, upon reaching full maturity, would go to jail for shooting a man in a cheese heist. Yes. Cheese. Mozzarella, parmesan and gorgonzola.) Rob's long hair flew like a lead guitarist on a psychedelic solo as he leapt and kneed that kid.

Then it came my turn to fight a dark and wordless wog named Ludo. Ludo was a dull-eyed pouter, in every bottom set and at the bottom of every bottom set. Seemingly scared of speech for its ability to unravel and leave him surrounded and swarmed over by a lot of half-sentences and random words. His silence, and the fact he ticked, gave him the air of a time bomb. His tic was facial, his right cheek leapt every thirty seconds, pulling his mouth corner into the subliminal suggestion of a smirk.

He came up to me at the bus stop after school where I was waiting with Bill Kuszcniacuk, a giant Russian, above all the racial argy-bargy and a member of no gang. Ludo's shirt was hanging out and his shoes unlaced, this scruffi-ness a blatant ad for the rebellious state of his mind. He was flanked by a couple of lesser wogs, Frankie Camarro and Joe Maloni, comedians not warriors, urgers and enablers of ticking malcontents.

He spat at my feet. 'I'm pickin' you.' I was alone, with no gang member in support, and suddenly frightened. Hundreds of kids were milling about here, waiting for buses, talking to girls, shouting to one another, jostling and laughing. This would be a massive audience. To fight and get beaten here would be an indelible stain on me and on my gang. To fight and be trounced. To fight and lose one's nerve and surrender. To fight badly and be thought a coward. To look ungainly, to make noises like a girl, to not live up to one's reputa-tion . . . Here was the possibility of a massive come down.

To refuse to fight was a more contained cowardice. Only those close by would bear witness. 'I don't want to fight. I'll miss my bus.' I threw this last in hoping it sounded a legiti-mate, even urgent, consideration. This dumbfounded Ludo, but, then, everything dumbfounded Ludo. He shook his head and stepped closer and poked a fist into my chest. 'I'm pickin' you.' I told myself he was a beast too dumb to know fear, or pain, and was beyond humiliation. I had everything to lose and he had nothing.

'I don't want to fight.'

'Fuck that.' He pushed me.

Bill Kuszcniacuk was, at thirteen, about the size of a VFL centre-half forward. He was affronted by this intrusion into his space. I had been quietly talking to him. He put his massive head up into Ludo's face and said, 'We're waiting for a bus here. Piss off.' You couldn't argue with that. Kuza would just pick you up and break bones. So Ludo backed off, promising to get me later, his sidekicks calling me a poof and a chicken and a sheila.

It was a long bus ride home. I'd done a shameful thing. A big moment had come and my warrior's heart had flipped and flopped as bewildered and panicked as a carp on a pier. The sudden gravity of Ludo's challenge had stripped me bare, there were no smart words, no will to fight, it had found me a coward, one of the quiet boys I preyed on, stole from, laughed at. Refusing to fight – that was an option for the boys who weren't in the gangs, not for us. What would happen when Hearts heard? Or Stowey, who couldn't consider not fighting when the chance came.

My reputation as a fighter was mostly undeserved, mostly bluff, made from my being able to talk shrewdly into the confusion all boys felt when violence was in the air. But this day even talk had deserted me. I didn't thank Kuza. When he got off the bus I felt less ashamed. But I knew this was all coming back to me, amplified in rumour and retelling, tomorrow.

When I got home I stripped down to my footy knicks and called Bindi, our terrier, and got in my dinghy and rowed downstream to a sand island and walked around alone thinking about what had just happened, who I was, and wondering what other horrors as well as cowardice lay inside me.

My reckoning of the shame grew greater and greater. The collective honour of Aussies had been defiled. It was as if I'd taken a tyre lever to the town cenotaph and smashed the brim of that marble digger's slouch hat. Over the next half hour I resolved to make this right. Tomorrow morning before school I would pick Ludo. The declaration of war would be mine. The pacifism of yesterday obliterated by my loud hostile challenges. Alone, the smell of our muddy river in my nostrils, I began to shadow-box. On my toes in the sand, throwing punches, skipping forward, left and right, kicking at air, bobbing and weaving. This wog was going to get a serious belting.

I would have to be at school early so news of the actual fight subsumed the shameful rumours of my refusal to fight. I would pick him as soon as he came through the school gate. I began to compose lines with which to call him out.

I was so ashamed I fought that fight all night. I whispered out loud in my half sleep, 'Come on, Ludo, you poofter wog fuckhead, let's go.' I was scared of losing . . . getting hurt. But even a loss was a win from the ground I now occupied. A loss at least rewrote my refusal to fight. A loss, if it had to be, was better than what I had now.

All night I fought. And despite making demands on my imagination, laying down rules and making threats to that black-toothed Lord Haw Haw that lived autonomously in my head, I lost as many times as I won.

Ludo came in on the bus from the small, post-war wog orchards to the east of town. As he stepped down I pushed off the school fence and shouted, 'Come on, you wog fuckstick. Let's go.' Sirens and war cries had been sounding in my head as I watched the bus drive toward me. I was at the adrenal pitch required for cannon fodder. There were plenty of other kids around, but of his mates only Frankie Camarro, a soft boy, a second-rate jester, worthless at war. Beside me Stowey smiled at Frankie, knowing if hostilities became general he would have one of those easy, show-boating victories that might enhance your reputation as a stylist.

As I stepped to him, yelling, surprise lit Ludo's habitually impassive face, and became shock, and maybe fear. 'Come on, fuckhead,' I shouted. He wouldn't raise his hands so I pushed him. Where was the coward of yesterday afternoon? My fists were up, ready to go.

'I don't want to fight.' He said it as if mistakenly giving speech to a mystifying thought.

'Pig's arse. Put 'em up, wog.'

'No. Piss off.' He shook his head, eyes down.

'He doesn't want to fight,' Frankie Camarro said. 'Leave him alone.' Seeing Ludo frightened and unwilling to fight made me a beast. 'You wog coward.' I slammed the heels of my hands into his chest. 'Poof won't fight,' I yelled to whoever might hear. Other, older boys got involved, pulled me away, while I strained to get at him. They told me to forget about it, you can't hit a wog who won't fight.

Were we back on equal terms? Had my cowardice been expunged by his? What happened to him, anyway? How could a kid be a serious goon one day and a chicken the next? He was weird.

At morning recess I received Ludo's challenge to fight, delivered by Camel. Ludo will fight you at lunchtime in the changing room. It seemed now that the shock of my ambush had worn off, and he had presumably trod the same path of shame and renewal as I had. He was ready to go.

Between recess and lunch, during Mrs Swaby's science class as we built potash volcanoes, I began to contemplate the downside again. Beating Ludo would profit me nothing. He was just the sort of troll who came wandering out of a forest in movies to commit gigantic vandalism. But he wasn't their famed warrior. The profit/loss balance wasn't right here. The risk/reward ratio stunk highly. To beat up a troll was no more than expected of me, and wouldn't lead on to fame. To be beaten up by a troll was a disgrace. If a protagonist is only ever as mighty as the antagonist he defeats, then I deserved a better adversary than Ludo, the very killing of whom might leave me a reputation as a hammer of dimwits. I couldn't see much possibility for enhancement of my status in fighting him.

But Ludo was what I had. So we fought in the changing room at the end of the male toilet at lunchtime. A small room, impenetrable to teachers when a fight was on, only one way in or out, choked off by jostling spectators, wogs and skips yelling a muddy brew of advice and abuse. We circled and threw punches. When I got hit sweetly, heard the crunch and saw the flash of light, I'd hang on to him, waiting for the world to come again, which it always did – the cheering came back first, then the exhaustion and maelstrom of thought. Sometimes I'd land a perfect punch on his head and he'd hang on to me while I tried to throw him off and work on him in his darkness. We circled around and swayed in front of each other in episodic consciousness sucking for breath and seeking an end.

When I took a punch and didn't fall it was because of guts and bravery. When I clocked him one and he stayed standing it was the Cro-Magnon brow, the dumb mulishness typical of a wog, bred like a beast of burden to take a beating, and not really an animal an Aussie should be fighting as much as shepherding through life with a bullwhip.

The baying of the crowd eventually brought teachers, who began to wrestle their way through the wall of fight fans. By the time they'd made it into the room it was a ruck of boys and Ludo and I hung our heads to hide our bloodied mouths and held our torn shirts closed. Someone had been fighting but they knew not who. Get out. Get out of here, you animals.

Outside in the breezeway, me doing a post-mortem with Stowey, Godden and Hearts, discussing missed opportunities and fine blows, Ludo came to me, stood outside our little circle until we noticed him and the talk stopped.

'What?' Hearts asked. 'Fuck do you want?'

He stepped to me and held out his hand. I took it and we shook. 'You fought good. You hurt me. I thought you would, and you did.'

'Thanks. You did too. You got me a good one. So ... yeah ... see you round.' I felt a moment of dizzying empathy for Ludo. With this fight we had freed each other from combat for a while. We shook hands. Hate was easily known. It was the rare moments of compatibility, even fraternity, that were truly confusing.

\* \* \*

The most bewildering rebuttal of the racial inferiority of wogs was the way desire flitted between our various ethnicities. I guess the problem, in a nutshell, was the loveliness of Italian girls. Wallster had an Italian girlfriend we nicknamed the Italian Job. She was a couple of years older than us. She would drift down from the senior areas of school, shyly, silently, to hang out with him, a short way from our gang. And if I have a vision of her batting her lashes as she looked at me over her shoulder, then that is the sort of fleeting, flirting presence she had, or the sort of hex-amore I was under. Cinnamon skin and brown eyes – she was a far-fetched beauty from the fairy tales and romances. Here was a reason to be a man. Here was a reason to fight wars and compose poems. Here was purpose beyond any other.

She was never mine. I was never hers. We were never a thing. There was never anything near so serious as one of those blurted contracts where you asked a girl to 'go with' you and she says, yeah, all right. She was Wallster's girl. But she flirted with me for a week or so, doubtless detecting my infatuation, thinking it cute, and feeding it a little, and walking it a little, and stroking it now and then with a wink or a blown kiss or a glimpse of bra strap. She ran her fingertips along my forearm once, held my chin between her fingers. To meet her gaze, and then to see her smile, set off a deep blue yearning in me.

It is strange to think of her now, as a man in my fifties, and feel an echo of the longing her beauty wrought in me, the billowing wonder at the thought of kissing her, and to realise I am thinking of a girl of, perhaps, fourteen. I must conclude that the boy of thirteen still lives in the man, quietly, unobtrusively, but ready always to honour the adumbration of that lovely girl. And that many differently aged iterations of self live on in the mind, the younger inside the older, like babushka dolls, each waiting their moment to salute a ghost as real as the Italian Job.

* * *

The teen society that was forming at high school began to break free of the campus and assert itself around town. We began to socialise, to sit with friends in parks and talk of songs, and to meet girls in shops and reveal who was keen on who. We played emissary for one another on little expeditions of romance. Kerryn told me she'd say yes if Goddo asked her. Goddo told me he'd probably ask her if he knew she'd say yes. Such laconic oil enabled Shepparton's young love to run smoothly.

When cafe society came to our town I embraced it as a new and exciting way to do nothing. I had mastered all previous methods, and was ready for this one. Sitting and talking while the latest pop tunes were disparaged by the cappuccino machine clearing its throat was suddenly an essential and meaningful pastime. It was ace to hang out. Other people, especially girls, had become exciting. We'd cram into a booth: Wallster, Hearts, Stowey, me, Sharon S, the Italian Job. And if I timed my entry right I might sit next to the Italian Job. In constant dance with those cinnamon eyes I couldn't look at and couldn't not look at. Inhaling the scent of her hair and ogling her olive skin surreptitiously. My thigh or forearm grazing hers set the rhino of adoration charging at the cage of my ribs and a mishmash of Dobie Gillis' many romantic soliloquies looped through my brain, jamming my syntax, purging my witticisms and making me the cafe cretin.

Everyone was in love, or they would have surely noticed I was in love. We had discovered a new capacity for romantic love, and like a new song, you would play it for a special someone to dig . . . and if they didn't dig it you'd play it to someone else tomorrow.

At the end of each booth was a wall-mounted jukebox. We'd flip through the hundreds of songs. 'Not "Goodbye to Jane", I'm sick of Slade.' 'Fuck Skyhooks, they're weird. Probly poofs.' Drop in your coin and press 3H, Gary Glitter. 'Do You Wanna Touch Me?' Gary Glitter wasn't a poof. No way. Not dressed in skin-tight spangle-suits and encased in make-up. We boys vamped along to the song's lyrics, happy to be given licence to chant lewd suggestions at girls as if we were just singers and not boys who wanted to actually do the things the singers were singing about: 'Do you wanna touch me there hair . . . yairhair?'

When the cappuccinos landed Sharon S would pull out the letter, moist from being tucked in her bra for safekeeping from the covetous moles round town who'd make off with it if they could. We'd been waiting for it while sipping our cappuccinos, wrestles breaking out among the boys as we swooped on our neighbours' choc-dusted froth with our teaspoons.

We'd heard the letter read before. But the thing was like a radio signal from an alien civilisation: its contents weren't so amazing as the very fact it existed. A higher, more advanced, life form had contacted Sharon S.

She held it close to her face and sniffed it and her eyes fluttered as if at some mind-altering myrrh from the frontier of cool. She would wait, inhaling, eyes fluttering, its magical presence killing off the banter until we were silent.

Slowly she'd open it, looking around at the other booths to see they were watching. They always were. Most of them had come here for the reading of the famous epistle from St Bon.

'Shazza, howzit, honey?' Or something like that. We listened hard, trying to glean more meaning from its words than was in them. The letter was flowery, gentle. It read like it was written by a thirteen-year-old C-grade English student who'd just worked her way through a foot-high stack of romance comics. Bon was bewitched by the light in Shazza's eyes. He was haunted by her fragrance. This was an unsettling communication from the leering frontman of Beelzebub's house band. I tried to imagine Bon Scott bewitched, haunted. The vision kept dissolving as he humped a microphone stand with his gourd of denim and waggled his tongue at the camera.

Sharon wasn't much to look at. But then, no girl was much to look at alongside the Italian Job. The Italian Job must have been a tough bestie to have at that skin-deep age. Luckily, miraculously, Sharon was the girl Bon Scott had written to. This gave her a wondrous allure you could neither demean nor deny. The girl was a hall-of-fame groupie, our own Helen of Shepp. And an AC/DC tour was headed our way.

The night of the concert we met to smoke beforehand among the rose bushes of Queen's Park across the road from the Civic Centre. The Italian Job wasn't there. Italian girls vanished at sundown and you fed them wild lies of the night next day. I wore beater boots and borrowed a sharpie cardigan. A boy soldier. Sharon was going to get us backstage. Sharon was going to introduce us to Bon. Where the hell was

Sharon? Sharon didn't show. AC/DC were brutal and we didn't understand what was being attempted, though we said we got it, loved it, wanted more.

Sharon had been laid low by a twenty-four-hour wog. A few days later when we assembled in our cafe she pulled the famous letter from her bra, sniffed it and fluttered her eyelids, waiting for silence. But it didn't bring silence now. We talked louder, faster, cracked jokes, flirted with the Italian Job, bewitched by the light in her eyes, haunted by her fragrance.

Despite no silence, despite what this meant, Sharon began reading. In a quavering zombie monotone she couldn't be stopped with a silver bullet or a stake through her heart. If she stopped reading before Bon told her he loved her and they'd catch up soon, then the show was dead. She kept reading until Hearts said to her, 'Shut up, Shaz. That letter's from you to you.' She stopped reading, folded the letter and put it away. She began to cry and jumped up from our booth and went to an empty one down the back, and sat by herself. We all felt bad. The Italian Job followed her, and put her arm around her, and I suppose that was just about the last thing she needed.

\*   \*   \*

I was swimming in Lucky Simson's pool the day Holt drowned. I remember that because I nearly drowned myself and had to be fished out by Dad, who spilt his beer saving me and made an observation in the form of a joke and sometimes just in the form of an observation that he didn't know if it was worth it or not. Holt drowned the day I didn't; that's all

I knew of politics. It was in woodwork class eight years and four PMs later that politics really broke on us.

I wasn't great at woodwork. If Frank Thring and I had each made a nut bowl and you were asked to choose one to take home for your mother you'd probably have chosen his. Our woodwork teacher, Mr Exeter, was a lanky member of the counterculture. A tottering hair ball conscripted annually to scamper along at the front of the school Easter pageant up a skate-ramp Calvary Hill with a papier-mâché cross over his shoulder while teenage Roman guards whanged away at him with binder-twine whips and he hissed, 'Guys, you're not really centurions. I'm not really Jesus. Hey. Hey. Go easy.'

He was a big-hearted hippy. There was constant speculation among us boys as to what variety of gore would be served up if he got his long beard or hair caught in the lathe. A schism developed in our woodwork class over this. One sect (we'll call them Cameronians) reckoned his flaccid face, still speaking of wood grain and chisels, would fly across the workshop and land in Bruce Stowe's lap, where it would sniff twice, grimace with incredulity, and die. The other sect believed his head would ping around the workshop like a soccer ball in a bar room of coked Brazilians. Each sect defended their theory as if they were legitimate speculations. Both parties watched him work the lathe, ready to erupt in triumph should he lean too close.

Mr Exeter was so late for class this day I'd started a rumour he'd been arrested for yelling lewd propositions at a war widow while on a marijuana binge. With hair like his virtually any slander got traction. Eventually he staggered in, pale with news, his voice brittle. 'The Prime Minister's . . . been dismissed . . . by the Governor-General.' We blinked, chewed our gum, listened to the watery music of our intestines. 'Gough . . . sacked by Kerr.' Again, we didn't react. He turned away from us and laid his head against the blackboard.

We knew nothing of politics. But we endorsed any constitutional turmoil powerful enough to make a sandal-wearing pinko stain a blackboard with his greasy brow and whimper about what a two-faced bitch Mother England was.

'*That's* why you're late?' I put enough amazement in my voice to let him know I thought it a paltry excuse. He turned to us, strained, shaking, a bewildered synthesis of despair and anger. 'Boys, the Tories have upended our democracy . . .'

'We heard you tried to upend some old duck and the fuzz nabbed you,' Clarky said.

'What? No. Boys, this is a really black day in our history. Really black.'

He struggled on, determined we see the gravity of this event. Sensing his pain, we naturally enough began to taunt him. 'Sacked? A poor man's assassination. Tell it to JFK.'

'Yeah, tell it to Harold Holt. He'd jump at a nice little sacking and a chance to sit next to Gough smelling old in an old fogies' home,' I said.

'Anyway, the Queen probably knows stuff about Gough we don't.'

'I bet she does. Reams of stuff. Eye-popping stuff.'

'It was an elected government, boys.'

'Elected by commos and potheads.'

Throughout the lesson teachers came and went at a hustle, their brows furrowed with martyrdom, whispering insurrection. Pretty soon Mr Exeter realised we weren't going to acknowledge this injury to civilisation. We were too young to care. Or maybe we were sons of rednecks who'd told us Gough was a crazy dreamer that deserved unique political afflictions. He was aghast at finding he didn't know us at all. 'We might have seen the best of Australia, boys. The best it will be.' The fact this thing had happened was bad enough. The fact we didn't care was worse.

I remember becoming more and more fascinated by his distress. According to him great treachery and calamity were afoot. Seeing his anguish was when I first realised politics touched real people. Politics was history in utero. History was politics in aspic.

\* \* \*

Our scruffy gang, wearing copper medallions on leather thongs, pants low, shoes gaping, hung round with an equivalent gang of short-skirted Anglo girls wearing copper and leather jewellery. Those girls were being dragged headlong into womanhood by a posse of confusing, and possibly shameful, inclinations. They were by turns astonished, proud and disgusted by their new selves and what their new selves made of us boys.

Our two gangs were overlapping carousels, and as they spun, powered by our chaotic requirements, we each took our turn being private with members of the other gang. Except Hearts and Ros, who were the King and Queen of each gang. They went out together and were a long way further down the road to sex than the rest of us. Hearts' mother was an usherette at the Capri Cinema and gave him free tickets. He told us that while in a theatre watching a kung fu movie it was easier to finger a girl if she was wearing jeans than if she was wearing a dress. It seemed unlikely. It seemed really unlikely. We were all hoping to test his assertion. But then Bruce Lee died.

For most of us 'mini-sex', or 'fumblings', or 'yes, no, fuck off', was a slow process surrounded by much flattery of the girl on the part of the boy. Our flattery wasn't poetic. It was experimental and sly. You watched the eyes. If a thing you said raised the lids you said more of that thing, improved on that thing. 'You get me better than the others do.' Her eyes opened a little, minimally happier than she was a moment ago and awaiting further hogwash. 'Somehow you know me . . . how hard it is to just . . . be me.' You would be inside her bra at this stage.

After school one night as the boy and girl gangs mingled on a vacant block waiting for their buses, I backed Anna McKendrick wordlessly up against a grey paling fence and kissed her. Then, because a few boys catcalled dirty things about me being an animal, I caught and kissed Heather Hall, Anna's best friend, who was loitering too close. The amazement of my mates and the lewdness of their catcalls amplified. Camo had gone mad. I liked being considered mad. Enjoyed the maverick status of the crazy cat. Two girls? That's nothing, man. Watch this. I continued kissing girls. Any I could catch. And I could catch them all.

No girl, perhaps, wanted to kiss me, but no girl wanted to be left as the sole representative of the unkissed, either. No girl wanted to be passed over. I tongue-kissed nine or ten girls in a kind of delirium. An event was taking place.

Performance art. I kissed them all again in sharpening confidence, holding them closer second time around.

My kissing so many girls was a phenomenon. At first each took part in a pantomime where I chased them, grabbed them, held them tight and writhed for their mouth with mine until our lips met, at which point the ritual resistance ended and the girl threw herself into the kiss and we relaxed into passionate smooching in front of twenty or so laughing, barracking onlookers.

Soon I didn't have to chase the girls to kiss them. They were waiting their turn. The thing had become an audition. Each girl was enjoying being on stage. Each girl, it occurred to me, was trying to out-kiss the other girls I had just kissed. It had become a talent quest. Some snaked the tongue, some sucked mine, some became fey and hollow mouthed, inviting me forward.

Since I was the only boy to kiss this group of girls sequentially, repeatedly, I was the sole earthly judge of their relative ability as kissers. And no one wanted to flunk. Each kiss might last a minute, and after each, like a sommelier, I adopted a reflective expression, waggled my jaw and weighed the worth of the kiss, spat into the long grass, before launching at another girl. Arm around her waist, hand on the back of her head, my stomach pressed flat on hers.

It was a time of our lives when kissing was a new and vital activity. But a mysterious one. No one knew how good you were at it, because no one could fairly compare. I kissed Sandy Taylor last month and she wasn't as good as Janice Hibbert who I kissed yesterday. But since I kissed Sandy she's been going with Jim Wilder and Bruce Pickworth. So she's obviously been schooled and had two new techniques added to the sum of her knowledge and is better now than she was then. People got ahead, slipped behind, high school girls kissed working men and came back with techniques, revelations and herpes to spread among their cohorts. Who could do the rankings? Only a boy who'd turned an idle, post-school hour into an audition. During that wild afternoon of kissing I kissed Gayle Simmons for half a minute. It was like someone had discovered soundtrack in an age of silent movies.

Gayle Simmons was lithe as a vine, with strong shoulders, high breasts, high buttocks and a handsome face of cheekbones and angles. The best-built girl in our year. She and I were not physically matched as the history of ardour suggests partners ought be. We were not champion and siren, choosing each other because our corresponding physical beauty meant each had a value commensurate with the other. No. She would need a full-grown centre-half forward for that contract. I was a cut-rate kid. Too skinny, big-nosed and big-eared to have any chance of cleaving her athletic thighs or getting my hands on her high breasts.

But after the night of the crazy kissing we became entangled in glances. In class we clasped hands while fighting for pencils and rulers neither of us wanted, and grimaced at each other keenly, not daring to smile, while wrestling over notes she had written that I wasn't allowed to read.

The buttons down the front of her dress were popped open to her bra and her socks pooled at her ankles the day I asked her to go with me. She was blink-thrice beautiful. I can't ever know why she stooped to say 'yes'.

So. She was my girlfriend. I was partnered with another person and, as was to become a lifelong pattern, a person who was too good for me. This exotic ownership made us suddenly shy with each other. How did you do this 'couple' thing?

We were in the corridor at recess, waiting to go into religious instruction. Seeing we wanted each other but couldn't quite get to each other my gang pulled a locker out of the row of lockers and thrust us in that space and trapped us there, pressing the displaced locker in on us. They put their shoulders to it and pushed us together, lobbing dirty suggestions over the locker into our space. No possibility of choice, of prevarication, of protocol, the world getting smaller, every part of her body would have to touch every part of mine.

We kissed. And kissing her usurped all existence. Take that, you hidebound days. Die, crawling happenstance, I'm gone to a better place. I've been promoted above and beyond whatever guy was the ring-a-ding-ding King of all life till now.

In close-up I watched her nostrils flare as she drew breath, our tongues fast and slow, fierce and tender, everything new. Our bodies were pressed hard on one another, and of all the new curves and sensations, our twinned desire was the newest part of the world. Her enthusiasm was the epiphany for me. Our culture, our provincial, religion-ridden era, hid the true psychology of the female from boys. I'd thought girls intrinsically reluctant. There was nothing in sex for girls. They had to be coerced into it with shiny trinkets and home loans. Sex was a joyous adventure for men that women agreed to participate in for being able to tag along to the bowling alley and, later, the great bounty of a Frigidaire with a double ice tray.

Up against Rev Wilson's office wall I was astounded to find this truth about the nature of women was, well . . . demonstrably, nostril-flaringly, untrue. Gayle Simmons needed no promise of white goods. She was driven by the same needs as me.

Through the wall I could hear Rev Wilson's claque of Christians applauding as he read them psalms. Christians. The point of psalms is to tell you that once, in a time of Holiness, humanity used to be smarter than it is these days. I couldn't believe that. Watching Gayle's eyes looking into my eyes I thought we'd about reached the apex of what was ever profound here and now. It was me grinding hard at her and her grinding hard back at me and no fibre or ligament at rest and no part of the mind partisan and the spectacular and revelatory migration of blood allowing me to hammer a proclamation of omnipotence all across her loins while inside that room, the wall of which I was humping her against, the Rev Wilson shouted hallelujah, and something about revelation and something about a flood.

\* \* \*

By my third year at high school I had a reputation among the staff as an insurrectionist. I'd walk into a new class at the start of the year and a new teacher would single me out with a hateful stare, 'Ahh, the infamous Mr Cameron.' They'd been prepped. The word was out. I was a known evil mega-clown and they spent time plotting against me in the staff room. Teachers fresh out of college, student teachers, female teachers – these vulnerable types had to be protected from me. The hard, bearded teachers with massive hairy thighs and skintight shorts, the apex predators, began to hunt me down. Lawson, Canning, Engstromme – the big hairy sheriffs formed plans.

The principal himself grabbed me by the back of the neck and threw me down the front steps of the main school building when he saw me drumming my fingers on Mrs Swaby's blue beehive because I had bet Rob Godden twenty cents that it was so lacquered up with hairspray that it would sound like a kettle drum.

I waited a while on the front steps, unsure if I was free for the day, or forever. Then I snuck around the building and in the back door and into Mrs Swaby's science class where Rob put his hand out to be paid his twenty cents because, he said, Old Swaby Baby's hair gave off no special resonance, though, he admitted, it was hard to be sure with the principal ranting serial falsetto threats like he had been.

I apologised to Mrs Swaby for the misunderstanding and told her I was removing a moth and that she might want to get her hairdo fumigated professionally to prevent further intrusions from good Samaritans like myself. This apology caused laughter and Mr Lawson to appear almost simultaneously, the latter red-eyed and vomiting threats at me. His anger was always so pungent he seemed to be geeing himself up for a physical assault of the holistic kind Killer Karl Kox and Mario Milano launched on each other on *World Championship Wrestling*.

I got the cuts. A leather strap hissing and biting and hissing and biting. I showed my hand around to the lads at lunchtime, casually, with a hero's disdain for fuss when a limb was lost. 'Nah, didn't hurt. Lawson's too fat to swing hard.' Then I showed it to Gayle who laid that superheated palm against her chest, proving women complicit in the foolery of agitators and egomaniacs.

But the bushy beards were on to me. In a room somewhere with 'Bushy-Bearded Staff Only' on its door they had decided war was declared on Anson John Cameron. And that letting me finish a sentence was as dangerous as letting the Russians go nuclear. Whenever there was a hassle and I would try to state my case the wonderbeards would appear and lean in close and shout me down. 'But Mr . . .' 'I DON'T WANT TO HEAR ONE WORD FROM YOU YOU LITTLE CREEP YOU ARE THE MEAT IN EVERY SANDWICH IN THIS SCHOOL BUT WE'RE ONTO YOU AND IF YOU THINK . . .' 'I didn't even . . .' '. . . A SELF-CENTRED EGO-TRIPPER WHO IMAGINES WE'RE ALL HERE FOR HIS AMUSEMENT, WELL LET ME TELL YOU . . .' I couldn't get heard. My days of smart-arsery and disruption were over. The tough guys were gunning for me and this was only going to end one way.

They began to haul me in and grill me. Long sessions in closed offices with loud bearded men leaning at me shouting questions whose only answers were that I was bad and going nowhere. The other beards stood around grim, watching, thinking, waiting to get tagged and take their turn up in my grill. Giving up their lunch hours for the divine mission of breaking me down. Who did I think I was? Where did I think this would end? Further you fall the bigger the splash, the greater the disgrace. Your father's a lawyer and you end up working at the cannery, the explanation isn't that you're too cool to conform, it's that you're a cretin, too dumb to know what dumb is. You're a retard that thinks he's a genius. Probably all retards do. I'm happy for you . . . being so stupid, so blind. Because if you could see what you really were you'd shoot yourself.

I realised they weren't just trying to reform me . . . they hated me. Making me pale and wordless was fun.

I'd been leading a double life, anyway. By day I was a hoodlum. At lunchtime we'd be over the back of the oval, smoking, carving our names in seats, chucking rocks at passing trains, smashing the odd window, pooling money to buy Marlboros, pants riding low and shirt buttons mostly gone. Transgression was the only way to manhood and honour. The pale cats over the school side of the oval were slaves to an adult world of fraud.

The tough life, the life of the hoodlum set against authority, was to be ours. We swore, shoplifted, spat continually, punched each other, and others, about a hundred times a day, handed in half-arsed schoolwork, bullied introverts and shrimps, vandalised indiscriminately, and spoke a nihilist patois. 'You fuckin' lookin' at?' I'd typically ask a boy I'd never met before.

At night I went home and talked in refined polysyllable without dropping my Gs and was a different boy. Dad and I spoke of Napoleon at Borodino and of Burke and Wills. Mum and I did the cryptic crossword. And when I went to bed I read novels and nodded my head quietly in appreciation of exotic cultures and heroic deeds until the neighbourhood slept. And this, it sometimes occurred to me, making me blink and pout, was me.

* * *

Out at Kialla I don't think anyone was as happy as they used to be. Mum and Dad now spoke to each other with the careful diplomacy of nations covertly spending half their GDP on armaments. You felt every sentence was a moment away from breaking into truth, and from there . . . unveil the new munitions.

Guy had left home and was somewhere in New South Wales jackarooing. He'd show up once a month in an electric purple V8 ute wearing a claw-hammer tuxedo jacket and a wide-brimmed akubra, cracking a stockwhip and denouncing Victoria as over-civilised and overrun with irrigators. He bought an elephant gun, a .458 Weatherby Magnum that fired a round like a railway spike, and he sometimes blasted bullets through steel power poles to win bets.

I rode into town with him to buy *Goodbye Yellow Brick Road* and Deep Purple's *Machine Head*. I treasured our time together because I knew he was doomed to die in a car crash. Recently he'd missed a turn doing one-eighty and sent his ute end-over-end off a bridge and landed in a dam and nearly drowned. Some nights he'd come flying down our gravel road with all his lights out and the cops not far behind sweeping the paddocks with a spotlight. He was, at eighteen, so loaded with risk Mum could hardly look at him without tears welling. She was right too. Before long he dived off a bridge in Deniliquin into the Edward River. Like most Australian rivers it was over-named. It should have been called a creek, or a dribble. It was only a metre deep and broke his back pretty thoroughly.

Debbie had disappeared into the wilds of Melbourne and was working for a major company in a skyscraper. She moved in some sort of society where it was acceptable to wear cork-soled platform shoes and arse-hugging satin flares and a matching silvery satin waistcoat. She had the zephyr-teased hair of a Bee Gee and another tough boyfriend. Half an hour after you met him you would be smoking a bong or explaining your inability or reluctance to do so. 'No, Cliffo, I've got a throat infection.' 'Cliffo, I feel a bit sick today.' Cliffo, I'm twelve, man.

Vicki was back from all the private schools, finishing her last year in ignominy in Shepp. Demoted back to a provincial facility she'd been freed from years before. How could she care about this life when she'd seen the other? She had a friend called Fat Harris, also an expellee, and they'd sit at the milk bar outside school smoking and going halvies in a hamburger contriving plans to get back to Melbourne ASAP while egg yolk dripped from their chins.

Halfway through the year she exploded into romance and freedom by eloping with an Italian chosen from a field of mulish applicants with sufficient spare cash for hamburgers and smokes. She was so romantically blinded she couldn't see the difference between high-school fellatio and lifelong happiness and had chosen to flee with a youth named Vince who, judging by the love letter we found, had to grit his teeth to write actual words and shake his head and growl like a hound to put those words one after another into a near sentence on a page.

Mum picked the hundred or so pieces of this torn-up love letter out of the wastepaper bin in Vicki's bedroom when she didn't come home one night. Mum and Dad grimly pieced them together while drinking whisky and breathing accusations at each other. It was no sonnet. But it was legible enough for us to find out that Vince thought Vicki was real cool and wanted to show her the good life in Quinlsand, which, according to Vince, was just forty miles away across the border where the VicPigs couldn't follow. I think by Quinlsand Vince meant Queensland and he had that state mixed up with New South Wales, which he mistakenly thought of as a type of Canada from which you could poke your tongue across the river at mainland Australia's southern-most cops with impunity and holler threats and taunts.

I was wearing a resolute pout as Mum read the letter aloud, showily affected by the gravity with which Mum and Dad were treating the emergency. But I secretly wanted Vicki to elope successfully. Ever since coming back from the last of her boarding schools she had been a sullen presence in the house and the mood could only lift with her gone. But this Quinlsand nonsense didn't fill me with any hope that Vince could elope with any efficiency. And as I suspected, they never got to make their run at whatever garbled version of Canada he carried in his head, because the lovelorn fool also included the intel in his love letter that he lived with three cousins on probation in a weatherboard rental on an orchard out at Shepp East – he gave its address so she could find him there.

Dad and I piled into the Fairlane. It was night and we travelled dirt roads cutting through small orchards that made a sea of apple trees. We pulled up outside a house shedding its weatherboards and sitting in a halo of junk and Dad said, 'You wait here, Ans.' I knew this was dangerous. Dad had silver cups from Melbourne University for boxing but . . . three Italians on probation. Probably hopped up on grappa and about to make an orgy of a white girl who aspired to the romantic heights of elopement.

'I'll come with you?'

'No. You stay here.' He walked into the darkness toward the house. Loud knocking and low voices and he came back out of the dark with Vicki in tow clutching a handbag puffed with the necessaries for life on the lam in no-star motels. She sat in the back, pretty morose to have her lifelong bliss nipped in the bud. From the front seat I stared over the back of the seat at her all the way home. I'd never seen anyone who'd eloped before. As we pulled into our driveway I said, 'You didn't get far.'

'Fuck off.'

'You going to try again?'

'Fuck off!!' She started crying. Some big collapse of some big romantic world she'd conjured up. From my experience of sisters their nights were pretty much a cacophony of collapsing romantic nirvanas. 'Don't *you* say another word,' Dad told me. He poked me in the ribs as he said 'you'.

* * *

315

Tina was, by then, the only spark of joy in the house and she was just a pot-bellied pet, a sort of self-glazing amphibian that drooled amply and smeared itself from hairline to toe until it smelt like a drunk licked by strays. You tickled it when you wanted it to laugh. You fed it when you wanted it to be quiet. You read it stories because, amazingly, kids' stories were fun to read. You bathed it when the smell got too bad. Then, by early arvo, everyone was sick of it so they put it away for a nap and eavesdropped through the door while it firstly cried and then wittered to itself of puppies and swished bright swatches of spittle-covered silk about its own head – two early behaviours that would become lifelong habits.

* * *

I knew the wonderbeards at high school were going to throw me out. Their mission was clear. And I knew my transfer to the next big school was in jeopardy because of it. My destiny was threatened by my delinquency. So halfway through the year I detached from my gang, from my mates, from Gayle, and from the low road. I quietened down in class, bit my lip, a champ hanging up the gloves. Countless times during an argument or a fracas when our rights were being impinged, the class would pause, silently waiting for me, but I never showed up.

It wasn't easy. I knew they needed my words, my shrill advocacy. When the shit hit the fan and big-faced adults were leaning close, shouting threats and vilifications, they needed my comebacks and deflections. They had none of worth themselves. They'd look across at me for deliverance, from the place it always came . . . but I just looked down at my desk and let the grown-up beasts roar on without stepping in. Let my friends lose the war. I was out of it. I wasn't going to risk my future Big Life at the grammar school by getting thrown out of this school, or arrested, or by becoming so debauched by our wastrel ethos that there was no coming back.

I stopped going over the far side of the oval. I stopped meeting my mates at the Star Bowl. I stopped stealing and vandalising, and I stopped hanging out. It was treachery. I was renouncing my mates to save myself. But I did it.

Sherman was my only friend who wasn't sold on daily misconduct, so I started hanging out with him. He read books and had a rare intelligence. His parents owned a pool and taught people to swim. His father had an Olympic bronze medal for water polo.

Being friends with him was a type of reform for me. He was a gentler soul than I normally hung around with, and we fell into a mutual awe of art. We discussed books and songs: *Papillon* by Henri Charrière, *Dark Side of the Moon* by Pink Floyd, *Jaws* by Benchley. We talked about how the Creedence track 'Long As I Can See the Light' gave us goose bumps and hollowed our guts into the loneliest of feelings. How? We shared our enthusiasm for plots and lyrics. We both had insights to declare to each other. We both discovered strange and magnificent things authors and musicians did, conjurings and deceits and echoes.

Sherman's observations were so good I started reading more closely so as not to miss what he might get. So as not to let him surprise me with his perspicacity, which he often did. We began to make each other good readers, good listeners.

Sure, when he came to visit at my place out on the river we shot at feral cats with broad-head arrows out of recurve hunting bows. Or if I went to his place at Bonnie Doon we'd roll rocks down hills to smash farmers' fences way below. Given easy access to gravity, rocks, feral cats and hunting bows, what boy wouldn't? But not counting these few run-of-the-mill atrocities, we were a partnership of the inner life.

He was the first person of my own age with whom I sat and listened deeply to music. 'Someone Saved My Life Tonight' by Elton John. 'The Wreck of the *Edmund Fitzgerald*' by Gordon Lightfoot. We listened and sang along, annexing these stories and making them ours. Enjoying being us, newly shipwrecked and heartbroken. All sorts of beautiful, sad stories could feel like your own story if you gave yourself over to them. It was empowering to find a kindred spirit, to explore emotions and admit to having a heart. It wasn't an act you could admit to in public in this town. It was clearly effeminate and wrong. But the last friendship I formed before I left was with a boy more likely to write an ode than vandalise a phone box.

At school, at the start of every recess or lunchtime, my gang broke away from the peaceable kids to go over the back of the oval and become grandees of rebellion. Over there moist packs of B&H that had nestled alongside scrotums all morning would be pulled from underwear and cigarettes so moist they needed lighting twice would be smoked.

They would ask me, 'Camo . . . you comin'?' 'Nah. I'm just goin' to hang here for a while.' They didn't abuse me outright. They shook their heads, spat, shrugged. What the hell was going on with Camo? Soon they stopped asking. One of their number had fallen.

Gayle would wait with me on the western side of the campus as her gang drifted over the back of the oval to join the hounds of rebellion, shouting at her to come on as they went. We held hands and talked, but the things we didn't say were suddenly louder than the things we did. She was confused, and hurt. Why was I refusing to go over the back of the oval? Why was I giving them up? What was wrong? Was I giving her up too? I couldn't explain it to her. I couldn't tell her I had a different path. That this world wasn't quite the real thing. That she wasn't quite . . . the real . . . that there would be princesses.

After a while she'd remember she had to swap some homework with Ros or return a hair-tie to Kerryn, and she'd kiss me on the lips and drift across the oval. I'd watch her walk through the paspalum to those swirling distant figures, my friends. She could drag her feet in parodied sadness and still have more spring in her step than any other girl in school. It broke my heart to give her up.

It made me feel empty to give them all up. But they didn't lug a deadweight of destiny like I did. They weren't burdened by being chosen. I had the Big Future to protect, and staying on track with them to where they were going was the sure-fire death of that.

It's nervous work having a Big Future hidden about you. It's like being a spy. I couldn't say anything to them about my unrevealed ethereal status. It would have come out wrong. They would have been jealous and stupefied. It would have been laughed at, remembered, repeated, used. Camo thinks he's a Prince or something. King Cameron. King Fucking Cameron. Heavy is the head that wears the erroneous and pitiful assumption he is bound for glory.

I tried to say goodbye to them all. But my school friends thought my going no big thing. I'd already stepped out of their circle, shunned them, and lost membership of that unique clan. I no longer fit there.

Last day of school I found Rob Godden at the bus stop waiting for his bus to Katandra West. I put my hand out for shaking – an overtly adult gesture. He smiled at me to try and crack this joke open, to test if I was kidding. Because . . . I'd opted out months ago . . . hadn't I? 'See ya, Rob. I'm not coming back.' He shook my hand half-heartedly, smiling, suspicious this was a pisstake, still not seeing the point. 'Yeah, I know.'

It was that way all round. I found Stowey at the bike sheds about to mount his yellow racer for home. 'See ya, knuckle-head. This is it for me. I'm goin' away next year.' I held out my hand. He slapped it away. 'You'll be back. None of your family last long at those schools. See ya in second term.' He rode away laughing. No one understood what a hit I was going to be in my second life. What they were about to lose. How much they'd miss me.

\* \* \*

When young you think of your family as an immemorial compact of souls that will journey through the universe together, without addition or subtraction. The family is at once the world in miniature and the self in glorious extension. The cast is as inflexible as the cast of *Hamlet*. You do not exile or kill Hamlet in Act I. Nor do you add another Queen or make the King a Prussian with Tourette's syndrome. The dramatis personae are unassailable, perfectly known, immortal. This wonderful world will go on forever, for there is no other world to come.

Yet all these additions and subtractions and transformations do occur. And year by year the range of your knowing extends and you see all the other possible worlds and realise this gallant symbiotic beast will soon die . . . must die, was born to die, is a convenience, a bunch of refugees who took shelter together from a storm. And now the sky is coming so blue . . .

I was ready to go. Damn these people. This world was played out and I was treading water, waiting for the next. I got the feeling Mum and Dad no longer believed in it. They had grim expressions and other projects. Dad took to breeding spotted horses. Mum opened a clothes shop. Guy was smirking from great days up north, reeking of girls and gun smoke. Debbie and Vicki had seen the El Dorado/ Gomorrah at the south end of the Hume Highway and were drawn to it like boho pilgrims fleeing puritanism to party. You could fetch them back to Shepparton daily and they'd have crawled to the fleshpots of Melbourne on their knees by sun-up. They were gone even when they were at home.

Mum took me down to Lunn & Fordyce where I was measured up with a tape measure and, according to the lady with the beehive hairdo taking the measurements, was beautifully proportioned, even manly. She was lying through the coloured pins she had clamped in her teeth.

I was fitted with a sports coat made of the type of triple-check tweed American ventriloquists favoured for their dummies. A Comanche at the Court of St James dressed in this vestment couldn't have looked, or felt, any sillier. I was a boy from a town, and now that they were fitting me up in raiment apt for a city I was sickened with the sudden knowledge that this better-life thing wasn't going to go as well as I'd always believed.

Looking at myself in the long mirror surrounded by caramel-coloured wood panels I was taken with the audacity of my fraudulence. I was so clearly not a boy who belonged in a sports coat . . . or to the life and tribe that wore sports coats. 'Oh, doesn't he look splendid? A gentleman,' the woman with the beehive hairdo comforted my mum. I was Mowgli in a petticoat. Malcolm Fraser was the Prime Minister at the time. He had a sports coat exactly the same as this. I was wearing the same sports coat as the fucking Prime Minister. The next life was going to be a fuck-up just like this one.

\* \* \*

I needed to pack my suitcase carefully. I was never coming home. I had to leave behind all the stuff that wasn't appropriate for a future in manor houses riding to hounds. Leave out the boyhood and the bogan, the toys and tools needed to live in a town that couldn't support an opera company. Just pack the stuff I'd need for a gilded adulthood. The world in which I'd befriend knights, ride with princes, romance actresses, beguile tycoons, catch planes

322

and own tall buildings – possibly without even knowing it, because . . . who can keep track of all one's real estate?

I snuck in a bottle of Dad's aftershave, though I didn't shave. One day it would be needed. I put in a stick deodorant, though I had no more body odour than a marble Medici. Before coming back here I would be a man, giving off a heavy musk like Dennis Lillee after destroying a top-order of hapless Pakistanis.

Mum was in a black-and-white print dress, lipsticked and nervous, breaking into hammy howls of grief every now and then and covering her face with her hands to be losing another child to the faraway schools that a child was required to go to if he was going to be a real adult appearing in newspapers and at ceremonies. Dad was in a checked sports coat and the old school tie; hair laid flat and swept over his head in a slurry of his lavender brilliantine. He would be meeting school friends he hadn't seen for years who would be dropping off their own sons and daughters. He was happy I was going to the place that had made him what he was so I could be made into whatever might be possible with the paltry ingredients provided. He knew I was wild, possibly mentally unstable and immoral. Now, let's see what the big school could do about that.

I hauled my tan suitcase out to the cavernous boot of the Fairlane and hoisted it inside. I left my guns and knives and my Alistair MacLean novels in the house. I guessed it would be Shakespeare and backgammon from hereon in. I bent down and scratched the dogs, under their chins, behind their ears. Goodbye, Snuff. See you, Sam. You, being Cameron dogs, being free and road-prone dogs, being snake dogs, will be dead before I return for holidays.

We drove with Mum periodically asking if I'd remembered this or that. Did I pack my runners? My toothbrush? 'Did you bring your toothbrush?' That was a question I'd heard a magistrate ask a burglar while watching Dad in court once. Mum asking it now made me feel as if I were headed for prison, an innocent man facing brave exile. Yeah, I brought my toothbrush. But I knew the other kids would have better toothbrushes. From the back seat I shook my head at my parents for their financial shortcomings and pictured myself brushing my teeth in a bathroom alongside kids with toothbrushes made of gold.

Forty years ago Dad had made this trip and he wanted to prepare me for what he'd encountered, for what I'd surely encounter. 'The other kids won't speak like you do. They won't drop their Gs. They'll say 'going' not 'goin'', 'coming' not 'comin''. 'I beg your pardon,' instead of 'What?' 'Carstle' not 'cassle.' But you're a chameleon. You'll soon adapt.'

'I beg your pardon; I'm *going* to the *carstle*. No way,' I laughed tightly, without humour.

'And there'll be snobbery. The kids of Toorak don't know or care where Shepparton is. They're rich and they'll think you pretty strange for not having a beach house and skiing in winter.' Snobbery had been my prerogative till now. But our future King had been schooled at this place, suggesting my opportunities for future snobbery would be slim. I was starting to dislike my new schoolmates already. 'I'm just letting you know it'll be different,' he said.

The road we drove toward the Alps was bordered by box trees, the remnants of the great forests that had covered Victoria's central plains. The February countryside was shimmering straw yellow. After an hour we began to climb into the high country and the paddocks tinged green. I'd travelled this road many times before, heading for the shack we stayed in on the Goulburn River outside the village of Jamieson in the mountains. This time we didn't turn south to that fibro hamlet. We followed the road toward Mount Buller and turned off at a place called Timbertop.

A camp-out campus of wooden barracks littered across a mountainside beneath towering eucalypts, all joined by gravel roads and walking tracks. Above it all sat an A-frame chapel, its triangular glass altar a diamond of modernity set in *terra nullius*. This place was where the plutocracy sent their offspring to toughen them up. To teach them the stuff the workers know; of cold nights under wet skies, and long distances and heavy weights and forking tracks and choices and blisters and a world without adults. But I figured I already knew all that. I'd been living as Lord of the Flies all my life. What did I need this place for?

We did a quick tour of the campus with a young rosy-faced Oxbridge master named Mr Polly. Dad shook hands with a few old friends and they fired reminiscence and laughter at one another. Mum smiled bravely through the coming loss. Guy used to bring brown snakes home from this campus in his suitcase, so she was watching where she trod.

The staff wanted the parents gone, so they could set about becoming the new parents. I kissed Mum quickly and broke her hug, not wanting my goodbyes to stand out as especially soppy among the many goodbyes that were going on around me. Veteran boarders waving parents away with faces that said 'Get gone' so they could re-meet friends after the long summer break. I shook Dad's hand. 'Righto, good luck,' he said.

'Yeah. Righto.'

When they got in the car – that was the end of child-hood. My ride back to that world was gone. The nooks and crannies in which my imaginary self had thrived suddenly vanished. No privacy anymore. Now I will sleep and shower in a dormitory alongside other boys. Strangers. I must start again. And hide my past.

I stood on the gravel turning circle out front of the dining room watching as their silver Fairlane wound out of sight downhill along the gravel driveway. And I must have stood there a while because everyone else was gone when a tall boy approached me and put out his hand. In his Harris Tweed sports coat he looked the sort of kid a filmmaker would choose to play a hick on holidays in the big smoke.

'G'day. Anson, is it?'

'Yeah. Yes.' We shook hands.

'My name's Will. Call me "Bum". Everyone calls me "Bum". Your old man and my old man were mates at school. You want me to show you round?'

'Yeah. Yes. Okay . . . Bum.'

I listened hard for the giveaway hint of grand houses in gilded suburbs, but heard none. Bum was straight off a farm. He had a farmer's drawl, which was somehow comforting. I felt a flush of gratitude. He was an old hand and had offered to show me around.

But Bum didn't seem much of a name for the first person I was to meet in this dignified world I'd waited so long to join. He was clearly a dag. And, you know . . . a farmer? Weren't farmers the sort of people I'd come here to get away from? I'd read my Unit list and knew I'd be sleeping alongside a Marquis. I wondered if mixing with Bum might handicap me with the cool kids, Marquises and the like, who probably smoked French cigarettes. Perhaps I ought to make some excuse, step away, scan the joint for some guy leaning up against a wall wearing a body shirt and flared jeans slung low and a Gauloise on his lip. Perhaps I should start again.

As I was weighing the value of Bum as an entry point to the New Big Life I heard gravel-crunch footsteps accelerating toward us and a boy came running from behind and launched into the air and hit Bum in the middle of the back with both knees, sending him sprawling face down across the gravel. The attacker lost balance in the collision and fell, coming to rest sitting, leaning back on his arms on the gravel in front of me. He was big and pale skinned with a bent nose, smiling happily with the outcome of his assault.

Everything I'd ever learnt told me I should kick him in the head. Here I stood above him. I could easily kick him under the chin and lay him out sobbing on his back in the gravel. It was normal schoolyard practice.

Or I could introduce myself to him. So, was Bum my friend or not? Mum and Dad weren't even off the mountain and already I was on the banks of a fairly frothy boyhood Rubicon, having to decide whether to assault this pale assailant or befriend him.

But I didn't come here to be that boyhoodlum. To be the prick I had been. I came here with a lifelong knowledge that metamorphosis was possible, and that this was it. Right here was the place, signposted from the beginning, where I turned from larvae to butterfly, from a grubby little solipsist to a gilded child who could parse Latin.

Yet . . . there sits the pale assailant, smiling at me as if we're conspirators. He will rise and introduce himself if I let him. Bum, my new friend, is sprawled and torn on the gravel. So all I've got to do now is all I've ever had to do – decide whether it's best for me to step forward and kick this guy in the face . . . or not to, and by letting him get away with an assault on a friend thereby signal an intention to ditch that friend and become his friend. To trade up to a tougher accomplice, as it were. Maybe this place isn't so different to where I'm from, I thought. Maybe metamorphosis is a myth. Maybe in a *carstle* the same wars are fought using better elocution.

From here, from this northern side of this mountain, if the day is clear, I can look across Victoria's central plains a hundred miles and detect a flaw in the horizon's light. A slight, perhaps imaginary, bruise on the far plain that lets me know I'm looking in the right direction.

It's a long way, and only a small clue to the past. But my yearning gaze, powered by all the memories I have, cuts through the intervening space and time and descends on that town. It flows down Wyndham Street and up Fraser Street into Cameron and Cameron where Dad is sitting at his desk, wrinkling his brow, nodding his wry pout to a new widow, sympathising with her that her dead husband had debts he hadn't owned up to. He surreptitiously checks his watch beneath the lip of the desk as the new widow catalogues the husband's failings as a man of business.

Then along Fryers Street to where Mum, having dropped Justina Gaye at kindergarten, is opening her new shop, ducking next door to get a cappuccino from the Taverna Café, batting away rude compliments from the round tables of Italian men gathered there in white singlets to play cards and backgammon.

Arriving late then for school, the bell for class already rung, everybody already seated, creeping in, listening to Mr Murray ask, 'Now, where did we leave off last week? Can anyone tell me?' Stowey makes a joke that the class, my audience, half laughs at. 'We were talking about the rebellion at . . . during the Gold Rush . . . Ballarat . . .'

Gayle Simmons, lithe, white socks cupping loose around sharp ankles, regally straight-backed, aware she's watched, on show, sitting up the back pulling the glances of boys who will never reach epiphany kissing her behind the lockers up against the wall of the school reverend's office.

Wallster passes her a note that flares a smile on her pretty face. Then his hand drops to her leg and he draws a heart on her thigh with a ballpoint pen and writes their initials inside the heart. She lets him. The heart is high enough above the hem of her dress to be invisible when she stands. That tribute drawn, Wallster begins stroking her thigh while Mr Murray asks for the two root causes of the rebellion at Eureka. How can I control this now? How can I take my friend's hand off my girl's thigh? How can I prevent this next step? How can I stop the excision of me from their lives?

Here on this mountainside, watching them in that town, in that class without me, I'm resenting them for going on living when the light, consciousness, raison d'être and puppeteer of that world has packed his tan suitcase and gone. They should have dropped like marionettes, those people I thought I could live so easily without. They don't seem to know I conjured them into being – that they don't exist without me.

Staring out through the vast air between us, between the me of now and the me of then, I feel the pulse of the town and realise with horror that it still lives, grows, loves, forgets . . . is drifting away with everyone on board beguiled by their own tomorrows.

My friends are there, now gripped in barter, now sliding free in laughter, now finding secrets in each other's eyes. My family is there in its hustle and pain and routine. And I can scream from this mountaintop till my lungs catch fire and those people won't stop living, dying, growing up, old, away, alien . . . Tomorrow they will be unrecognisable as the commemorated cast I hold captive in my boyhood head. Tomorrow the people who are living in that town will smile at, laugh at, sneer at, and regret those younger selves I hold in memorial stasis. The place I know and love is being razed by a banal blur of days. There's no past to go back to. To leave is to destroy the place you leave.

It's alive for minutes at a time in the first year – the past. The rooms, sounds, sayings and smells. Purpled with yearning, but real. On your bike you ride that bare path through the vacant block dodging potholes to the pool, where you see that girl, her way of walking and smiling, marvel at her little revelations, the taste of a spearmint malted milk-shake on her lips, the first rain of autumn called in by the currawongs, a new emotion, the arc of jealousy when a friend turns away from you to another friend, the proud moments alone underwater after a perfect dive from the three-metre board when your world was watching . . . then the laundry truck shifts down a gear to climb the mountain to the school and its engine snarls and the past yields all and the here and now is cruelly true again. And, lying in your bed with the old world lost again, you reach upward into the dark of the dormitory for those waning times.

In the second year the past is rarer and its lifespan shorter. Its moments are as infrequent, unplanned and disconcerting as meteor-strike. Dad's beer-laugh watching TV movies on Friday night. The triangle of streetlight that hung above my boyhood bed. The knothole in a fence through which we passed coded notes. The scream of Pigsy falling from the silky oak. The tiny wart on Debby Neeld's thumb as she ventured her hand to be held.

And the intrusions that drag you back to the present are heartbreakingly small . . . a boy coughs in his bed, a car passes, time-beeps mark the hour on a radio somewhere . . . and that gust of past has passed.

Eventually there is only an occasional ephemeral image, surfacing greyly in the coloured tumult of now, igniting a throb of reminiscence. A peripheral glimpse of a half-known somebody such as you might see when running past a warped mirror. That boy was tangled in that town as it crossed the frontier moment of now into the past. That kid is dead for all but a few unplanned flashes a year, and even in those moments of reincarnation is a stranger.

# Acknowledgements

Acknowledgement is made to Fairfax Media, in which the initial incarnation of some of these episodes appeared. Also to Martin Summons for permission to reprint my, somewhat changed, Endnote to his historical work, *Water: The Vital Element*.

**Anson Cameron** has written six critically acclaimed novels, *Silences Long Gone*, *Tin Toys*, *Confessin' the Blues*, *Lies I Told About a Girl*, *Stealing Picasso* and *The Last Pulse*, as well as two collections of short stories, *Nice Shootin' Cowboy* and *Pepsi Bears and Other Stories*. He was born in Shepparton, Victoria in 1961 and lives in Melbourne where he currently writes a column for *The Age*.

## ALSO BY ANSON CAMERON

### THE LAST PULSE

*A blackly funny novel about an unlikely hero, and his misadventures on the flood he has created*

In the drought-stricken Riverland town of Bartel in South Australia, after the suicide of his wife, Merv Rossiter has an epiphany. He trucks north with his eight-year-old daughter, Em, into Queensland. There he blows the dam at Karoo Station sky high, releasing a surging torrent through outback New South Wales into South Australia.

As the authorities frantically search for the culprits, Merv and Em ride the flood south in a stolen boat, rescuing a bedraggled Queensland Minister from her floating portaloo, and an indignant young blackfella who fancies he sang the river to life all by himself.

Meanwhile, in Canberra, the political flotsam carried by Merv's renegade ocean brings the Federal Government to its knees.

Wryly humorous, poignant, timely, *The Last Pulse* is one of Anson Cameron's finest works.

**PEPSI BEARS**

*Daring and provocative short stories from one of Australia's best comic writers*

A cola company uses the last wild polar bears as billboards. A boy is forced to compose poems for cats. A dog starts a race riot. A zebra shames two armies. A zoologist vivisects a gorilla to disprove evolution and has his own brain placed in the ape's head. In New Guinea, zookeepers eat their exhibits. In Gippsland, the face of the Lord appears on dairy cows. In the Western Desert, mummified egg-bandits hang from trees . . .

*Pepsi Bears* hilariously exposes the nature of man as he pilots Mother Earth into oblivion, while the other species wryly look on.

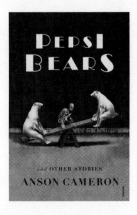